P9-AFP-395

Treat this book with care and respect.

It should become part of your personal
and professional library. It will
serve you well at any number
of points during your
professional career.

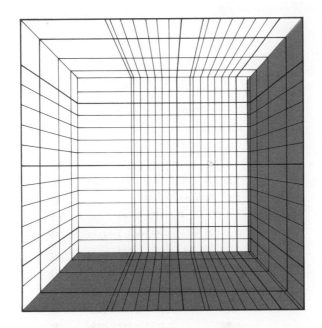

COLLEGE
ACCOUNTING
10th Edition PART 1

A. B. CARSON, PhD, CPA
Professor Emeritus of Accounting
University of California, Los Angeles

ARTHUR E. CARLSON, PhD
Professor of Accounting
School of Business Administration
Washington University, St. Louis

Published by

A51 **SOUTH-WESTERN PUBLISHING CO.**

CINCINNATI   WEST CHICAGO, ILL.   DALLAS   PELHAM MANOR, N.Y.
PALO ALTO, CALIF.   BRIGHTON, ENGLAND

ISBN: 0-538-01510-1

Library of Congress Catalog Card Number: 74-81824

1 2 3 4 5 6 7 8 9 K 2 1 0 9 8 7

Printed in the United States of America

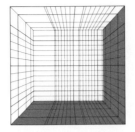 # PREFACE

College Accounting is for students of accounting, business administration, and secretarial science. An understanding of the principles of business accounting is essential for anyone who aspires to a successful career in business, in many of the professions, and in numerous branches of government. Those who manage or operate a business, its owners, its prospective owners, its present and prospective creditors, governmental taxing authorities, and other government agencies have need for various types of information. Accounting systems are designed to fill such needs. The particular practices followed are tailored to meet the requirements and the circumstances in each case. However, the same accounting principles underlie the practices—just as the same principles of structural engineering apply to the construction of a one-car frame garage and of a fifty-floor steel and concrete office building.

This tenth edition of *College Accounting* continues the pattern of earlier editions — explanations of principles with examples of practices. Numerous forms and documents are illustrated. Because the terminology of accounting is undergoing gradual change, the currently preferred terms are used throughout the textbook. Diagrams and color are used both to facilitate understanding and, in the case of many of the color illustrations, to conform to practice. Because the discussion of accounting practices involves several references to computers, an appendix entitled "Computer-Based Accounting Systems — Design and Use" is included.

The textbook is organized to facilitate the use of various supplementary learning aids. Each chapter consists of one or more sections. A workbook containing correlated study assignments is available. Each workbook study assignment (called a *report*) includes an exercise on principles and one or more problems bearing on the material discussed in the related section of the textbook. A compilation of check figures for selected workbook problems is available for distribution to students. Additional accounting problems to be used for either supplementary or remedial work are included following Chapters 5 and 10. Two entirely new practice sets are available: the first involves the accounting records of a professional man (John H. Roberts, a management consultant); the second involves the accounting records of a retail clothing store (Boyd's Clothiers). These sets provide realistic work designed to test the student's ability to apply the knowledge of the principles of accounting which has been gained from studying the textbook and completing the workbook assignments. Upon completion of each practice set, a test is used to determine the student's ability to interpret intelligently the records and financial statements of the enterprise. New with this tenth edition is a learning aid entitled Self-Paced Learning Activity Guides (SPLAGs). The SPLAGs were developed to **(1)** provide guides for the completion of the accounting course with minimal instructor direction, and **(2)** provide remedial work whenever trouble spots emerge in the learning process. A comprehensive testing program is provided. Tests are available for use following completion of Chapters 2, 5, and 10.

The authors acknowledge their indebtedness and express their appreciation to the considerable number of accounting instructors, business executives, accountants, and other professional people whose suggestions contributed to the preparation of this textbook.

A. B. Carson

A. E. Carlson

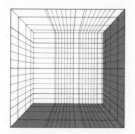

CONTENTS
PART 1

Chapter 1

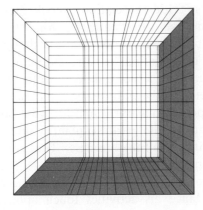

THE NATURE OF BUSINESS ACCOUNTING

The purpose of business accounting is to provide information about the financial operations and condition of an enterprise to the individuals, agencies, and organizations who have the need and the right to be so informed. These interested parties normally include the following:

(a) The **owners** of the business — both present and prospective.

(b) The **managers** of the business. (Often, but not always, the owners and the managers are the same persons.)

(c) The **creditors** of the business — both present and prospective. (*Creditors* are those who furnish or supply goods and services "on credit" — meaning that payment need not be made immediately. The creditor category also includes banks and individuals who lend money to the business.)

(d) **Government agencies** — local, state, and national. (For purposes of either regulation or taxation — sometimes both — various governmental agencies must be given certain financial information.)

The preceding four classes of users of information relate to virtually every business enterprise. In connection with many businesses, some or all of the following also make use of relevant information: customers or clients, labor unions, competitors, trade associations, stock exchanges, commodity exchanges, financial analysts, and financial journalists.

The information needed by all of the users is not identical, though most want data regarding either results of operations for a recent period — net income or loss — or financial status as of a recent date, or both. In addition to these requirements, a variety of other information may be wanted. The exact requirement depends upon who wants it and for what purpose. As might be expected, the demand for the greatest quantity and variety of information comes from the managers of the business. They constantly need up-to-the-minute information about many things.

The accountant has the task of accumulating and dispensing needed financial information to users. Since his activities touch upon nearly every phase of business operation and since financial information is communicated in accounting terms, accounting is said to be the "language of business." Anyone intending to engage in any type of business activity is well advised to learn this language.

Since accounting relates to so many phases of business, it is not surprising that there are several fields of specialization in accounting. Some major special fields are tax work, cost accounting, information systems design and installation, and budget preparation. Many accountants have but one employer; whereas others become qualified as public accountants and offer their services as independent contractors or consultants. Some states license individuals as *Public Accountants* or *Registered Accountants*. All states grant the designation *Certified Public Accountant* (CPA) to those who meet various prescribed requirements, including the passing of a uniform examination prepared by the American Institute of Certified Public Accountants. Public accountants perform various functions. One of their major activities is *auditing*. This involves testing and checking the records of an enterprise to be certain that acceptable policies and practices have been consistently followed. In recent years, public accountants have been extending their activities into what is called "management services" — a term that covers a variety of specialized consulting assignments. Specialization is common among members of the accounting profession. Tax work is one important example of specialization. Management services is another.

All of the foregoing comments have related to accounting and accountants in connection with profit-seeking organizations. Since there are thousands of not-for-profit or nonprofit organizations (such as governments, educational institutions, churches, and hospitals) that also need to accumulate information, thousands of accountants are in their employ. These organizations also engage public accountants. While the "rules of the game" are somewhat different for not-for-profit organizations, much of the record keeping is identical with that found in business.

THE ACCOUNTING PROCESS

Business accounting may be defined as the art of analyzing and recording financial transactions and certain business-related economic events in a manner that facilitates classifying and summarizing the information, and reporting and interpreting the results.

Analyzing is the first step. There may be more than one way of looking at something that has happened. The accountant must determine the fundamental significance to the business of each transaction or event in order to record it properly.

Recording traditionally has meant writing something by hand. Much of the record keeping in accounting still is manual, but for years typewriters and many varieties of so-called "bookkeeping machines" (which typically combine the major attributes of typewriters and adding machines or desk calculators) have been in use. Today the recording sometimes takes the form of holes punched in certain places on a card or a paper tape, or of invisible magnetized spots on a special type of tape used to feed information into an electronic computer.

Classifying relates to the process of sorting or grouping like things together rather than merely keeping a simple, diary-like narrative record of numerous and varied transactions and events.

Summarizing is the process of bringing together various items of information to determine or explain a result.

Reporting refers to the process of attempting to communicate the results. In accounting, it is common to use tabular arrangements rather than narrative-type reports. Sometimes, a combination of the two is used.

Interpreting refers to the steps taken to direct attention to the significance of various matters and relationships. Percentage analyses and ratios often are used to help explain the meaning of certain related bits of information. Footnotes to financial reports may also be valuable in the interpreting phase of accounting.

Accounting and bookkeeping

Accounting involves forms and records design, policy making, data analysis, report preparation, and report interpretation. A person involved with or responsible for these functions may be referred to as an accountant. Bookkeeping is the recording phase of the accounting process. The person who records the information in the accounting records may be referred to as a bookkeeper. That term goes back to the time when formal accounting records were in the form of books — pages bound together. While this still is sometimes the case, modern practice favors the use of loose-leaf records and cards and, in some instances, computers. When the language catches up with practice, the designation "record keeper" will replace "bookkeeper." Sometimes the accountant also serves as the bookkeeper — an experience that may be of great value to him.

Accounting elements

If complete accounting records are to be maintained, all transactions and events that affect the basic accounting elements must be recorded. The basic accounting elements are *assets*, *liabilities*, and *owner's equity*.

Assets. Properties of value that are owned by a business are called assets. Properties such as money, accounts receivable, merchandise, furniture, fixtures, machinery, buildings, and land are common examples of business assets. *Accounts receivable* are unwritten promises by customers to pay at a later date for goods sold to them or for services rendered.

It is possible to conduct a business or a professional practice with very few assets. A dentist, for example, may have relatively few assets, such as money, instruments, laboratory equipment, and office equipment. But in many cases, a variety of assets is necessary. A merchant must have merchandise to sell and store equipment on which to display the merchandise, in addition to other assets. A manufacturer must have materials, tools, and various sorts of machinery, in addition to other assets.

Liabilities. An obligation of a business to pay a debt is a business liability. The most common liabilities are accounts payable and notes payable. *Accounts payable* are unwritten promises to pay creditors for property (such as merchandise, supplies, and equipment) purchased on credit or for services rendered. *Notes payable* are formal written promises to pay creditors or lenders specified sums of money at some future time. A business also may have one or more types of *taxes payable*.

Owner's Equity. The amount by which the business assets exceed the business liabilities is termed the owner's equity in the business. The word "equity" used in this sense means "interest in" or "claim of." It would be quite reasonable to call liabilities "creditors' equity," but this is not customary. The terms *proprietorship*, *net worth*, or *capital* are sometimes used as synonyms for owner's equity. If there are no business liabilities, the owner's equity in the business is equal to the total amount of the assets of the business.

In visualizing a business that is owned and operated by one person (traditionally called the proprietor), it is essential to realize that a distinction must be made between his *business* assets and liabilities and any *non-*

business assets and liabilities that he may have. The proprietor will certainly have various types of personal property, such as clothing; it is probable that he will have a home, furniture, and a car. He may own a wide variety of other valuable properties quite apart from his business. Likewise, the proprietor may owe money for reasons that do not pertain to his business. Amounts owed to merchants from whom food and clothing have been purchased and amounts owed to doctors and dentists for services received are common examples. Legally there is no distinction between the proprietor's business and nonbusiness assets nor between the business and nonbusiness liabilities; but since it is to be expected that the formal accounting records for the enterprise will relate to the business only, any nonbusiness assets and liabilities should be excluded. While the term "owner's equity" can be used in a very broad sense, its use in accounting is nearly always limited to the meaning: business assets minus business liabilities.

Frequent reference will be made to the owner's acts of investing money or other property in the business, or to his withdrawal of money or other property from the business. All that is involved in either case is that some property is changed from the category of a nonbusiness asset to a business asset or vice versa. It should be apparent that these distinctions are important if the owner is to be able to judge the financial condition and results of the operations of his business apart from his nonbusiness affairs.

The accounting equation

The relationship between the three basic accounting elements can be expressed in the form of a simple equation:

ASSETS = LIABILITIES + OWNER'S EQUITY

When the amounts of any two of these elements are known, the third can always be calculated. For example, Donna Musgrave has business assets on December 31 in the sum of $28,400. Her business debts on that date consist of $800 owed for supplies purchased on account and $1,000 owed to a bank on a note. The owner's equity element of her business may be calculated by subtraction ($28,400 − $1,800 = $26,600). These facts about her business can be expressed in equation form as follows:

ASSETS	= LIABILITIES	+ OWNER'S EQUITY
$28,400	$1,800	$26,600

In order to increase her equity in the business, Ms. Musgrave must either increase the assets without increasing the liabilities, or decrease the liabilities without decreasing the assets. In order to increase the assets and owner's equity without investing more money or other property in the business, she will have to operate the business at a profit.

For example, if one year later the assets amount to $42,300 and the liabilities to $2,100, the status of the business would be as follows:

ASSETS	=	LIABILITIES	+	OWNER'S EQUITY
$42,300		$2,100		$40,200

However, the fact that Ms. Musgrave's equity in the business had increased by $13,600 (from $26,600 to $40,200) does not prove that she had made a profit (often called *net income*) equal to the increase. She might have invested additional money or other property in the business. Suppose, for example, that she invested additional money during the year in the amount of $6,000. In that event the remainder of the increase in her equity ($7,600) would have been due to profit (net income).

Another possibility could be that she had a very profitable year and withdrew assets in an amount less than the amount of profit. For example, her equity might have been increased by $22,000 as a result of profitable operation; and during the year she might have withdrawn a total of $8,400 in cash for personal use. This series of events could account for the $13,600 increase. It is essential that the business records show the extent to which the change in owner's equity is due to the regular operation of the business and the extent to which increases and decreases in owner's equity are due to the owner's acts of investing and withdrawing assets.

Transactions

Any activity of an enterprise which involves the exchange of values is usually referred to as a *transaction*. These values usually are expressed in terms of money. Buying and selling property and services are common transactions. The following typical transactions are analyzed to show that each one represents an exchange of values.

TYPICAL TRANSACTIONS	ANALYSIS OF TRANSACTIONS
(a) Purchased equipment for cash, $950.	Money was exchanged for equipment.
(b) Received cash in payment of professional fees, $250.	Professional service was rendered in exchange for money.
(c) Paid office rent, $200.	Money was exchanged for the right to use property.
(d) Paid an amount owed to a creditor, $575.	Money was given in settlement of a debt that may have resulted from the purchase of property on account or from services rendered by a creditor.
(e) Paid wages in cash, $125.	Money was exchanged for services rendered.
(f) Borrowed $2,500 at a bank giving an 8 percent interest-bearing note due in 30 days.	A liability known as a note payable was incurred in exchange for money.

(g) Purchased office equipment on account, $400.

A liability known as an account payable was incurred in exchange for office equipment.

Effect of transactions on the accounting equation

Each transaction affects one or more of the three basic accounting elements. For example, the purchase of equipment for cash represents both an increase and a decrease in assets. The assets increased because equipment was acquired; the assets decreased because cash was disbursed. If the equipment had been purchased on account, thereby incurring a liability, the transaction would result in an increase in assets (equipment) with a corresponding increase in liabilities (accounts payable). Neither of these transactions has any effect upon the owner's equity element of the equation.

The effect of any transaction on the basic accounting elements may be indicated by addition and subtraction. To illustrate: assume that Stanley Jones, an attorney, decided to go into business for himself. During the first month of this venture (June, 1977), the following transactions relating to his business took place:

An Increase in an Asset Offset by an Increase in Owner's Equity

Transaction (a). Mr. Jones opened a bank account with a deposit of $6,000. This transaction caused his new business to receive the asset cash; and since no business liabilities were involved, the owner's equity element was increased by the same amount. As a result of this transaction, the equation for the business would appear as follows:

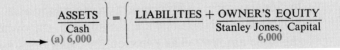

ASSETS	=	LIABILITIES + OWNER'S EQUITY
Cash		Stanley Jones, Capital
(a) 6,000		6,000

An Increase in an Asset Offset by an Increase in a Liability

Transaction (b). Mr. Jones purchased office equipment (desk, chairs, file cabinet, etc.) for $3,500 on 30 days' credit. This transaction caused the asset office equipment to increase by $3,500 and resulted in an equal increase in the liability accounts payable. Updating the foregoing equation by this (b) transaction gives the following result:

ASSETS		=	LIABILITIES	+ OWNER'S EQUITY
Cash +	Office Equipment		Accounts Payable	Stanley Jones, Capital
Bal. 6,000				6,000
(b)	+3,500		+3,500	
Bal. 6,000	3,500		3,500	6,000

An Increase in One Asset Offset by a Decrease in Another Asset

Transaction (c). Mr. Jones purchased office supplies (stationery, carbon paper, pencils, etc.) for cash, $530. This transaction caused a $530 increase in the asset office supplies that exactly offset the $530 decrease in the asset cash. The effect on the equation is as follows:

	ASSETS				LIABILITIES + OWNER'S EQUITY	
	Cash +	Office Equipment +	Office Supplies		Accounts Payable	Stanley Jones, Capital
Bal.	6,000	3,500		=	3,500	6,000
(c)	−530		+530			
Bal.	5,470	3,500	530		3,500	6,000

A Decrease in an Asset Offset by a Decrease in a Liability

Transaction (d). Mr. Jones paid $2,000 on account to the company from which the office equipment was purchased. (See Transaction (b).) This payment caused the asset cash and the liability accounts payable both to decrease $2,000. The effect on the equation is as follows:

	ASSETS				LIABILITIES + OWNER'S EQUITY	
	Cash +	Office Equipment +	Office Supplies		Accounts Payable	Stanley Jones, Capital
Bal.	5,470	3,500	530	=	3,500	6,000
(d)	−2,000				−2,000	
Bal.	3,470	3,500	530		1,500	6,000

An Increase in an Asset Offset by an Increase in Owner's Equity Resulting from Revenue

Transaction (e). Mr. Jones received $1,500 cash from a client for professional services. This transaction caused the asset cash to increase $1,500, and since the liabilities were not affected, the owner's equity increased by the same amount. The effect on the equation is as follows:

	ASSETS				LIABILITIES + OWNER'S EQUITY	
	Cash +	Office Equipment +	Office Supplies		Accounts Payable	Stanley Jones, Capital
Bal.	3,470	3,500	530	=	1,500	6,000
(e)	+1,500					+1,500
Bal.	4,970	3,500	530		1,500	7,500

A Decrease in an Asset Offset by a Decrease in Owner's Equity Resulting from Expense

Transaction (f). Mr. Jones paid $300 for office rent for June. This transaction caused the asset cash to be reduced by $300 with an equal reduction in owner's equity. The effect on the equation is as follows:

ASSETS				LIABILITIES + OWNER'S EQUITY	
	Office	Office		Accounts	Stanley Jones,
Cash +	Equipment +	Supplies		Payable	Capital
Bal. 4,970	3,500	530	=	1,500	7,500
(f) −300					−300
Bal. 4,670	3,500	530		1,500	7,200

Transaction (g). Mr. Jones paid a bill for telephone service, $35. This transaction, like the previous one, caused a decrease in the asset cash with an equal decrease in the owner's equity. The effect on the equation is as follows:

ASSETS				LIABILITIES + OWNER'S EQUITY	
	Office	Office		Accounts	Stanley Jones,
Cash +	Equipment +	Supplies		Payable	Capital
Bal. 4,670	3,500	530	=	1,500	7,200
(g) − 35					− 35
Bal. 4,635	3,500	530		1,500	7,165

The financial statements

A set of accounting records is maintained to fill a variety of needs. Foremost is its use as source data in preparing various reports including those referred to as *financial statements*. The two most important of these are the *income statement* and the *balance sheet*.

The Income Statement. The income statement, sometimes called a *profit and loss statement* or *operating statement*, shows the *net income* (*net profit*) or *net loss* for a specified period of time and how it was calculated. A very simple income statement relating to the business of Stanley Jones for the first month's operation, June, 1977, is shown below. The information it contains was obtained by analysis of the changes in the owner's equity element of the business for the month. This element went from zero to $7,165. Part of this increase, $6,000, was due to the investment of Mr. Jones. The remainder of the increase, $1,165, must have been due to net income, since Mr. Jones had made no withdrawals. Transaction (e) involved revenue of $1,500; transactions (f) and (g) involved expenses of $300 and $35, respectively. Taken together, these three transactions explain the net income of $1,165.

```
                  STANLEY JONES, ATTORNEY
                       Income Statement
                  For the Month of June, 1977

    Professional fees.....................         $1,500

    Expenses:
        Rent expense........................  $300
        Telephone expense...................    35    335

    Net income for month..................           $1,165
```

The Balance Sheet. The balance sheet, sometimes called a *statement of financial condition* or *statement of financial position*, shows the assets, liabilities, and owner's equity of a business at a specified date. A balance sheet for Mr. Jones' business as of June 30, 1977, is shown below. The information it contains was obtained from the accounting equation after the last transaction (g).

STANLEY JONES, ATTORNEY

Balance Sheet

June 30, 1977

Assets			Liabilities		
Cash...................	$4,635		Accounts payable.......	$1,500	
Office supplies.........	530				
Office equipment........	3,500		Owner's Equity		
			Stanley Jones, capital..	7,165	
Total assets...........	$8,665		Total liabilities and owner's equity........	$8,665	

NOTE: In order to keep the illustrations of transaction analysis, the income statement, and the balance sheet as simple as possible at this point, two expenses were ignored; namely, office supplies used and depreciation of office equipment.

Report No. 1-1

A workbook of study assignments is provided for use with this textbook. Each study assignment is referred to as a report. The work involved in completing Report No. 1-1 requires a knowledge of the principles developed in the preceding textbook discussion. Before proceeding with the following discussion, complete Report No. 1-1 in accordance with the instructions given in the study assignments.

THE DOUBLE-ENTRY MECHANISM

The meanings of the terms asset, liability, and owner's equity were explained in the preceding pages. Examples were given to show how each business transaction causes a change in one or more of the three basic accounting elements. The first transaction (a) shown on page 7 involved an increase in an asset with a corresponding increase in owner's equity. In the second transaction (b), an increase in an asset caused an equal increase in a liability. In the third transaction (c), an increase in one asset was offset by a decrease in another. In each of the transactions illustrated, there was this *dual effect*. This is always true. A change (increase or decrease) in any asset, any liability, or in owner's equity is always accompanied by an offsetting change within the basic accounting elements.

The fact that each transaction has two aspects — a dual effect upon the accounting elements — provides the basis for what is called *double-entry bookkeeping*. This phrase describes a recording system that involves the making of a record of each of the two aspects that are involved in every transaction. Double entry does not mean that a transaction is recorded twice; instead, it means that both of the two aspects of each transaction are recorded.

The technique of double entry is described and illustrated in the following pages. This method of recording transactions is not new. Double entry is known to have been practiced for at least 500 years. This long popularity is easily explained since the method has several virtues. It is orderly, fairly simple, and very flexible. There is no transaction that cannot be recorded in a double-entry manner. Double entry promotes accuracy. Its use makes it impossible for certain types of errors to remain undetected for very long. For example, if one aspect of a transaction is properly recorded but the other part is overlooked, it will soon be found that the records are "out of balance." The bookkeeper then knows that something is wrong and can check his work to discover the trouble and can make the needed correction.

The account   It has been explained previously that the assets of a business may consist of a number of items, such as money, accounts receivable, merchandise, equipment, buildings, and land. The liabilities may consist of one or more items, such as accounts payable and notes payable. A separate record should be kept of each asset and of each liability. Later it will be shown that a separate record should also be kept of the increases and decreases in owner's equity. The form or record kept for each item is known as an *account*. There are many types of account forms in general use. They may be ruled on sheets of paper and bound in book form or kept in a loose-leaf binder, or they may be ruled on cards and kept in a file of some sort. An illustration is shown on page 12 of a *standard form of account* that is widely used.

ACCOUNT _____   ACCOUNT NO. _____

DATE	ITEM	POST. REF.	DEBIT	DATE	ITEM	POST. REF.	CREDIT

Standard Form of Account

This account form is designed to facilitate the recording of the essential information regarding each transaction that affects the account. Before any entries are recorded in an account, the title and number of the account should be written on the horizontal line at the top of the form. Each account should be given an appropriate title that will indicate whether it is an asset, a liability, or an owner's equity account. The standard account form is divided into two equal parts or sections which are ruled identically to facilitate recording increases and decreases. The left side is called the debit side, while the right side is called the credit side. The columnar arrangement and headings of the columns on both sides are the same except that the amount column on the left is headed "Debit" while that on the right is headed "Credit." The Date columns are used for recording the dates of transactions. The Item columns may be used for writing a brief description of a transaction when deemed necessary. The Posting Reference columns will be discussed later. The Debit and Credit columns are used for recording the amounts of transactions.

The three major parts of the standard account form are **(1)** the title (and, usually, the account number), **(2)** the debit side, and **(3)** the credit side. To determine the balance of an account at any time, it is necessary only to total the amounts in the Debit and Credit columns, and calculate the difference between the two totals. To save time, a "T" form of account is commonly used for instructional purposes. It consists of a two-line drawing resembling the capital letter T and is sometimes referred to as a skeleton form of account.

TITLE	
Debit side	Credit side

"T" Account Form

Debits and credits

To debit an account means to record an amount on the left or debit side of the account. To credit an account means to record an amount on the right or credit side of the account. The abbreviation for debit is Dr. and for credit Cr. (based on the Latin terms *debere* and *credere*). Sometimes the word *charge* is used as a substitute for debit. Increases in assets are recorded on the left side of the accounts; increases in liabilities and in owner's equity are recorded on the right side of the accounts. Decreases in assets are recorded on the right side of the accounts; decreases in liabilities and in owner's equity are recorded on the left side of the accounts. Recording increases and decreases in the accounts in this manner will reflect the basic equality of assets to liabilities plus owner's equity; at the same time it will maintain equality between the total amounts debited to all accounts and the total amounts credited to all accounts. These basic relationships may be illustrated in the following manner:

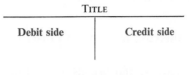

ASSETS	=	LIABILITIES + OWNER'S EQUITY
DEBITS	=	**CREDITS**

ALL ASSET ACCOUNTS		ALL LIABILITY ACCOUNTS	
Debit to record increases (+)	Credit to record decreases (−)	Debit to record decreases (−)	Credit to record increases (+)

ALL OWNER'S EQUITY ACCOUNTS	
Debit to record decreases (−)	Credit to record increases (+)

Use of asset, liability, and owner's equity accounts

To illustrate the application of the double-entry process, the transactions discussed on pages 7–9 will be analyzed and their effect on the accounting elements will be indicated by showing the proper entries in "T" accounts. As before, the transactions are identified by letters; dates are omitted intentionally.

An Increase in an Asset Offset by an Increase in Owner's Equity

Transaction (a). Stanley Jones, an attorney, started a business of his own and invested $6,000 in cash.

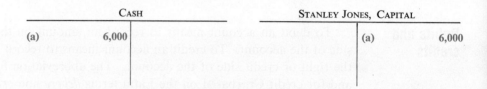

CASH		STANLEY JONES, CAPITAL	
(a)	6,000	(a)	6,000

Analysis: As a result of this transaction the business acquired an asset, cash. The amount of money invested by Mr. Jones represents his equity in the business; thus the amount of the asset cash is equal to the owner's equity in the business. Separate accounts are kept for the asset cash and for the owner. To record the transaction properly, the cash account was debited and Stanley Jones' capital account was credited for $6,000.

An Increase in an Asset Offset by an Increase in a Liability

Transaction (b). Purchased office equipment (desk, chairs, file cabinet, etc.) for $3,500 on 30 days' credit.

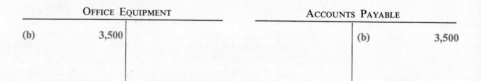

OFFICE EQUIPMENT		ACCOUNTS PAYABLE	
(b)	3,500	(b)	3,500

Analysis: As a result of this transaction the business acquired a new asset, office equipment. The debt incurred as a result of purchasing the office equipment on 30 days' credit is a liability, accounts payable. Separate accounts are kept for office equipment and for accounts payable. The purchase of office equipment caused an increase in the assets of the business. Therefore, the asset account Office Equipment was debited for $3,500. The purchase also caused an increase in a liability. Therefore, the liability account Accounts Payable was credited for $3,500.

An Increase in One Asset Offset by a Decrease in Another Asset

Transaction (c). Purchased office supplies (stationery, carbon paper, pencils, etc.) for cash, $530.

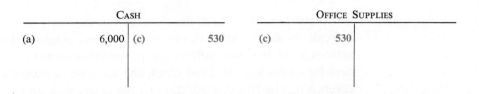

	CASH			OFFICE SUPPLIES	
(a)	6,000	(c) 530	(c)	530	

Analysis: As a result of this transaction the business acquired a new asset, office supplies. However, the addition of this asset was offset by a decrease in the asset cash. To record the transaction properly, Office Supplies was debited and Cash was credited for $530. (It will be noted that this is the second entry in the cash account; the account was previously debited for $6,000 when Transaction (a) was recorded.)

It is proper to record office supplies as an asset at time of purchase even though they will become an expense when consumed. (The procedure in accounting for supplies consumed will be discussed later.)

A Decrease in an Asset Offset by a Decrease in a Liability

Transaction (d). Paid $2,000 "on account" to the company from which the office equipment was purchased. (See Transaction (b).)

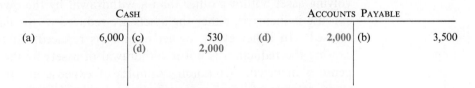

	CASH			ACCOUNTS PAYABLE	
(a)	6,000	(c) 530	(d)	2,000	(b) 3,500
		(d) 2,000			

Analysis: This transaction resulted in a decrease in the liability accounts payable with a corresponding decrease in the asset cash; hence, it was recorded by debiting Accounts Payable and by crediting Cash for $2,000. (It will be noted that this is the second entry in the accounts payable account and the third entry in the cash account.)

Revenue and expense
The owner's equity element of a business or professional enterprise may be increased in two ways as follows:

(a) The owner may invest additional money or other property in the enterprise. Such investments result in an increase both in the assets of the enterprise and in the owner's equity, but they do not further enrich the owner; he merely has more property invested in the enterprise and less property outside of the enterprise.

(b) Revenue may be derived from sales of goods or services, or from other sources.

As used in accounting, the term *revenue* in nearly all cases refers to an increase in the owner's equity in a business resulting from any transactions involving asset inflows except the investment of assets in the business by its owner. In most cases, the increase in owner's equity due to revenue results from an addition to the assets without any change in the liabilities. Often it is cash that is increased. However, an increase in cash and other assets can occur in connection with several types of transactions that do not involve revenue. For this reason, revenue is defined in terms of the change in owner's equity rather than the change in assets. Any transaction that causes owner's equity to increase, except investments in the business by its owner, involves revenue.

The owner's equity element of a business or professional enterprise may be decreased in two ways as follows:

(a) The owner may withdraw assets (cash or other property) from the business enterprise.

(b) Expenses may be incurred in operating the enterprise.

As used in accounting, the term *expense* in nearly all cases means a decrease in the owner's equity in a business caused by any transactions involving asset outflows other than a withdrawal by the owner. When an expense is incurred, either the assets are reduced or the liabilities are increased. In either event, owner's equity is reduced. If the transaction causing the reduction is not a withdrawal of assets by the owner, an expense is incurred. Common examples of expense are rent of office or store, salaries of employees, telephone service, supplies consumed, and many types of taxes.

If, during a specified period of time, the total increases in owner's equity resulting from revenue exceed the total decreases resulting from expenses, it may be said that the excess represents the *net income* or net profit for the period. On the other hand, if the expenses of the period exceed the revenue, such excess represents a *net loss* for the period. The time interval used in the measurement of net income or net loss can be chosen by the owner. It may be a month, a quarter (three months), a year, or some other period of time. If the accounting period is a year, it is usually referred to as a *fiscal year*. The fiscal year frequently coincides with the *calendar year*.

Transactions involving revenue and expense always cause a change in the owner's equity element of an enterprise. Such changes could be recorded by debiting the owner's equity account for expenses and crediting it for revenue. If this practice were followed, however, the credit side of the owner's equity account would contain a mixture of increases due to revenue and to the investment of assets in the business by the owner, while the debit side would contain a mixture of decreases due to expenses and to the withdrawal of assets from the business by the owner. In order to calculate the net income or the net loss for each accounting period, a careful analysis of the owner's equity account would be required. It is, therefore, better practice to record revenue and expenses in separate accounts. These are called *temporary* owner's equity accounts because it is customary to close them at the end of each accounting period by transferring their balances to a *summary* account. The balance of this summary account then represents the net income or net loss for the period. The summary account is also a temporary account which is closed by transferring its balance to the owner's equity account.

A separate account should be kept for each type of revenue and for each type of expense. When a transaction produces revenue, the amount of the revenue should be credited to an appropriate revenue account. When a transaction involves expense, the amount of the expense should be debited to an appropriate expense account. The relationship of these temporary accounts to the owner's equity account and the application of the debit and credit theory to the accounts are indicated in the following diagram:

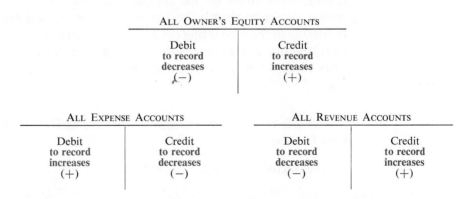

It is important to recognize that the credit side of each revenue account is serving temporarily as a part of the credit side of the owner's equity account. Increases in owner's equity are recorded as credits. Thus, increases in owner's equity resulting from revenue should be credited to revenue accounts. The debit side of each expense account is serving temporarily as a part of the debit side of the owner's equity account. Decreases in owner's equity are recorded as debits. Thus, decreases in owner's equity resulting from expense should be debited to expense accounts.

Use of revenue and expense accounts

To illustrate the application of the double-entry process in recording transactions that affect revenue and expense accounts, the transactions that follow will be analyzed and their effect on the accounting elements will be indicated by showing the proper entries in "T" accounts. These transactions represent a continuation of the transactions completed by Stanley Jones, an attorney, in the conduct of his business. (See pages 14 and 15 for Transactions (a) to (d).)

An Increase in an Asset Offset by an Increase in Owner's Equity Resulting from Revenue

Transaction (e). Received $1,500 in cash from a client for professional services rendered.

CASH					PROFESSIONAL FEES	
(a)	6,000	(c)	530		(e)	1,500
(e)	1,500	(d)	2,000			

Analysis: This transaction resulted in an increase in the asset cash with a corresponding increase in owner's equity because of revenue from professional fees. To record the transaction properly, Cash was debited and an appropriate account for the revenue was credited for $1,500. Accounts should always be given a descriptive title that will aid in classifying them in relation to the accounting elements. In this case the revenue account was given the title Professional Fees. (It will be noted that this is the fourth entry in the cash account and the first entry in the account Professional Fees.)

A Decrease in an Asset Offset by a Decrease in Owner's Equity Resulting from Expense

Transaction (f). Paid $300 for office rent for one month.

CASH					RENT EXPENSE	
(a)	6,000	(c)	530	(f)	300	
(e)	1,500	(d)	2,000			
		(f)	300			

Analysis: This transaction resulted in a decrease in the asset cash with a corresponding decrease in owner's equity because of expense. To record the transaction properly, Rent Expense was debited and Cash was credited for $300. (This is the first entry in the rent expense account and the fifth entry in the cash account.)

Transaction (g). Paid bill for telephone service, $35.

	CASH			TELEPHONE EXPENSE	
(a)	6,000	(c)	530	(g)	35
(e)	1,500	(d)	2,000		
		(f)	300		
		(g)	35		

Analysis: This transaction is identical with the previous one except that telephone expense rather than rent expense was the reason for the decrease in owner's equity. To record the transaction properly, Telephone Expense was debited and Cash was credited for $35.

The trial balance

It is a fundamental principle of double-entry bookkeeping that the sum of the assets is always equal to the sum of the liabilities and owner's equity. In order to maintain this equality in recording transactions, the sum of the debit entries must always be equal to the sum of the credit entries. To determine whether this equality has been maintained, it is customary to take a trial balance periodically. A *trial balance* is a list of all of the accounts showing the title and balance of each account. The balance of any account is the amount of difference between the total debits and the total credits to the account. Preliminary to taking a trial balance, the debit and credit amounts in each account should be totaled. This is called *footing* the amount columns. If there is only one item entered in a column, no footing is necessary. To find the balance of an account it is necessary only to determine the difference between the footings by subtraction. Since asset and expense accounts are debited for increases, these accounts normally have *debit balances*. Since liability, owner's equity, and revenue accounts are credited to record increases, these accounts normally have *credit balances*. The balance of an account should be entered on the side of the account that has the larger total. The footings and balances of accounts should be written in small figures just below the last entry. A pencil is generally used for this purpose. If the footings of an account are equal in amount, the account is said to be *in balance*.

The accounts of Stanley Jones are reproduced on page 20. To show the relationship to the fundamental accounting equation, the accounts are arranged in three columns under the headings of Assets, Liabilities, and Owner's Equity. It will be noted that the cash account has been footed and the balance inserted on the left side. The two debits totaled $7,500; the four credits totaled $2,865. Thus, the debit balance was $4,635. The footings and the balance are printed in italics. It was not necessary to foot any of the other accounts because none of them contained more than one entry on either side. The balance of the accounts payable account is shown on the credit side in italics. It was not necessary to enter the balances of the other accounts because there were entries on only one side of those accounts.

ASSETS	=	LIABILITIES	+	OWNER'S EQUITY

CASH

(a)	6,000	(c)	530
(e)	1,500	(d)	2,000
4,635	*7,500*	(f)	300
		(g)	35
			2,865

ACCOUNTS PAYABLE

(d)	2,000	(b)	3,500
			1,500

STANLEY JONES, CAPITAL

(a)	6,000

PROFESSIONAL FEES

(e)	1,500

OFFICE SUPPLIES

(c)	530

OFFICE EQUIPMENT

(b)	3,500

RENT EXPENSE

(f)	300

TELEPHONE EXPENSE

(g)	35

A trial balance of Stanley Jones' accounts is shown below. The trial balance was taken on June 30, 1977; therefore, this date is shown in the third line of the heading. The trial balance reveals that the debit and credit totals are equal in amount. This is proof that in recording Transactions (a) to (g) inclusive the total of the debits was equal to the total of the credits.

Stanley Jones, Attorney
Trial Balance
June 30, 1977

Account	Dr. Balance	Cr. Balance
Cash	4 635 00	
Office Supplies	530 00	
Office Equipment	3 500 00	
Accounts Payable		1 500 00
Stanley Jones, Capital		6 000 00
Professional Fees		1 500 00
Rent Expense	300 00	
Telephone Expense	35 00	
	9 000 00	9 000 00

Stanley Jones' Trial Balance

A trial balance is not a formal statement or report. Normally, it is never seen by anyone except the accountant or bookkeeper. It is used to aid in preparing the income statement and the balance sheet. If the trial balance on the preceding page is studied in conjunction with the income statement and balance sheet shown on pages 9 and 10, it will be seen that those statements could have been prepared quite easily from the information that this trial balance provides.

**Report
No. 1-2**

Refer to the study assignments and complete Report No. 1-2 in accordance with the instructions given therein. The work involved in completing the assignment requires a knowledge of the principles developed in the preceding discussion. Any difficulty experienced in completing the report will indicate a lack of understanding of these principles. In such event further study should be helpful. After completing the report, you may continue with the textbook discussion in Chapter 2 until the next report is required.

Chapter 2

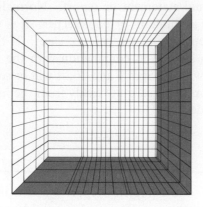

ACCOUNTING PROCEDURE

The principles of double-entry bookkeeping were explained and illustrated in the preceding chapter. To avoid distraction from the fundamentals, the mechanics of collecting and classifying information about business transactions were ignored. In actual practice the first record of a transaction (sometimes called the "source document") is made in the form of a business paper, such as a check stub, receipt, cash register tape, sales ticket, or purchase invoice. The information supplied by source documents is an aid in analyzing transactions to determine their effect upon the accounts.

JOURNALIZING TRANSACTIONS

The first formal double-entry record of a transaction is usually made in a record called a *journal* (frequently in book form). The act of recording transactions in a journal is called *journalizing*. It is necessary to analyze each transaction before it can be journalized properly. The purpose of the journal entries is to provide a chronological record of all transactions completed showing the date of each transaction, titles of accounts to be debited and credited, and amounts of the debits and credits. The journal then provides all the information needed to record the debits and credits in the proper accounts. The flow of data concerning transactions can be illustrated in the following manner:

Transactions are evidenced
by various
SOURCE DOCUMENTS———→ The source documents provide   the   information
needed   to   record   the
transactions in a
JOURNAL————————————→ The journal provides the
information needed to re-
cord the debits and credits
in the accounts which
collectively comprise a
LEDGER

**Source
documents**

The term source document covers a wide variety of forms and papers. Almost any document that provides information about a business transaction can be called a source document.

SOURCE DOCUMENTS

Examples:	Provide information about:
(a) Check stubs or carbon copies of checks	Cash disbursements
(b) Receipt stubs, or carbon copies of receipts, cash register tapes, or memos of cash register totals	Cash receipts
(c) Copies of sales tickets or sales invoices issued to customers or clients	Sales of goods or services
(d) Purchase invoices received from vendors	Purchases of goods or services

The journal

While the original record of a transaction usually is a source document as explained above, the first formal double-entry record of a transaction is made in a journal. For this reason a journal is commonly referred to as a *book of original entry*. The ruling of the pages of a journal varies with the type and size of an enterprise and the nature of its operations. The simplest form of journal is a *two-column journal*. A standard form of such a journal is illustrated on page 24. It is referred to as a two-column journal because it has only two amount columns, one for debit amounts and one for credit amounts. In the illustration the columns have been numbered as a means of identification in connection with the following discussion.

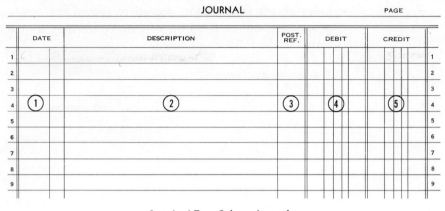

Standard Two-Column Journal

Column No. 1 is a date column. The year should be written in small figures at the top of the column immediately below the column heading and need only be repeated at the top of each new page unless an entry for a new year is made farther down on the page. The date column is a double column, the perpendicular single rule being used to separate the month from the day. Thus in writing June 20, the name of the month should be written to the left of the single line and the number designating the day of the month should be written to the right of this line. The name of the month need only be shown for the first entry on a page unless an entry for a new month is made farther down on the page.

Column No. 2 is generally referred to as a description or an explanation column. It is used to record the titles of the accounts affected by each transaction, together with a description of the transaction. Two or more accounts are affected by each transaction, and the titles of all accounts affected must be recorded. Normally the titles of the accounts debited are written first and then the titles of the accounts credited. A separate line should be used for each account title. The titles of the accounts to be debited are generally written at the extreme left of the column, while the titles of the accounts to be credited are usually indented about one-half inch (about 1.3 centimeters). The description should be written immediately following the credit entry, and usually is indented an additional one-half inch. Reference to the journal reproduced on pages 31 and 32 will help to visualize the arrangement of the copy in the Description column. An orderly arrangement is desirable.

Column No. 3 is a posting reference column — sometimes referred to as a folio column. No entries are made in this column at the time of journalizing the transactions; such entries are made only at the time of posting (which is the process of entering the debits and credits in the proper accounts in the ledger). This procedure will be explained in detail later in this chapter.

Column No. 4 is an amount column in which the amount that is to be debited to any account should be written on the same line on which the title of that account appears. In other words, the name of the account to be debited should be written in the Description column and the amount of the debit entry should be written on the same line in the Debit column.

Column No. 5 is an amount column in which the amount that is to be credited to any account should be written on the same line on which the title of that account appears. In other words, the name of the account to be credited should be written in the Description column and the amount of the credit entry should be written on the same line in the Credit column.

Journalizing

Journalizing involves recording the significant information concerning each transaction either **(1)** at the time the transaction occurs or **(2)** subsequently, but in the chronological order in which it and the other transactions occurred. For every transaction the entry should record the date, the title of each account affected, the amounts, and a brief description. The only effect a transaction can have on any account is either to increase or to decrease the balance of the account. Before a transaction can be recorded properly, therefore, it must be analyzed in order to determine:

> **(a)** Which accounts are affected by the transaction.
> **(b)** What effect the transaction has upon each of the accounts involved; that is, whether the balance of each affected account is increased or decreased.

The chart of accounts

In analyzing a transaction preparatory to journalizing it, the accountant or bookkeeper must know which accounts are being kept. When an accounting system is being established for a new business, the first step is to decide which accounts are required. The accounts used will depend upon the information needed or desired. Ordinarily it will be found desirable to keep a separate account for each type of asset and each type of liability, since it is certain that information will be desired in regard to what is owned and what is owed. A permanent owner's equity or capital account should be kept in order that information may be available as to the owner's interest or equity in the business. Furthermore, it is advisable to keep separate accounts for each type of revenue and each kind of expense. The revenue and expense accounts are the temporary accounts that are used in recording increases and decreases in owner's equity from asset movements apart from changes caused by the owner's investments and withdrawals. The specific accounts to be kept for recording the increases and the decreases in owner's equity depend upon the nature and the sources of the revenue and the nature of the expenses incurred in earning the revenue.

A professional person or an individual engaged in operating a small enterprise may need to keep relatively few accounts. On the other hand, a large manufacturing enterprise, a public utility, or any large business may need to keep a great many accounts in order that the information required or desired may be available. Regardless of the number of accounts kept, they can be segregated into the three major classes and should be grouped according to these classes in the ledger. The usual custom is to place the asset accounts first, the liability accounts second, and the owner's equity accounts, including the revenue and the expense accounts, last. It is common practice to prepare a list of the accounts that are to be kept. This list, often in the form of an outline, is called a *chart of accounts*. It has become a general practice to give each account a number and to keep the accounts in numerical order. The numbering usually follows a consistent pattern and becomes a *code*. For example, asset accounts may be assigned numbers that always start with "1," liability accounts with "2," owner's equity accounts with "3," revenue accounts with "4," and expense accounts with "5."

To illustrate: Suppose that on December 1, 1977, L. A. Eason enters the employment agency business under the name of The Eason Employment Agency. He decides to keep his accounts on the calendar-year basis; therefore, his first accounting period will be for one month only, that is, the month of December. It is decided that a two-column journal and a ledger with the standard form of account will be used. Mr. Eason realizes that he will not need many accounts at present because the business is new. He also realizes that additional accounts may be added as the need arises. Following is a chart of the accounts to be kept at the start:

THE EASON EMPLOYMENT AGENCY

CHART OF ACCOUNTS

*Assets**
111 Cash
112 Office Supplies
121 Office Equipment

Liabilities
211 Accounts Payable

Owner's Equity
311 L. A. Eason, Capital
312 L. A. Eason, Drawing

Revenue
411 Placement Fees

Expenses
511 Rent Expense
512 Salary Expense
513 Traveling Expense
514 Telephone Expense
515 Office Supplies Expense
516 Miscellaneous Expense

Words in italics represent headings and not account titles.

**Journalizing
procedure
illustrated**

To illustrate journalizing procedure, the transactions completed by The Eason Employment Agency through December 31, 1977, will be journalized. A *narrative* of the transactions follows. It provides all of the information that is needed in journalizing the transactions. Some of the transactions are analyzed to explain their effect upon the accounts, with the journal entry immediately following the explanation of the entry. The journal of The Eason Employment Agency with all of the entries recorded is reproduced on pages 31 and 32.

THE EASON EMPLOYMENT AGENCY

NARRATIVE OF TRANSACTIONS

Thursday, December 1, 1977

Mr. Eason invested $3,000 cash in a business enterprise to be known as The Eason Employment Agency.

As a result of this transaction, the business acquired the asset cash in the amount of $3,000. Since neither a decrease in any other asset nor an increase in any liability was involved, the transaction caused an increase of $3,000 in owner's equity. Accordingly, the entry to record the transaction is a debit to Cash and a credit to L. A. Eason, Capital, for $3,000.

JOURNAL   PAGE *1*

	DATE	DESCRIPTION	POST. REF.	DEBIT	CREDIT	
1	*1977 Dec. 1*	*Cash*		*300000*		1
2		*L. A. Eason, Capital*			*300000*	2
3		*Original investment*				3
4		*in employment agency.*				4

Note that the following steps were involved:

(a) Since this was the first entry on the journal page, the year was written at the top of the Date column.

(b) The month and day were written on the first line in the Date column.

(c) The title of the account to be debited, Cash, was written on the first line at the extreme left of the Description column. The amount of the debit, $3,000, was written on the same line in the Debit column.

(d) The title of the account to be credited, L. A. Eason, Capital, was written on the second line indented one-half inch from the left side of the Description column. The amount of the credit, $3,000, was written on the same line in the Credit column.

(e) The explanation of the entry was started on the next line indented an additional one-half inch. The second line of the explanation was also indented the same distance as the first.

Friday, December 2

Paid office rent for December, $350.

> This transaction resulted in a decrease in owner's equity because of expense, with a corresponding decrease in the asset cash. The transaction is recorded by debiting Rent Expense and by crediting Cash for $350.

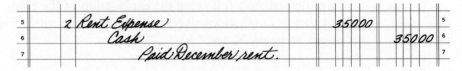

> Note: Mr. Eason ordered several pieces of office equipment. Since the dealer did not have in stock what Mr. Eason wanted, the articles were ordered from the factory. Delivery is not expected until the latter part of the month. Pending arrival of the equipment, the dealer loaned Mr. Eason some used office equipment. No entry is required until the new equipment is received.

Monday, December 5

Purchased office supplies from the Adams Supply Co. on account, $261.41.

> In this transaction the business acquired a new asset which represented an increase in the total assets. A liability was also incurred because of the purchase on account. The transaction is recorded by debiting Office Supplies and by crediting Accounts Payable for $261.41. As these supplies are consumed, the amount will become an expense of the business.

Tuesday, December 6

Paid the Consolidated Telephone Co. $32.50 covering the cost of installing a telephone in the office, together with the first month's service charges payable in advance.

> This transaction caused a decrease in owner's equity because of expense and a corresponding decrease in the asset cash. The transaction is recorded by debiting Telephone Expense and by crediting Cash for $32.50.

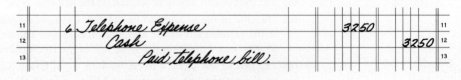

Wednesday, December 7

Paid $8 for a subscription to a trade journal.

> This transaction resulted in a decrease in owner's equity due to expense and a corresponding decrease in the asset cash. The transaction is recorded by debiting Miscellaneous Expense and by crediting Cash for $8.

14	7 Miscellaneous Expense	800		14
15	Cash		800	15
16	Trade journal sub.			16

Thursday, December 8

Received $200 from James Paynter for placement services rendered.

This transaction resulted in an increase in the asset cash with a corresponding increase in owner's equity because of revenue from placement fees. The transaction is recorded by debiting Cash and by crediting Placement Fees for $200. In keeping his accounts, Mr. Eason follows the practice of not recording revenue until it is received in cash. This practice is common to professional and personal service enterprises.

17	8 Cash	200 00		17
18	Placement Fees (OE)		200 00	18
19	James Paynter.			19

Friday, December 9

Paid the World Travel Service $145.30 for an airplane ticket to be used the next week for an employment agency convention trip.

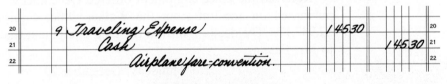

20	9 Traveling Expense	145 30		20
21	Cash		145 30	21
22	Airplane fare—convention.			22

Friday, December 16

Paid Carol Hogan $225 covering her salary for the first half of the month.

Miss Hogan is employed by Mr. Eason as his secretary and bookkeeper at a salary of $450 a month. The transaction resulted in a decrease in owner's equity because of salary expense with a corresponding decrease in the asset cash. The transaction is recorded by debiting Salary Expense and by crediting Cash for $225. (The matter of payroll taxes is purposely ignored at this point. These taxes will be discussed in detail in Chapter 4.)

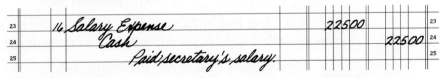

23	16 Salary Expense	225 00		23
24	Cash		225 00	24
25	Paid secretary's salary.			25

Note: The Posting Reference column has been left blank in the eight preceding journal entry illustrations. This is because the column is not used until the amounts are posted to the accounts in the ledger, a process to be described starting on page 33. Account numbers are shown in the Posting Reference column of the journal illustrated on pages 31 and 32, since the illustration shows how the journal appears *after* the posting has been completed.

The journal entries for the following transactions (as well as for those to this point) are illustrated on pages 31 and 32.

Monday, December 19

Received $500 from Timothy Willis for placement services rendered.

Wednesday, December 21

Mr. Eason withdrew $600 for personal use.

Amounts of cash withdrawn for personal use by the owner of a business enterprise represent a decrease in owner's equity. Although amounts withdrawn might be recorded as debits to the owner's capital account, it is better practice to record withdrawals in a separate account. Doing it in this way makes it a little easier to summarize the decreases in owner's equity caused by the owner's withdrawals. This transaction is recorded in the journal by debiting L. A. Eason, Drawing, and by crediting Cash for $600.

Friday, December 23

Received $650 from Susan Taylor for services rendered.

Tuesday, December 27

Paid $50 membership dues in the American Association of Employment Agencies.

Wednesday, December 28

Received the office equipment ordered December 2. These items were purchased on account from the Walker Office Equipment Co. Cost: $2,948.17. The dealer removed the used equipment that had been loaned to Mr. Eason.

Thursday, December 29

Paid the Adams Supply Co. $261.41 for the office supplies purchased on December 5.

This transaction caused a decrease in the liability accounts payable with a corresponding decrease in the asset cash. The transaction was recorded by debiting Accounts Payable and by crediting Cash for $261.41.

Received $500 from Bradford Davis for placement services rendered.

Friday, December 30

Paid Carol Hogan $225 covering her salary for the second half of the month. (Paid this day since it is the last working day of the month.)

Office supplies used during the month, $45.

By referring to the transaction of December 5 it will be noted that office supplies amounting to $261.41 were purchased and were recorded as an asset. By taking an inventory, counting the supplies in stock at the end of the month, Mr. Eason was able to determine that the cost of supplies used during the month amounted to $45. The expenses for the month of December would not be reflected properly in the accounts if the supplies used during the month were not taken into consideration. Therefore, the cost of supplies used was recorded by debiting the expense account, Office Supplies Expense, and by crediting the asset account, Office Supplies, for $45.

JOURNAL   PAGE *1*

	DATE		DESCRIPTION	POST. REF.	DEBIT	CREDIT	
1	1977 Dec.	1	Cash	111	3000 00		1
2			L. A. Eason, Capital	311		3000 00	2
3			Original investment				3
4			in employment agency.				4
5		2	Rent Expense	511	350 00		5
6			Cash	111		350 00	6
7			Paid December rent.				7
8		5	Office Supplies	112	261 41		8
9			Accounts Payable	211		261 41	9
10			Adams Supply Co.				10
11		6	Telephone Expense	514	32 50		11
12			Cash	111		32 50	12
13			Paid telephone bill.				13
14		7	Miscellaneous Expense	516	8 00		14
15			Cash	111		8 00	15
16			Trade journal sub.				16
17		8	Cash	111	200 00		17
18			Placement Fees	411		200 00	18
19			James Paynter.				19
20		9	Traveling Expense	513	145 30		20
21			Cash	111		145 30	21
22			Airplane fare-convention.				22
23		16	Salary Expense	512	225 00		23
24			Cash	111		225 00	24
25			Paid secretary's salary.				25
26		19	Cash	111	500 00		26
27			Placement Fees	411		500 00	27
28			Timothy Willis.				28
29		21	L. A. Eason, Drawing	312	600 00		29
30			Cash	111		600 00	30
31			Withdrawn for personal use.				31
32		23	Cash	111	650 00		32
33			Placement Fees	411		650 00	33
34			Susan Taylor.				34
35		27	Miscellaneous Expense	516	50 00		35
36			Cash	111		50 00	36
37			A. A. E. A. dues.				37
38		28	Office Equipment	121	2948 17		38
39			Accounts Payable	211		2948 17	39
40			Walker Office Equip. Co.				40
41					8970 38	8970 38	41

The Eason Employment Agency Journal

(*continued on next page*)

JOURNAL   PAGE 2

DATE	DESCRIPTION	POST. REF.	DEBIT	CREDIT	
1977 Dec. 29	Accounts Payable	211	26141		1
	Cash	111		26141	2
	Adams Supply Co.				3
29	Cash	111	50000		4
	Placement Fees	411		50000	5
	Bradford Davis				6
30	Salary Expense	512	22500		7
	Cash	111		22500	8
	Paid secretary's salary				9
30	Office Supplies Expense	515	4500		10
	Office Supplies	112		4500	11
	Cost of supplies used				12
	during December				13
			103141	103141	14

The Eason Employment Agency Journal (*concluded*)

Note: Some bookkeepers leave a blank line after the explanation of each entry. This practice is acceptable though not recommended.

Proving the journal

Because a double entry is made for each transaction, the equality of debit and credit entries on each page of the journal may be proved merely by totaling the amount columns. The total of each column is usually entered as a footing immediately under the last entry. When a page of the journal is filled, the footings may be entered just under the last single horizontal ruled line at the bottom of the page as shown in the illustration on page 31. When the page is not filled, the footings should be entered immediately under the last entry as shown in the illustration above.

Report No. 2-1

Refer to the study assignments and complete Report No. 2-1. To complete this assignment correctly, the principles developed in the preceding discussion must be understood. Review the text assignment if necessary. After completing the report, continue with the following textbook discussion until the next report is required.

POSTING TO THE LEDGER; THE TRIAL BALANCE

The purpose of a journal is to provide a chronological record of financial transactions expressed as debits and credits to accounts. These accounts are kept to supply desired information. Collectively the accounts are described as the *general ledger* or, often, simply as "the ledger." (Frequently, so-called "subsidiary" ledgers are also used. These will be explained and illustrated in Chapter 8.) The account forms may be on sheets of paper or on cards. When on sheets of paper, the sheets may be bound in book form or they may be kept in a loose-leaf binder. Usually a separate page or card is used for each account. The accounts should be classified properly in the ledger; that is, the asset accounts should be grouped together, the liability accounts together, and the owner's equity accounts together. Proper grouping of the accounts in the ledger is an aid in preparing the various reports desired by the owner. Mr. Eason decided to keep all of the accounts for The Eason Employment Agency in a loose-leaf ledger. The numbers shown in the agency's chart of accounts on page 26 were used as a guide in arranging the accounts in the ledger. The ledger of The Eason Employment Agency is reproduced on pages 35–37. Note that the accounts are in numerical order.

Since Mr. Eason makes few purchases on account, he does not keep a separate account for each creditor. When invoices are received for items purchased on account, the invoices are checked and recorded in the journal by debiting the proper accounts and by crediting Accounts Payable. The credit balance of Accounts Payable indicates the total amount owed to creditors. After each invoice is recorded, it is filed in an unpaid invoice file, where it remains until it is paid in full. When an invoice is paid in full, it is removed from the unpaid invoice file and is then filed under the name of the creditor for future reference. The balance of the accounts payable account may be proved at any time by determining the total of the unpaid amounts of the invoices.

Posting

The process of transcribing (often called "entering") information in the ledger from the journal is known as *posting*. All amounts entered in the journal should be posted to the accounts kept in the ledger in order to summarize the results. Such posting may be done daily or at frequent intervals. The ledger is not a reliable source of information until all of the transactions recorded in the journal have been posted.

Since the accounts provide the information needed in preparing financial statements, a posting procedure that insures accuracy in maintaining the accounts must necessarily be followed. Posting from the journal to the ledger involves recording the following information in the accounts:

(a) The date of each transaction.

(b) The amount of each transaction.

(c) The page of the journal from which each transaction is posted.

As each amount in the journal is posted to the proper account in the ledger, the number of that account should be entered in the Posting Reference column in the journal so as to provide a cross-reference between the journal and the ledger. The first entry to be posted from the journal (a segment of which is reproduced below) required a debit to Cash of $3,000. This was accomplished by entering the year, "1977," the month, abbreviated "Dec.," and the day, "1," in the Date column of the cash account (reproduced below); the number "1" in the Posting Reference column (since the posting came from Page 1 of the journal); and the amount, "$3,000.00" in the Debit column. Inasmuch as the number of the cash account is 111, that number was entered in the Posting Reference column of the journal on the same line as the debit of $3,000.00 that was just posted to Cash. The same pattern was followed in posting the credit part of the entry — $3,000 to L. A. Eason, Capital, Account No. 311 (reproduced below).

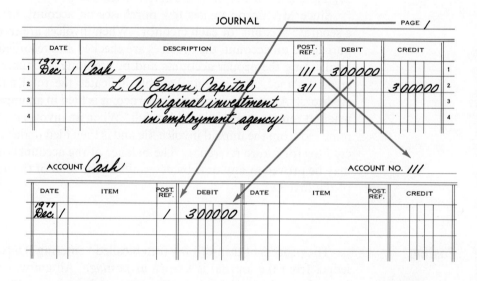

Reference to the journal of The Eason Employment Agency (reproduced on pages 31 and 32) and its ledger (reproduced below and on pages 36 and 37) will indicate that a similar procedure was followed in posting every amount from the journal. Note also that in the ledger, the year "1977" was entered only at the top of each Date column, and that the month "Dec." was entered only with the first posting to an account.

ACCOUNT *Cash*   ACCOUNT NO. *111*

DATE	ITEM	POST. REF.	DEBIT	DATE	ITEM	POST. REF.	CREDIT
1977 Dec. 1		1	3000 00	1977 Dec. 2		1	350 00
8		1	200 00	6		1	32 50
19		1	500 00	7		1	8 00
23		1	650 00	9		1	145 30
29		2	500 00	16		1	225 00
	2,952.79		4850 00	21		1	600 00
				27		1	50 00
				29		2	261 41
				30		2	225 00
							1897 21

ACCOUNT *Office Supplies*   ACCOUNT NO. *112*

DATE	ITEM	POST. REF.	DEBIT	DATE	ITEM	POST. REF.	CREDIT
1977 Dec. 5		1	261 41	1977 Dec. 30		2	45 00
	216.41						

ACCOUNT *Office Equipment*   ACCOUNT NO. *121*

DATE	ITEM	POST. REF.	DEBIT	DATE	ITEM	POST. REF.	CREDIT
1977 Dec 28		1	2948 17				

ACCOUNT *Accounts Payable*   ACCOUNT NO. *211*

DATE	ITEM	POST. REF.	DEBIT	DATE	ITEM	POST. REF.	CREDIT
1977 Dec. 29		2	261 41	1977 Dec. 5		1	261 41
				28	2,948.17	1	2948 17
							3209 58

The Eason Employment Agency Ledger
(continued on next page)

ACCOUNT *L. A. Eason, Capital*   ACCOUNT NO. *311*

DATE	ITEM	POST REF.	DEBIT	DATE	ITEM	POST REF.	CREDIT
				1977 Dec. 1		1	3 000 00

ACCOUNT *L. A. Eason, Drawing*   ACCOUNT NO. *312*

DATE	ITEM	POST REF.	DEBIT	DATE	ITEM	POST REF.	CREDIT
1977 Dec. 21		1	600 00				

ACCOUNT *Placement Fees*   ACCOUNT NO. *411*

DATE	ITEM	POST REF.	DEBIT	DATE	ITEM	POST REF.	CREDIT
				1977 Dec. 8		1	200 00
				19		1	500 00
				23		1	650 00
				29		2	500 00
							1 850 00

ACCOUNT *Rent Expense*   ACCOUNT NO. *511*

DATE	ITEM	POST REF.	DEBIT	DATE	ITEM	POST REF.	CREDIT
1977 Dec. 2		1	350 00				

ACCOUNT *Salary Expense*   ACCOUNT NO. *512*

DATE	ITEM	POST REF.	DEBIT	DATE	ITEM	POST REF.	CREDIT
1977 Dec. 16		1	225 00				
30		2	225 00				
			450 00				

ACCOUNT *Traveling Expense*   ACCOUNT NO. *513*

DATE	ITEM	POST REF.	DEBIT	DATE	ITEM	POST REF.	CREDIT
1977 Dec. 9		1	145 30				

The Eason Employment Agency Ledger (*continued*)

ACCOUNT *Telephone Expense*							ACCOUNT NO. *514*
DATE	ITEM	POST. REF.	DEBIT	DATE	ITEM	POST. REF.	CREDIT
1977 Dec. 6		1	3250				

ACCOUNT *Office Supplies Expense*							ACCOUNT NO. *515*
DATE	ITEM	POST. REF.	DEBIT	DATE	ITEM	POST. REF.	CREDIT
1977 Dec. 30		2	4500				

ACCOUNT *Miscellaneous Expense*							ACCOUNT NO. *516*
DATE	ITEM	POST. REF.	DEBIT	DATE	ITEM	POST. REF.	CREDIT
1977 Dec. 7		1	8 00				
27		1	50 00				
			58 00				

The Eason Employment Agency Ledger (*concluded*)

It will be seen from the preceding discussion that there are four steps involved in posting — three involving information to be recorded in the ledger and one involving information to be recorded in the journal. The date, the amount, and the effect of each transaction are first recorded in the journal. The same information is later posted to the ledger. Posting does not involve an analysis of each transaction to determine its effect upon the accounts. Such an analysis is made at the time of recording the transaction in the journal, and posting is merely transcribing the same information in the ledger. In posting, care should be used to record each debit and each credit entry in the proper columns so that the entries will reflect correctly the effects of the transactions on the accounts.

When the posting is completed, the same information is provided in both the journal and the ledger as to the date, the amount, and the effect of each transaction. A cross-reference from each book to the other book is also provided. This cross-reference makes it possible to trace the entry of December 1 on the debit side of the cash account in the ledger to the journal by referring to the page indicated in the Posting Reference column. The entry of December 1 on the credit side of the account for L. A. Eason, Capital, may also be traced to the journal by referring to the page indicated in the Posting Reference column. Each entry in the journal may be traced to the ledger by referring to the account numbers indicated in the Posting

Reference column of the journal. By referring to pages 31 and 32, it will be seen that the account numbers were inserted in the Posting Reference column. This was done as the posting was completed.

The trial balance

The purpose of a trial balance is to prove that the totals of the debit and credit balances in the ledger are equal. In double-entry bookkeeping, equality of debit and credit balances in the ledger must be maintained. A trial balance may be taken daily, weekly, monthly, or whenever desired. Before taking a trial balance, all transactions previously completed should be journalized and the posting should be completed in order that the effect of all transactions will be reflected in the ledger accounts.

Footing Accounts. When an account form similar to the one illustrated on page 36 is used, it is necessary to foot or add the amounts recorded in each account preparatory to taking a trial balance. The footings should be recorded immediately below the last item in both the debit and credit amount columns of the account. The footings should be written in small figures close to the preceding line so that they will not interfere with the recording of an item on the next ruled line. At the same time, the balance, the difference between the footings, should be computed and recorded in small figures in the Item column of the account on the side with the larger footing. In other words, if an account has a debit balance, the balance should be written in the Item column on the debit or left side of the account. If the account has a credit balance, the balance should be written in the Item column on the credit or right side of the account. The balance or difference between the footings should be recorded in the Item column just below the line on which the last regular entry appears and in line with the footing.

Reference to the accounts kept in the ledger shown on pages 35–37 will reveal that the accounts have been footed and will show how the footings and the balances are recorded. When only one item has been posted to an account, regardless of whether it is a debit or a credit amount, no footing is necessary.

Care should be used in computing the balances of the accounts. If an error is made in adding the columns or in determining the difference between the footings, the error will be carried to the trial balance; and considerable time may be required to locate the mistake. Most accounting errors result from carelessness. For example, a careless bookkeeper may write an account balance on the wrong side of an account or may enter figures so illegibly that they may be misread later. Neatness in writing the amounts is just as important as accuracy in determining the footings and the balances.

Preparing the Trial Balance. It is important that the following procedure be followed in preparing a trial balance:

    (a) Head the trial balance, being certain to show the name of the individual, firm, or organization, the title, "Trial Balance," and the date. (The date shown is the day of the last transaction that is included in the accounts — usually the last day of a month. Actually, the trial balance might be prepared on January 3, but if the accounts reflected only transactions through December 31, this is the date that should be used.)

    (b) List the account titles in order, showing each account number.

    (c) Record the account balances in parallel columns, entering debit balances in the left amount column and credit balances in the right amount column.

    (d) Add the columns and record the totals, ruling a single line across the amount columns above the totals and a double line below the totals in the manner shown in the illustration below.

A trial balance is usually prepared on ruled paper (though it can be written on plain paper if desired). An illustration of the trial balance, as of December 31, 1977, of the ledger of The Eason Employment Agency is shown below.

Even though the trial balance indicates that the ledger is in balance, there still may be errors in the ledger. For example, if a journal entry has been made in which the wrong accounts were debited or credited, or if an

The Eason Employment Agency
Trial Balance
December 31, 1977

Account	Acct. No.	Dr. Balance	Cr. Balance
Cash — Balance Sheet account	111	2952 79	
Office Supplies	112	216 41	
Office Equipment	121	2948 17	
Accounts Payable	211		2948 17
L. A. Eason, Capital	311		3000 00
L. A. Eason, Drawing	312	600 00	
Placement Fees	411		1850 00
Rent Expense	511	350 00	
Salary Expense	512	450 00	
Traveling Expense	513	145 30	
Telephone Expense	514	32 50	
Office Supplies Expense	515	45 00	
Miscellaneous Expense	516	58 00	
		7798 17	7798 17

Model Trial Balance

item has been posted to the wrong account, the ledger will still be in balance. It is important, therefore, that extreme care be used in preparing the journal entries and in posting them to the ledger accounts.

<table>
<tr><td>Report
No. 2-2</td><td>Refer to the study assignments and complete Report No. 2-2. To complete this assignment correctly, the principles developed in the preceding discussion must be understood. Review the text assignment if necessary. After completing the report, continue with the following textbook discussion until the next report is required.</td></tr>
</table>

THE FINANCIAL STATEMENTS

The transactions completed by The Eason Employment Agency during the month of December were recorded in a two-column journal (see pages 31 and 32). The debits and credits were subsequently posted to the proper accounts in a ledger (see pages 35–37). At the end of the month a trial balance was taken as a means of proving that the equality of debits and credits had been maintained throughout the journalizing and posting procedures (see page 39).

Although a trial balance may provide much of the information that the owner of a business may desire, it is primarily a device used by the bookkeeper for the purpose of proving the equality of the debit and credit account balances. Although the trial balance of The Eason Employment Agency taken as of December 31 contains a list of all of the accounts and shows the amounts of their debit and credit balances, it does not clearly present all of the information that Mr. Eason may need or desire regarding either the results of operations during the month or the status of his business at the end of the month. To meet these needs it is customary to prepare two types of *financial statements*. One is known as an income statement and the other as a balance sheet or statement of financial position.

The income statement

The purpose of an *income statement* is to provide information regarding the results of operations *during a specified period of time*. It is an itemized statement of the changes in owner's equity resulting from the revenue and expenses of a specific period (month, quarter, year). Such changes are recorded in temporary owner's equity accounts known as revenue and expense accounts. Changes in owner's equity resulting from investments or withdrawals of assets by the owner are not included in the income statement because they involve neither revenue nor expense.

A model income statement for The Eason Employment Agency showing the results of operations for the month ended December 31, 1977, is reproduced below. The heading of an income statement consists of the following:

(a) The name of the business
(b) The title of the statement — Income Statement
(c) The period of time covered by the statement

The Eason Employment Agency
Income Statement
For the Month Ended December 31, 1977

Revenue:			
Placement fees			#185000
Expenses:			
Rent expense		#35000	
Salary expense		45000	
Traveling expense		14530	
Telephone expense		3250	
Office supplies expense		4500	
Miscellaneous expense		5800	
Total expenses			108080
Net income			#76920

Model Income Statement

The body of an income statement consists of **(1)** an itemized list of the sources and amounts of revenue received during the period and **(2)** an itemized list of the various expenses incurred during the period. It is said that the "heart" of income measurement is the process of *matching* on a *periodic basis* the revenue and expenses of a business. The income statement carries out this matching concept.

The financial statements usually are prepared first on ruled paper. Such handwritten copies may then be typed so that a number of copies will be available for those who are interested in examining the statements. Since the typewritten copies are not on ruled paper, dollar signs are included in the handwritten copy so that the typist will understand just where they are to be inserted. Note that a dollar sign is placed beside the first amount in each column and the first amount below a ruling in each column. The income statement illustrated on page 41 is shown on two-column ruled paper; however, the columns do not have any debit-credit significance.

In the case of The Eason Employment Agency, the only source of revenue was placement fees that amounted to $1,850. The total expenses for the month amounted to $1,080.80. The revenue exceeded the expenses by $769.20. This represents the amount of the net income for the month. If the total expenses had exceeded the total revenue, the excess would have represented a net loss for the month.

The trial balance supplied the information needed in preparing the income statement. However, it can be seen readily that the income statement provides more information concerning the results of the month's operations than was supplied by the trial balance.

The Eason
Balance
December

Assets		
Cash	$ 2952 79	
Office supplies	216 41	
Office equipment	2948 17	
Total assets	$ 6117 37	

Model Balance Sheet — Account Form (Left Page)

**The balance
sheet**

The purpose of a *balance sheet* is to provide information regarding the status of the assets, liabilities, and owner's equity of a business enterprise *as of a specified date.* It is an itemized statement of the respective amounts of these basic accounting elements at the close of business on the date indicated in the heading.

A model balance sheet for The Eason Employment Agency showing the status of the business when it closed on December 31, 1977, is reproduced below and on page 42. The heading of a balance sheet contains the following:

(a) The name of the business.

(b) The title of the statement — Balance Sheet.

(c) The date of the statement (as of the close of business on that day).

The body of a balance sheet consists of an itemized list of the assets, the liabilities, and the owner's equity, the latter being the difference between the total amount of the assets and the total amount of the liabilities. The balance sheet illustrated is arranged in account form. Note the similarity of this form of balance sheet to the standard account form illustrated on page 12. The assets are listed on the left side and the liabilities and owner's equity are listed on the right side. The information provided by the balance sheet of The Eason Employment Agency may be summarized in equation form as follows:

> **ASSETS = LIABILITIES + OWNER'S EQUITY**
> **$6,117.37 $2,948.17 $3,169.20**

Employment Agency
Sheet
31, 1977

Liabilities			
Accounts payable	$2948 17		
Total liabilities		$2948 17	
Owner's Equity			
L. A. Eason, capital			
Capital, Dec. 1, 1977		$300000	
Net income	$769.20		
Less withdrawals	600.00		
Net increase		169 20	
Capital, Dec. 31, 1977			3169 20
Total liabilities and owner's equity			$6117 37

Model Balance Sheet — Account Form (Right Page)

The trial balance was the source of the information needed in listing the assets and liabilities in the balance sheet. The amount of the owner's equity may be calculated by subtracting the total liabilities from the total assets. Thus, Mr. Eason's equity as of December 31, 1977, is as follows:

Total assets.	$6,117.37
Less total liabilities	2,948.17
Owner's equity.	$3,169.20

Proof of the amount of the owner's equity as calculated above may be determined by taking into consideration the following factors:

(a) The amount invested in the enterprise by Mr. Eason on December 1 as shown by his capital account.

(b) The amount of the net income of The Eason Employment Agency for December as shown by the income statement.

(c) The total amount withdrawn for personal use during December as shown by Mr. Eason's drawing account.

The trial balance on page 39 shows that Mr. Eason's equity in The Eason Employment Agency on December 1 amounted to $3,000. This is indicated by the credit balance of his capital account. The income statement on page 41 shows that the net income of The Eason Employment Agency for December amounted to $769.20. The trial balance shows that the amount withdrawn by Mr. Eason for personal use during the month amounted to $600. This is indicated by the debit balance of his drawing account. On the basis of this information, Mr. Eason's equity in The Eason Employment Agency as of December 31, 1977, is as follows:

Amount of capital December 1		$3,000.00
Net income for December	$769.20	
Less amount withdrawn for personal use during the month	600.00	169.20
Capital at close of business December 31		$3,169.20

Report No. 2-3

Refer to the study assignments and complete Report No. 2-3. This assignment provides a test of your ability to apply the principles developed in Chapters 1 and 2 of this textbook. The textbook and the study assignments go hand in hand, each serving a definite purpose in the learning process. Inability to solve correctly any problem included in the report indicates that you have failed to master the principles developed in the textbook. After completing the report, you may proceed with Chapter 3 until the next report is required.

Chapter 3

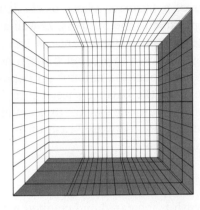

ACCOUNTING FOR CASH

In the preceding chapters the purpose and nature of business accounting, transaction analysis, and the mechanics of double-entry bookkeeping were introduced. Explanations and illustrations were given of **(1)** *journalizing* (recording transactions in a *general journal* — a "book of original entry"), **(2)** *posting* (transcribing the entries to the accounts that, all together, comprise the *general ledger*), **(3)** taking a *trial balance*, and **(4)** using the latter to prepare an *income statement* and a *balance sheet* (two basic and important *financial statements*). This chapter is devoted to a discussion of the handling of and accounting for cash receipts and disbursements, including various considerations that are involved when cash is kept in a commercial bank. (The use of bank "checking accounts" is a near-universal business practice.)

RECORDS OF CASH RECEIPTS AND DISBURSEMENTS; PETTY CASH

The term *cash* has several different, though not totally dissimilar, meanings. In a very narrow sense, cash means currency and coin. In a broader sense, cash includes checks, drafts, and money orders. All of these, as well as currency and coin, are sometimes called "cash items." Usually any reference to the *cash receipts* of a business relates to the receipt of checks, drafts, and money orders payable to the business, as well as to the receipt of currency and coin. The amount of the balance of the cash account, as well as the amount shown for cash in a balance sheet, normally includes cash and cash items on hand plus the amount on deposit in a bank checking account. In some cases the balance sheet figure for cash includes amounts on deposit in more than one bank. In accounting for cash, it is rather rare to make a distinction between "cash on hand" and "cash in bank," but sometimes this is done.

The cash account

This account is debited when cash is increased and credited when cash is decreased. This means that the cash account has a debit balance unless the business has no cash. In the latter case, the account will be *in balance* — meaning that the account has no balance since the total of the debits is equal to the total of the credits.

Cash Receipts. It is vital that an accurate and timely record be kept of cash receipts. When the volume of the receipts is large in both number and amount, a practice designed to reduce the danger of mistake and embezzlement may be followed. When there are numerous receipts of currency and coin from customers paying in person for goods or services just received, it is customary to use a cash register. Such a machine usually provides a listing of amounts recorded as the money is received. A cash register may have the capability of accumulating subtotals that permit classification of amounts — sales by departments, for example. When money comes in by mail (nearly always checks), it is usual for the one remitting to enclose a presupplied form showing name, address, and the amount on the enclosed check or money order. A good example is the top part of a monthly statement the customer has received. (An illustration of such a statement appears on page 194.) Sometimes a written receipt must be prepared. A carbon copy of the receipt provides the initial record of the cash received.

In any case, a record of each amount received should be prepared by someone other than the bookkeeper. The money received (including checks and money orders) is placed in the custody of whoever handles bank deposits and cash on hand. The bookkeeper gets the records to use in preparing proper journal entries for cash receipts. Under such a plan the bookkeeper does not actually handle any cash; instead he enters cash receipts from records prepared by other persons. The procedure of having transactions involving cash handled by two or more persons reduces the danger of fraud and is one of the important features of a system of internal control.

Cash Disbursements. Disbursements may be made in cash or by bank check. When a disbursement is made in cash, a receipt or a receipted voucher should be obtained as evidence of the payment. When a disbursement is made by bank check, it is not necessary to obtain a receipt since the canceled check that is returned by the bank serves as a receipt.

Recording Cash Receipts and Disbursements. In the preceding chapter, transactions involving the receipt and disbursement of cash were recorded in a two-column general journal along with other transactions. If the number of cash transactions is relatively small, the manner of recording that was illustrated is quite satisfactory. If, however, the number of such transactions is large, the repetition entailed in making numerous debit postings or credit postings to the cash account is time-consuming, tedious, and burdensome. A discussion of a journal with special columns is deferred until Chapter 5, and the use of *special journals* is discussed in Chapter 6.

Proving Cash. The process of determining whether the amount of cash (on hand and in the bank) is the amount that should be there according to the records is called *proving cash*. Cash should be proved at least once a week and, perhaps, more often if the volume of cash transactions is large. The first step is to determine from the records what amount of cash should be on hand. The cash balance should be calculated by adding the total of the receipts to the opening balance and subtracting the total of the payments. The result should be equal to the amount of cash on deposit in the bank plus the total of currency, coins, checks, and money orders on hand. Normally, an up-to-date record of cash in bank is maintained — often by using stubs in a checkbook for this purpose. There is space provided on the stubs to show deposits as well as the record of checks drawn, and the resulting balance after each deposit made or check drawn. (See check stubs illustrated on page 60.) The amount of cash and cash items on hand must be determined by actual count.

Cash Short and Over. If the effort to prove cash is not successful, it means that either **(1)** the records of receipts, disbursements, and cash on deposit contain one or more errors, **(2)** the count of cash and cash items was incorrect, or **(3)** a "shortage" or an "overage" exists. If a verification of the records and the cash count does not uncover any error, it is evident that due to some mistake in handling cash, either not enough or too much cash is on hand.

Finding that cash is slightly short or over is not unusual. If there are numerous cash transactions, it is difficult to avoid occasional errors in making change. (There is always the danger of shortages due to dishonesty, but most discrepancies are the result of mistakes.) Many businesses have a ledger account entitled *Cash Short and Over*. If, in the effort to prove cash, it is found that a shortage exists, its amount is treated as a cash disbursement transaction involving a debit to Cash Short and Over. Any overage discovered is regarded as a cash receipt transaction involving a credit to Cash Short and Over. By the end of the fiscal year it is likely that the cash short and over account will have both debits and credits. If the total of the debits exceeds the total of the credits, the balance represents an expense or loss; if the reverse is the case, the balance represents revenue.

The petty cash fund

A good policy for a business enterprise to adopt is one which requires that all cash and cash items which it receives shall be deposited in a bank. When this is done, its total cash receipts will equal its total deposits in the bank. It is also a good policy to make arrangements with the bank so that all checks and other cash items received by the business from customers or others in the usual course of business will be accepted by the bank for deposit only. This will cause the records of cash receipts and disbursements of the business to agree exactly with the bank's record of deposits and withdrawals.

When all cash and cash items received are deposited in a bank, an office fund or *petty cash fund* may be established for paying small items. ("Petty" means small or little.) Such a fund eliminates the necessity of writing checks for small amounts.

Operating a Petty Cash Fund. To establish a petty cash fund, a check should be drawn for the amount that is to be set aside in the fund. The amount may be $25, $50, $100, or any amount considered necessary. The check may be made payable to "Cash," "Petty Cash," "Office Fund," or to the person who will have custody of the fund. When the check is cashed by the bank, the money is placed in a cash drawer, a cash register, or a safe at the depositor's place of business; and a designated individual in the office is authorized to make payments from the fund. The one who is responsible for the fund should be able to account for the full amount of the fund at any time. Disbursements from the fund should not be made without obtaining a voucher or a receipt. A form of petty cash voucher is shown on page 49. Such a voucher should be used for each expenditure unless a receipt or receipted invoice is obtained.

The check drawn to establish the petty cash fund may be recorded in the journal by debiting Petty Cash Fund and by crediting Cash. When it is necessary to replenish the fund, the petty cashier usually prepares a statement of the expenditures, properly classified. A check is then drawn for the exact amount of the total expenditures. This check is recorded in the

```
┌─────────────────────────────────────────────────────────────┐
│              PETTY CASH VOUCHER                               │
│                                                               │
│   No.    4              Date  December 12, 1977              │
│                                          ┌──────────────────┐ │
│   Paid To  J. L. Porter                  │    Amount        │ │
│                                          ├──────────┬───────┤ │
│   For  Red Cross                         │   10     │  00   │ │
│                                          └──────────┴───────┘ │
│   Charge To  Donations Expense                               │
│                                                               │
│   Payment Received:                                           │
│                                                               │
│   J. L. Porter          Approved By  Arthur Cobb             │
└─────────────────────────────────────────────────────────────┘
```

Petty Cash Voucher

journal by debiting the proper accounts indicated in the statement and by crediting Cash.

The petty cash fund is a revolving fund that does not change in amount unless the fund is increased or decreased. The actual amount of cash in the fund plus the total of the petty cash vouchers or receipts should always be equal to the amount originally charged to the petty cash fund.

This method of handling a petty cash fund is sometimes referred to as the *imprest method*. It is the method most commonly used.

Petty Cash Disbursements Record. When a petty cash fund is maintained, it is good practice to keep a formal record of all disbursements from the fund. Various types of records have been designed for this purpose. One of the standard forms is illustrated on pages 50 and 51. The headings of the Distribution columns may vary with each enterprise, depending upon the desired classification of the expenditures. It should be remembered that the headings represent accounts that eventually are to be charged for the expenditures. The desired headings may either be printed on the form or they may be written in. Often the account numbers instead of account titles are used in the headings to indicate the accounts to be charged.

The petty cashier should have a document for each disbursement made from the petty cash fund. Unless a receipt or receipted invoice is obtained, the petty cashier should prepare a voucher. The vouchers should be numbered consecutively.

A model petty cash disbursements record is reproduced on pages 50 and 51. It is a part of the records of Arthur Cobb, an attorney. Since Mr. Cobb is out of the office much of the time, he considers it advisable to provide a petty cash fund from which his secretary is authorized to make petty cash disbursements not to exceed $20 each. A narrative of the petty cash transactions completed by Dorothy Melvin, Mr. Cobb's secretary, during the month of December follows on page 50.

ARTHUR COBB

NARRATIVE OF PETTY CASH TRANSACTIONS

Dec. 1. Issued check for $100 payable to Dorothy Melvin. She cashed the check, and placed the proceeds in a petty cash fund.

> This transaction was recorded in the journal by debiting Petty Cash Fund and by crediting Cash. A memorandum entry was also made in the Description column of the petty cash disbursements record reproduced below and on page 51.

During the month of December the following disbursements were made from the petty cash fund:

6. Gave Mr. Cobb $14.60 to reimburse him for the amount spent in having his automobile serviced. Petty Cash Voucher No. 1.
7. Gave Mr. Cobb $10 to reimburse him for the amount spent in entertaining a client at lunch. Petty Cash Voucher No. 2.
12. Gave Mr. Cobb $20 for personal use. Petty Cash Voucher No. 3.

> This item was entered in the Amount column provided at the extreme right of the petty cash disbursements record since no special distribution column had been provided for recording amounts withdrawn by the owner for personal use.

12. Gave the Red Cross a $10 donation. Petty Cash Voucher No. 4.
15. Paid $7.50 for typewriter repairs. Petty Cash Voucher No. 5.

PAGE *1*   PETTY CASH DISBURSEMENTS

	DAY	DESCRIPTION		VOU. NO.	TOTAL AMOUNT	Tel. Exp.	Auto. Exp.	
1		AMOUNTS FORWARDED						1
2	1	Received in fund	100.00	✓				2
3	6	Automobile repairs		1	14 60		14 60	3
4	7	Client luncheon		2	10 00			4
5	12	Arthur Cobb, personal use		3	20 00			5
6	12	Red Cross		4	10 00			6
7	15	Typewriter repairs		5	7 50			7
8	19	Traveling expense		6	7 80			8
9	20	Washing automobile		7	1 75		1 75	9
10	22	Postage expense		8	1 25			10
11	23	Salvation Army		9	5 00			11
12	26	Postage stamps		10	10 00			12
13	27	Long distance call		11	3 20	3 20		13
14					91 10 / 91 10	3 20 / 3 20	16 35 / 16 35	14
15	30	Balance	8.90					15
16	30	Received in fund	91.10					16
17		Total	100.00					17
18								18

Arthur Cobb's Petty Cash Disbursements Record (Left Page)

19. Gave Mr. Cobb $7.80 to reimburse him for traveling expenses. Petty Cash Voucher No. 6.
20. Gave Mr. Cobb $1.75 to reimburse him for the amount spent in having his automobile washed. Petty Cash Voucher No. 7.
22. Paid $1.25 for mailing a package. Petty Cash Voucher No. 8.
23. Donated $5 to the Salvation Army. Petty Cash Voucher No. 9.
26. Paid $10 for postage stamps. Petty Cash Voucher No. 10.
27. Gave Mr. Cobb $3.20 to reimburse him for a long distance telephone call made from a booth. Petty Cash Voucher No. 11.
30. Issued check for $91.10 payable to Dorothy Melvin to replenish the petty cash fund.

This transaction was recorded in the journal by debiting the proper accounts and by crediting Cash for the total amount of the expenditures.

Proving the Petty Cash Disbursements Record. To prove the petty cash disbursements record, it is first necessary to foot all of the amount columns. The sum of the footings of the Distribution columns should equal the footing of the Total Amount column. After proving the footings, the totals should be recorded and the record should be ruled as shown in the illustration. The illustration shows that a total of $91.10 was paid out during December. Since it was desired to replenish the petty cash

FOR MONTH OF *December* 19 77   PAGE *1*

	Post. Exp.	Don. Exp.	Travel Exp.	Misc. Exp.		ACCOUNT	AMOUNT	
1								1
2								2
3								3
4				10 00				4
5						Arthur Cobb, Drawing	20 00	5
6		10 00						6
7				7 50				7
8			7 80					8
9								9
10	1 25							10
11		5 00						11
12	10 00							12
13								13
14	11 25 11 25	15 00 15 00	7 80 7 80	17 50 17 50			20 00 20 00	14
15								15
16								16
17								17
18								18

Arthur Cobb's Petty Cash Disbursements Record (Right Page)

fund at this time, the following statement of the disbursements for December was prepared:

STATEMENT OF PETTY CASH DISBURSEMENTS FOR DECEMBER

Telephone Expense	$ 3.20
Automobile Expense	16.35
Postage Expense	11.25
Donations Expense	15.00
Traveling Expense	7.80
Miscellaneous Expense	17.50
Arthur Cobb, Drawing	20.00
Total disbursements	$91.10

The statement of petty cash disbursements provides the information for the issuance of a check for $91.10 to replenish the petty cash fund. After footing and ruling the petty cash disbursements record, the balance in the fund and the amount received to replenish the fund may be recorded in the Description column below the ruling as shown in the illustration. It is customary to carry the balance forward to the top of a new page before recording any of the transactions for the following month.

The petty cash disbursements record reproduced on pages 50 and 51 is an *auxiliary record* that supplements the regular accounting records. No posting is done from this auxiliary record. The total amount of the expenditures from the petty cash fund is entered in the journal at the time of replenishing the fund by debiting the proper accounts and by crediting Cash. A *compound entry* (one that affects more than two accounts, though the sum of the debits is equal to the sum of the credits) is usually required. The statement of petty cash disbursements provides the information needed in recording the check issued to Dorothy Melvin to replenish the petty cash fund. The entry is posted from the journal.

	JOURNAL			PAGE 15	
	DATE	DESCRIPTION	POST. REF.	DEBIT	CREDIT
1	1977 Dec. 30	Telephone Expense		3 20		1
2		Automobile Expense		16 35		2
3		Postage Expense		11 25		3
4		Donations Expense		15 00		4
5		Traveling Expense		7 80		5
6		Miscellaneous Expense		17 50		6
7		Arthur Cobb, Drawing		20 00		7
8		Cash			91 10	8
9		Reimbursement of				9
10		petty cash fund.				10
11						11

The method of recording the check issued by Arthur Cobb on December 30 to replenish the fund is illustrated on the bottom of page 52.

<table>
<tr><td>

**Report
No. 3-1**

</td><td>

Refer to the study assignments and complete Report No. 3-1. After completing the report, proceed with the textbook discussion until the next report is required.

</td></tr>
</table>

BANKING PROCEDURE

A bank is a financial institution that receives deposits, lends money, makes collections, and renders other services, such as providing vaults for the safekeeping of valuables and handling trust funds for its customers. Most banks offer facilities for both checking accounts and savings accounts.

**Checking
account**

It is estimated that 90–95 percent of all money payments in the United States are made by checks. A *check*, a piece of commercial paper, is drawn on a bank and payable on demand. It involves three original parties: **(1)** the *drawer*, the depositor who orders the bank to pay; **(2)** the *drawee*, the bank in which the drawer has money on deposit in a so-called "commercial" account; and **(3)** the *payee*, the person directed to receive the money. The drawer and payee may be the same person, though the payee named in such case usually is "Cash."

A check is *negotiable* (meaning that the right to receive the money can be transferred to someone else) because it complies with the following requirements; it is in writing, is signed by the drawer, contains an unconditional order to pay a specified amount of money, is payable on demand, and is payable to order or bearer. The payee transfers his right to receive the money by *indorsing* the check. If the payee simply signs his name on the back of the check (customarily near the left end), it is called a *blank* indorsement. (This makes the check payable to bearer.) If, as is very common, there are added such words as "For deposit," "Pay to any bank or banker," or "Pay to J. Doe only," it is called a *restrictive* indorsement. A widely used business practice when indorsing checks for deposit is to use a rubber stamp similar to that illustrated on page 55.

Important factors in connection with a checking account are **(1)** opening the account, **(2)** making deposits, **(3)** making withdrawals, and **(4)** reconciling the bank statement.

Opening a Checking Account. To open a checking account with a bank, it is necessary to obtain the approval of an official of the bank and to make an initial deposit. Money, checks, bank drafts, money orders, and other cash items usually will be accepted for deposit, subject to their verification as to amount and validity.

Signature Card. Banks require a new depositor to sign his name on a card or form as an aid in verifying the depositor's signature on checks that he may issue, on cash items that he may indorse for deposit, and on other business papers that he may present to the bank. The form a depositor signs to give the bank a sample of his signature is called a *signature card*. To aid in identification, the depositor's social security number (if any) may also be shown. If desired, a depositor may authorize others to sign his name to checks and to other business forms. Each person who is so authorized is required to sign the depositor's name along with his own signature on a signature card. A signature card is one of the safeguards that a bank uses to protect its own interests as well as the interests of its depositors.

Deposit Ticket. Banks provide depositors with a printed form to use for a detailed listing of items being deposited. This form is called a *deposit ticket*. A model filled-in deposit ticket is reproduced on page 55. This illustration is typical of the type of ticket that most banks provide. Note that the number of the depositor's account is preprinted at the bottom in so-called "MICR" numbers (meaning *magnetic ink character recognition*) that can be "read" by a type of electronic equipment used by banks. This series of digits (which also is preprinted at the bottom of all of the depositor's checks) is actually a code used in sorting and routing deposit slips and checks. In the first set of digits, 0420-0003, the "4" indicates that the bank is in the Fourth Federal Reserve District. The "20" following is what is called a "routing" number. The "3" is a number assigned to the Kenwood National Bank. This numbering method was established by the American Bankers Association (ABA). The second set of digits, 136-92146, is the number assigned by the Kenwood National Bank to the Miller Company's account.

It is very common practice to prepare deposit tickets in duplicate so that one copy, when receipted by the bank teller, may be retained by the depositor. In preparing a deposit ticket, the date should be written in the space provided. Currency (paper money) should be arranged in the order of the denominations, the smaller denominations being placed on top. The bills should all be faced up and top up. Coins (pennies, nickels, dimes, quarters, and half dollars) that are to be deposited in considerable quantities should be wrapped in coin wrappers, which the bank will provide. The name and account number of the depositor should be written

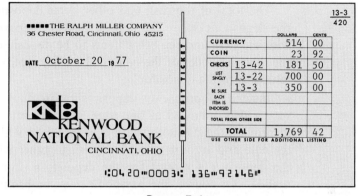

		DOLLARS	CENTS
CURRENCY		514	00
COIN		23	92
CHECKS	13-42	181	50
LIST SINGLY	13-22	700	00
BE SURE EACH ITEM IS ENDORSED	13-3	350	00
TOTAL FROM OTHER SIDE			
TOTAL		1,769	42

Deposit Ticket

on the outside of each coin wrapper as a means of identification in the event that a mistake has been made in counting the coins. The amounts of cash represented by currency and by coins should be entered in the amount column of the deposit ticket on the lines provided for these items.

Each additional item to be deposited should be listed on a separate line of the deposit ticket as shown in the illustration above. In listing checks on the deposit ticket, the instructions of the bank should be observed in describing the checks for identification purposes. Banks usually prefer that depositors identify checks being deposited by showing the ABA number of the bank on which the check is drawn. The ABA number for the first check listed on the deposit ticket above is $\frac{13-42}{420}$. The number 13 is the number assigned to the city in which the bank is located and the number 42 is assigned to the specific bank. The 420 is the check routing symbol, but only the numerator is used in identifying the deposit.

All checks being deposited must be indorsed. The indorsement on the check illustrated below was by means of a rubber stamp.

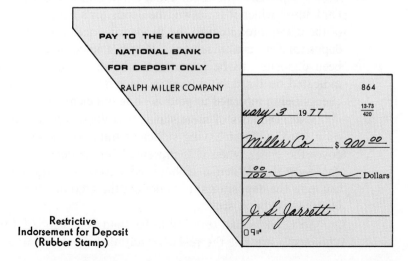

Restrictive
Indorsement for Deposit
(Rubber Stamp)

The total of the cash and other items deposited should be entered on the deposit tickets. The deposit tickets, prepared in duplicate, together with the cash and the other items to be deposited, should be delivered to the receiving teller of the bank. The teller receipts the duplicate copy and returns it to the depositor.

Instead of preparing deposit slips in duplicate, another practice — very widely followed at one time, and still often used — is for the bank to provide the depositor with a *passbook* in which the bank teller enters the date and amount of each deposit together with his initial. This gives the depositor a receipt for the deposit; a duplicate deposit slip is not needed. Of course, the passbook must be brought in (or sent in) to the bank with each deposit.

Instead of providing the depositor with either duplicate deposit tickets or a passbook, the bank may provide him with a machine-printed receipt for each deposit. Some banks use *automatic teller machines* in preparing the receipts. The use of such machines saves the time required to make manual entries in a passbook and eliminates the need for making duplicate copies of deposit tickets. Such machines are not only timesaving, but they also promote accuracy in the handling of deposits. The deposits handled by each teller during the day may be accumulated so that at the end of the day the total amount of the deposits received by a teller is automatically recorded by the machine. This amount may be proved by counting the cash and cash items accepted by a teller for deposit during the day.

Dishonored Checks. A check that a bank refuses to pay is described as a *dishonored check*. A depositor guarantees all items that he deposits and is liable to the bank for the amount involved if, for any reason, any item is not honored when presented for payment. When a check or other cash item is deposited with a bank and is not honored upon presentation to the bank upon which it is drawn, the depositor's bank may charge the amount of the dishonored item to the depositor's account or may present it to the depositor for reimbursement. It is not uncommon for checks that have been deposited to be returned to the depositor for various reasons, as indicated on the debit advice on page 57. The most common reason for checks being returned unpaid is "not sufficient funds" (NSF).

Under the laws of most states, it is illegal for anyone to issue a check on a bank without having sufficient funds on deposit with that bank to cover the check when it is presented for payment. This action is called an *overdraft*. When a dishonored check is charged to the depositor's account, the depositor should deduct the amount from the balance shown on his checkbook stub.

Most checks that turn out to be "bad" or "rubber" (meaning that they "bounce") are not the result of any dishonest intent on the part of the

ADVICE OF CHARGE   KN8 KENWOOD   CINCINNATI, OHIO
                                        NATIONAL BANK

TO __The Ralph Miller Company__
       __Account No. 136-92146__   DATE __June 16__ 19 __77__

WE HAVE TODAY CHARGED YOUR ACCOUNT AS FOLLOWS:
Dishonored check--not sufficient funds

$ __48.75__

BY _ℒℊℐ_

Debit Advice

drawers of such checks. Either the depositor thought that he had enough money in his account when the check was written, or he expected to get a deposit to the bank in time to "cover" the check before it reached the bank for payment. It is commonly considered to be something of a disgrace to the drawer of a check if the bank will not honor (pay) it. In recent years, many banks have made available (for a fee) plans that guarantee that all checks, within prescribed limits as to amount, will be honored even if the depositor's balance is too low. This amounts to a prearrangement with the bank to make a loan to the depositor. These plans have been given names such as "Ready Reserve Account," "Instant Cash," and others. Sometimes arrangements of this sort are parts of larger plans that involve such things as picture checks, no minimum balance, bank statements that list checks paid in numerical order, "check guarantee cards," travelers checks without fee, safe-deposit boxes, and even bank credit cards (discussed in Chapter 6). The bank charges a monthly fee for any or all of these services. Such comprehensive plans are not widely subscribed to by businesses (in contrast to individuals.)

Postdated Checks. Checks dated subsequent to the date of issue are known as *postdated checks*. For example, a check that is issued on March 1 may be dated March 15. The recipient of a postdated check should not deposit it before the date specified on the check. One reason for issuing a postdated check may be that the maker does not have sufficient funds in his bank at the time of issuance to pay it, but he may expect to have a sufficient amount on deposit by the time the check is presented for payment on or after the date of the check. When a postdated check is presented to the bank on which it is drawn and payment is not made, it is handled by the bank in the same manner as any other dishonored check and the payee should treat it as a dishonored check. Generally, it is not considered good practice to issue postdated checks.

Making Deposits by Mail. Bank deposits may be made either over the counter or by mail. The over-the-counter method of making deposits is generally used. It may not always be convenient, however, for a depositor to make his deposits over the counter, especially if he lives at a great distance from the bank. In such a case it may be more convenient for him to make his deposits by mail. When a depositor makes his deposits by mail, the bank may provide him with a special form of deposit ticket, and a form for him to self address which is subsequently returned to him with a receipt for his deposit.

Night Deposits. Some banks provide night deposit service. While all banks do not handle this in the same way, a common practice is for the bank to have a night safe with an opening on the exterior of the bank building. Upon signing a night depository contract, the bank supplies the depositor with a key to the outside door of the safe, together with a bag that has an identifying number and in which valuables may be placed, and two keys to the bag itself. Once the depositor places his bag in the night deposit safe it cannot be retrieved because it moves to a vault in the bank that is accessible to bank employees only. Since only the depositor is provided with keys to his bag, he or his authorized representative must go to the bank to unlock the bag. At that time the depositor may or may not deposit in his account in the bank the funds that he had placed previously in the night deposit safe.

Night deposit banking service is especially valuable to those individuals and concerns that do not have safe facilities in their own places of business and that accumulate cash and other cash items which they cannot take to the bank during regular banking hours.

Making Withdrawals. The amount deposited in a bank checking account may be withdrawn either by the depositor himself or by any other person who has been properly authorized to make withdrawals from the depositor's account. Such withdrawals are accomplished by the use of checks signed by the depositor or by others having the authority to sign checks drawn on the account.

Checkbook. Checks used by businesses commonly come bound in the form of a book with two or three blank checks to a page, perforated so that they may be removed singly. To the left of each one is a *check stub* containing space to record all relevant information about the check (check number, date, payee, amount, the purpose of the check and often the account to be charged, along with the bank balance before the check was issued, current deposits if any, and the resulting balance after the check). The depositor's name and address normally are printed on each check and the MICR numbers are shown along the bottom edge. Often the checks are prenumbered — commonly in the upper right corner.

Sometimes checks come bound in the form of a pad. There may be a blank page after each check for use in making a carbon copy of the check. (The carbon copy is not a check; it is merely a copy of what was typed or written on the check. However, the essential information is supplied to be entered in the formal records.) Sometimes the depositor is provided with a checkbook that, instead of stubs, is accompanied by a small register in which the relevant information is noted. Checks may be provided by the bank (often for a charge) or purchased directly from firms that specialize in the manufacture of check forms.

Writing a Check. If the check has a stub, the latter should be filled in at the time the check is written. If, instead of a stub, a checkbook register is used, an entry for the check should be made therein. This plan insures that the drawer will retain a record of each check issued.

A depositor may personally obtain cash at the time of making a deposit by indicating on the deposit slip the portion of the total of the items listed to be returned to him, with the remainder to constitute the deposit. Alternatively, he may draw a check payable to himself or, usually, just to "Cash."

The purpose for which a check is drawn is often noted in some appropriate area of the check itself. Indicating the purpose on the check provides information for the benefit of the payee and provides a specific receipt for the drawer.

The amount of the check is stated on the check in both figures and words. If the amount shown on the check in figures does not agree with the amount shown in words, the bank usually will contact the drawer for the correct amount or will return the check unpaid.

Care must be used in writing the amount on the check in order to avoid any possibility that the payee or a subsequent holder may change the amount. If the instructions given below are followed in the preparation of a check, it will be difficult to change the amount.

    (a) The amount shown in figures should be written so that there is no space between the dollar sign and the first digit of the amount.

    (b) The amount stated in words should be written beginning at the extreme left on the line provided for this information. The cents should be written in the form of a common fraction; if the check is for an even number of dollars, use two ciphers or the word "no" as the numerator of the fraction. If a vacant space remains, a line should be drawn from the amount stated in words to the word "Dollars" on the same line with it, as illustrated on the next page.

A machine frequently used to write the amount of a check in figures and in words is known as a *checkwriter*. The use of a checkwriter is desirable because it practically eliminates the possibility of a change in the amount of a check.

Each check issued by a depositor will be returned to him by the bank on which it is drawn after the check has been paid. Canceled checks are returned to the depositor with the bank statement, which is usually rendered each month. Canceled checks will have been indorsed by the payee

	DOLLARS	CENTS
NO 105		
DATE *April 4* 19 *77*		
TO *Ridley Bros.*		
FOR *April rent*		
ACCT. *Rent Expense*		
BAL. BRO'T FOR'D	2,226	34
AMT. DEPOSITED		
TOTAL		
AMT. THIS CHECK	225	00
BAL. CAR'D FOR'D	2,001	34

THE RALPH MILLER COMPANY
36 Chester Road, Cincinnati, Ohio 45215   no. **105**   13-3 / 420

April 4 19 *77* ← PAYEE

pay to the order of *Ridley Bros.* $225 00

Two hundred twenty-five 00/100 dollars

KNB
KENWOOD
NATIONAL BANK
CINCINNATI, OHIO   by *Ralph Miller*

⑆0420⑆0003⑈ 136⑈92146⑈

← DRAWEE

← DRAWER

	DOLLARS	CENTS
NO. 106		
DATE *April 5* 19 *77*		
TO *Patrick Mfg. Co.*		
FOR *Inv. March 31*		
ACCT. *Accounts Payable*		
BAL. BRO'T FOR'D	2,001	34
AMT. DEPOSITED	893	50
TOTAL	2,894	84
AMT. THIS CHECK	742	18
BAL. CAR'D FOR'D	2,152	66

THE RALPH MILLER COMPANY
36 Chester Road, Cincinnati, Ohio 45215   no. **106**   13-3 / 420

April 5 19 *77*

pay to the order of *Patrick Manufacturing Co.* $742 18

Seven hundred forty-two 18/100 dollars

KNB
KENWOOD
NATIONAL BANK
CINCINNATI, OHIO   by *Ralph Miller*

⑆0420⑆0003⑈ 136⑈92146⑈

Checks and Stubs

and any subsequent holders. They constitute receipts that the depositor should retain for future reference. They may be attached to the stubs from which they were removed originally or they may be filed.

Electronic Processing of Checks. It is now nearly universal practice to use checks that can be processed by MICR (magnetic ink character recognition) equipment. The unique characteristic of such checks is that there is imprinted in magnetic ink along the lower margin of the check a series of numbers or digits in the form of a code that indicates **(1)** the identity of the Federal Reserve district in which the bank is located and a routing number, **(2)** the identity of the bank, and **(3)** the account number assigned to the depositor. Sometimes the check number is also shown. In processing checks with electronic equipment, the first bank that handles a check will imprint its amount in magnetic ink characters to further aid in the processing of the check. The amount will be printed directly below the signature line in the lower right-hand corner of the check.

Checks imprinted with the bank's number and the depositor's number can be fed into MICR machines which will "read" the numbers and cause the checks to be sorted in the desired fashion. If the amounts of the checks are printed thereon in magnetic ink, such amounts can be totaled, and each check can be posted electronically to the customer's account. This process can be carried on at extremely high speed with almost no danger of error.

The two checks reproduced at the top of the preceding page illustrate the appearance of the magnetic ink characters that have been printed at the bottom, as well as check stubs properly completed. (For a further discussion of electronic processing of checks, see Appendix, pages A-11 — A-13.)

Recording Bank Transactions. A depositor should keep a record of the transactions he completes with his bank. The usual plan is to keep this record on the checkbook stubs as shown in the illustration on page 60. It will be noted that the record consists of detailed information concerning each check written and an amount column in which should be recorded **(1)** the balance brought forward or carried down, **(2)** the amount of deposits to be added, and **(3)** the amount of checks to be subtracted. The purpose is to keep a detailed record of deposits made and checks issued and to indicate the balance in the checking account after each check is drawn.

As the amount of each check is recorded in the journal, a check mark may be placed immediately after the account title written on the stub to indicate that it has been recorded. When the canceled check is subsequently received from the bank, the amount shown on the stub may be checked to indicate that the canceled check has been received.

Records Kept by a Bank. The usual transactions completed by a bank with a depositor are:

    (a) Accepting deposits made by the depositor.
    (b) Paying checks issued by the depositor.
    (c) Lending money to the depositor.
    (d) Collecting the amounts of various kinds of commercial paper, such as matured bonds, for the account of the depositor.

The bank keeps an account for each depositor. Each transaction affecting a depositor's account is recorded by debiting or crediting his account, depending upon the effect of the transaction. When a bank accepts a deposit, the account of the depositor is credited for the amount of the deposit. The deposit increases the bank's liability to the depositor.

When the bank pays a check that has been drawn on the bank, it debits the account of the depositor for the amount of the check. If the bank makes a collection for a depositor, the net amount of the collection is credited to his account. At the same time the bank notifies the depositor on a form similar to the one shown below that the collection has been made.

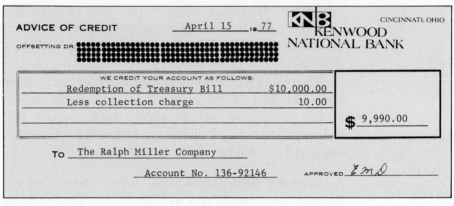

Credit Advice

Bank Statement. Once each month a bank renders a statement of account to each depositor. An illustration of a widely used form of bank statement is shown on the next page. It may be mentioned that some banks provide statements that also present information about savings accounts, loan accounts, etc., for those depositors that have such additional accounts. Very commonly, however, a separate statement is furnished for each type of account.

The statement illustrated is for a checking account. It is a report showing **(1)** the balance on deposit at the beginning of the period, **(2)** the amounts of deposits made during the period, **(3)** the amounts of checks honored during the period, **(4)** other items charged to the depositor's account during the period, and **(5)** the balance on deposit at the end of the period. With his bank statement, the depositor also receives all checks paid by the bank during the period, together with any other vouchers representing items charged to his account.

Reconciling the Bank Statement. When a bank statement is received, the depositor should check it immediately with the bank balance record kept on his check stubs. This procedure is known as *reconciling the bank statement*, sometimes called "balancing the statement." The balance shown on the bank statement may not be the same as the amount shown on the check stubs for one or more of the following reasons:

   (a) Some of the checks issued during the period may not have been presented to the bank for payment before the statement was prepared. These are known as *outstanding checks*.

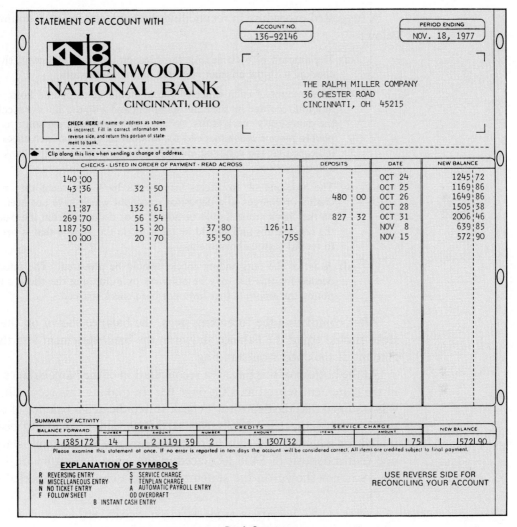

STATEMENT OF ACCOUNT WITH

ACCOUNT NO.
136–92146

PERIOD ENDING
NOV. 18, 1977

KNB
KENWOOD
NATIONAL BANK
CINCINNATI, OHIO

THE RALPH MILLER COMPANY
36 CHESTER ROAD
CINCINNATI, OH 45215

CHECK HERE if name or address as shown is incorrect. Fill in correct information on reverse side, and return this portion of statement to bank.

◄ Clip along this line when sending a change of address.

CHECKS · LISTED IN ORDER OF PAYMENT · READ ACROSS					DEPOSITS	DATE	NEW BALANCE
140 00						OCT 24	1245 72
43 36	32 50					OCT 25	1169 86
					480 00	OCT 26	1649 86
						OCT 28	1505 38
11 87	132 61				827 32	OCT 31	2006 46
269 70	56 54						
1187 50	15 20	37 80	126 11			NOV 8	639 85
10 00	20 70	35 50	75S			NOV 15	572 90

SUMMARY OF ACTIVITY

BALANCE FORWARD	DEBITS		CREDITS		SERVICE CHARGE		NEW BALANCE
	NUMBER	AMOUNT	NUMBER	AMOUNT	ITEMS	AMOUNT	
1385 72	14	2119 39	2	1307 32	1	75	572 90

Please examine this statement at once. If no error is reported in ten days the account will be considered correct. All items are credited subject to final payment.

EXPLANATION OF SYMBOLS

R REVERSING ENTRY	S SERVICE CHARGE
M MISCELLANEOUS ENTRY	T TENPLAN CHARGE
N NO TICKET ENTRY	A AUTOMATIC PAYROLL ENTRY
F FOLLOW SHEET	OD OVERDRAFT
	B INSTANT CASH ENTRY

USE REVERSE SIDE FOR
RECONCILING YOUR ACCOUNT

Bank Statement

(b) Deposits made by mail may have been in transit, or a deposit placed in the night depository may not have been recorded by the bank until the day following the date of the statement.

(c) The bank may have credited the depositor's account for an amount collected for him but the depositor may not as yet have noted it on his check stubs — possibly the credit advice had not yet been received.

(d) Service charges or other charges may appear on the bank statement that the depositor has not recorded on the check stubs.

(e) The depositor may have erred in keeping the bank record.

(f) The bank may have erred in keeping its account with the depositor.

If a depositor is unable to reconcile the bank statement, a report on the matter should be made to the bank immediately.

A suggested procedure in reconciling the bank statement is enumerated below:

(a) The amount of each deposit recorded on the bank statement should be checked with the amount recorded on the check stubs.

(b) The amount of each canceled check should be compared both with the amount recorded on the bank statement and with the amount recorded on the depositor's check stubs. When making this comparison it is a good plan to place a check mark by the amount recorded on each check stub to indicate that the canceled check has been returned by the bank and its amount verified.

(c) The amounts of any items listed on a bank statement that represent credits or charges to a depositor's account which have not been entered on the check stubs should be added to or deducted from the balance on the check stubs and should be recorded in the journal that is being used to record cash disbursements.

(d) A list of the outstanding checks should be prepared. The information needed for this list may be obtained by examining the check stubs and noting the amounts that have not been check marked.

After completing the foregoing steps, the balance shown on the check stubs should equal the balance shown in the bank statement less the total amount of the checks outstanding.

At the bottom of this page is a reconciliation of the bank balance shown in the statement reproduced on page 63. In making this reconciliation it was assumed that the depositor's check stub indicated a balance of $757.22 on November 18, that Checks Nos. 416, 419, and 421 had not been presented for payment and thus were not returned with the bank statement, and that a deposit of $456.13 placed in the night depository on November 18 is not shown on the statement. In matching the canceled checks

THE RALPH MILLER COMPANY
Reconciliation of Bank Statement
November 18, 1977

Balance, November 18, per bank statement............			$ 572.90
Add: Deposit, November 18.........................			456.13
			$1,029.03
Less checks outstanding, November 18:			
No. 416.......................................		$ 85.00	
No. 419.......................................		17.40	
No. 421.......................................		170.25	272.65
Adjusted bank balance, November 18.................			$ 756.38
Check stub balance, November 18....................			$ 757.22
Less: Bank service charge...........................	$	.75	
Error on stub for Check No. 394................		.09	.84
Adjusted check stub balance, November 18............			$ 756.38

that were returned with the bank statement against the check stubs, an error on the stub for Check No. 394 was discovered. That check was for $11.87. On its stub, the amount was shown as $11.78. This is called a *transposition* error. The "8" and the "7" were transposed (order reversed). On Stub No. 394 and the others that followed, the bank balance shown was 9 cents too large. The correct amount, $11.87, should be shown on Stub No. 394, and the bank balance shown on the stub of the last check used should be reduced $.09. If Check No. 394 was in payment of, say, a telephone bill, an entry should be made debiting Telephone Expense and crediting Cash. (Alternatively, since such a small amount was involved, the debit might be made to Miscellaneous Expense.)

Service Charges. A service charge may be made by a bank for the handling of checks and other items. The basis and the amount of such charges vary with different banks in different localities. Sometimes a rather elaborate *deposit activity analysis* is involved.

When a bank statement indicates that a service charge has been made, the depositor should record the amount of the service charge by debiting an expense account, such as Miscellaneous Expense, and by crediting Cash. He should also deduct the amount of such charges from the check stub balance.

Keeping a Ledger Account with the Bank. As explained previously, a memorandum account with the bank may be kept on the depositor's checkbook stub. The depositor may also keep a ledger account with the bank if desired. The title of such an account usually is the name of the bank. Sometimes more than one account is kept with a bank in which case each account should be correctly labeled. Such terms as "commercial," "executive," and "payroll" are used to identify the accounts.

The bank account should be debited for the amount of each deposit and should be credited for the amount of each check written. The account should also be credited for any other items that may be charged to the account by the bank, including service charges.

When both a cash account and a bank account are kept in the ledger, the following procedure should be observed in recording transactions affecting these accounts:

CASH		KENWOOD NATIONAL BANK	
Debit	Credit	Debit	Credit
For all receipts of cash and cash items.	(a) For all payments in cash, (b) For all bank deposits.	(a) For all deposits. (b) For collection of amounts for the depositor.	(a) For all checks written, (b) For all service charges, (c) For all other charges, such as for dishonored checks.

Under this method of accounting for cash and banking transactions, the cash account will be in balance when all cash on hand has been deposited in the bank. To prove the balance of the cash account at any time, it is necessary only to count the cash and cash items on hand and to compare the total with the cash account balance. To prove the bank account balance, it will be necessary to reconcile the bank balance in the same manner in which it is reconciled when only a memorandum record of bank transactions is kept on the check stubs.

The cash account can be dispensed with when a bank account is kept in the ledger and all cash receipts are deposited in the bank. When this is done, all disbursements (except small expenditures made from a petty cash fund) are made by check. Daily, or at frequent intervals, the receipts are deposited in the bank. If all cash received during the month has been deposited before the books are closed at the end of the month, the total amount of the bank deposits will equal the total cash receipts for the month. If all disbursements during the month are made by check, the total amount of checks issued will be the total disbursements for the month.

Savings account

When a savings account is opened in a bank, a signature card must be signed by the depositor. A passbook is given to the depositor that must be presented at the bank when making deposits or when making withdrawals. By signing the signature card, the depositor agrees to abide by the rules and the regulations of the bank. These rules and regulations vary with different banks and may be altered and amended from time to time. The principal differences between a savings account and a checking account are that interest is paid by the bank on a savings account and withdrawals from a savings account may be made at the bank or by mail by the depositor or his authorized agent. Interest usually is computed on a quarterly basis. The passbook must be presented or mailed along with a withdrawal slip when money is withdrawn from the account. Banks do not pay interest on the balances in checking accounts. Depositors use checking accounts primarily as a convenient means of making payments, while savings accounts are used primarily as a means of accumulating funds with interest.

Savings accounts are not too frequently used by businesses. If the assets of a business include money in a bank savings account, there should be a separate account in the ledger with a title and a number that indicate the nature of the deposit. Sometimes the name of the bank is in the title, as, for example, "Kenwood National Bank — Savings Account." When the bank credits interest to the account, the depositor should record the amount in his accounts by a debit to the savings account and by a credit to Interest Earned. The interest is revenue whether withdrawn or not (and is taxed to the depositor when earned).

Report **No. 3-2**	Refer to the study assignments and complete Report No. 3-2. This assignment provides a test of your ability to apply the principles developed in the first three chapters of the textbook. After completing the report, you may proceed with the textbook discussion in Chapter 4 until the next report is required.

Chapter 4

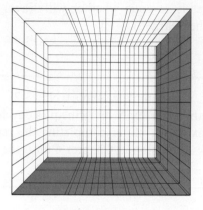

PAYROLL ACCOUNTING

Employers need to maintain detailed and accurate payroll accounting records. Accurate accounting for employees' earnings preserves the legal and moral right of each employee to be paid according to his employment contract and the laws governing such contracts.

Payroll accounting records also provide information useful in the analysis and classification of labor costs. At the same time, payroll accounting information is invaluable in contract discussions with labor unions, in the settlement of company-union grievances, and in other forms of collective bargaining. Clearly, there is virtually no margin for error in payroll accounting.

EARNINGS AND DEDUCTIONS

The first step in determining the amount to be paid to an employee is to calculate the amount of his total or gross earnings for the pay period. The second step is to determine the amounts of any deductions that are required either by law or by agreement. Depending upon a variety of circumstances, either or both of these steps may be relatively simple or quite complicated. An examination of the factors that are involved follows.

Employer-employee relationships

Not every individual who performs services for a business is considered to be an employee. A public accountant, lawyer, or management consultant who sells his services to a business does not become its employee. Neither does a plumber nor an electrician who is hired to make specific repairs or installations on business property. These people are told what to do, but not how to do it, and the compensation that they receive for their services is called a *fee*. Any person who agrees to perform a service for a fee and is not subject to the control of those whom he serves is called an *independent contractor*.

In contrast, an employee is one who is under the control and direction of his employer with regard to the performance of services. The difference between an independent contractor and an employee is an important legal distinction. The nature and extent of the responsibilities of a contractor and a client to each other and to third parties are quite different from the mutual obligations of an employer and any one of his employees.

Types of compensation

Compensation for managerial or administrative services usually is called *salary*. A salary normally is expressed in terms of a month or a year. Compensation either for skilled or for unskilled labor usually is referred to as *wages*. Wages ordinarily are expressed in terms of hours, weeks, or pieces of accomplishment. The terms salaries and wages often are used interchangeably in practice.

Supplements to basic salaries or wages of employees include bonuses, commissions, cost-of-living adjustments, pensions, and profit sharing plans. Compensation also may take the form of goods, lodging, meals, or other property, and as such is measured by the fair market value of the property or service given in payment for the employee's efforts.

Determination of total earnings

An employee's earnings commonly are based on the time worked during the payroll period. Sometimes earnings are based on units of output or of sales during the period. Compensation based on time requires a record of the time worked by each employee. Where there are only a few employees, a record of times worked kept in a memorandum book may suffice. Where there are many employees, time clocks commonly are used to record time spent on the job each day. With time clocks, a clock card is provided for each employee and the clock is used to record arrival and departure times. Alternatively, plastic cards or badges with holes punched in them for basic employee data are now being used in computer-based timekeeping systems. Whatever method is used, the total time worked during the payroll period must be computed.

Employees often are entitled to compensation at more than their regular rate of pay for work during certain hours or on certain days. If the employer is engaged in Interstate Commerce, the Federal Fair Labor Standards Act (commonly known as the Wages and Hours Law) provides that all employees covered by the Act must be paid one and one-half times the regular rate for all hours worked over 40 per week. Labor-management agreements often require extra pay for certain hours or days. In such cases, hours worked in excess of eight per day or work on Sundays and specified holidays may be paid for at higher rates.

To illustrate, assume that the company which employs Ronald Slone pays time and a half for all hours worked in excess of 40 per week and double time for work on Sunday. Slone's regular rate is $6 per hour; and during the week ended April 15, he worked nine hours each day Monday through Friday, six hours on Saturday, and four on Sunday. Slone's total earnings for the week ended April 15 would be computed as follows:

40 hours @ $6.00	$240.00
11 hours @ $9.00	99.00
(Slone worked 9 hours each day Monday through Friday and 6 hours on Saturday — a total of 51 hours. Forty hours would be paid for at the regular rate and 11 hours at time and a half.)	
4 hours (on Sunday) @ $12.00	48.00
Total earnings for the week	$387.00

An employee who is paid a regular salary may be entitled to premium pay for any overtime. If this is the case, it is necessary to compute the regular hourly rate of pay before computing the overtime rate. To illustrate, assume that Bessie Smith receives a regular salary of $1,000 a month. Ms. Smith is entitled to overtime pay at the rate of one and one-half times her regular hourly rate for any time worked in excess of 40 hours per week. Her overtime pay may be computed as follows:

$1,000 \times 12$ months $= $12,000 annual pay
$12,000 \div 52$ weeks $= $230.77 per week
$230.77 \div 40$ hours $= $5.77 per regular hour
$5.77 \times 1\frac{1}{2} = $8.65 per overtime hour

Deductions from total earnings

With few exceptions, employers are required to withhold portions of each employee's total earnings both for federal income tax and for social security taxes. Certain states and cities also require income or earnings tax withholding on the part of employers. Besides these deductions, an agreement between the employer and the employee may call for amounts to be withheld for any one or more of the following reasons:

(a) To purchase United States savings bonds for the employee.
(b) To pay a life, accident, or health insurance premium for the employee.
(c) To pay the employee's union dues.
(d) To add to a pension fund or profit sharing fund.
(e) To pay to some charitable organization.
(f) To repay a loan from the company or from the company credit union.

**Social
security and
tax account
number**

Each employee is required to have a social security account and tax account number for payroll accounting purposes. A completed Form SS-5, the official form to be used in applying for an account number, follows:

APPLICATION FOR A SOCIAL SECURITY NUMBER   270   DO NOT WRITE IN THE ABOVE SPACE
See Instructions on Back.   Print in Black or Dark Blue Ink or Use Typewriter.

1 Print FULL NAME YOU WILL USE IN WORK OR BUSINESS   (First Name)   (Middle Name or Initial – if none, draw line ___)   (Last Name)
   Ronald   Marlin   Lee

2 Print FULL NAME GIVEN YOU AT BIRTH   Ronald Marlin Lee
6 YOUR DATE OF BIRTH   (Month) (Day) (Year) July 30, 1948

3 PLACE OF BIRTH   (City)   (County if known)   (State)
   Minneapolis   Hennepin   Minnesota
7 YOUR PRESENT AGE (Age on last birthday)   19

4 MOTHER'S FULL NAME AT HER BIRTH (Her maiden name)
   Lorraine E. Quist
8 YOUR SEX   MALE FEMALE   X

5 FATHER'S FULL NAME (Regardless of whether living or dead)
   Marlin D. Lee
9 YOUR COLOR OR RACE   WHITE NEGRO OTHER   X

10 HAVE YOU EVER BEFORE APPLIED FOR OR HAD A SOCIAL SECURITY, RAILROAD, OR TAX ACCOUNT NUMBER?   NO DON'T KNOW YES   (If "YES" Print STATE in which you applied and DATE you applied and SOCIAL SECURITY NUMBER if known)   X

11 YOUR MAILING ADDRESS   (Number and Street, Apt. No., P.O. Box, or Rural Route)   (City)   (State)   (Zip Code)
   502 Kingsland Avenue   St. Louis,   Missouri   63130

12 TODAY'S DATE   Jan. 2, 1968
14 Sign YOUR NAME HERE (Do Not Print)   Ronald Marlin Lee
   NOTICE: Whoever, with intent to falsify his or someone else's true identity, willfully furnishes or causes to be furnished false information in applying for a social security number, is subject to a fine of not more than $1,000 or imprisonment for up to 1 year, or both.

13 TELEPHONE NUMBER   862-1673

TREASURY DEPARTMENT Internal Revenue Service   RESCREEN ASSIGN DUP ISSUED
FORM SS-5   Return completed application to nearest SOCIAL SECURITY ADMINISTRATION OFFICE

Completed Application for Social Security and Tax Account Number (Form SS-5)

**Employees'
income tax
withheld**

Under federal law, employers are required to withhold certain amounts from the total earnings of each employee to be applied toward the payment of the employee's federal income tax. The amount to be withheld is governed by **(1)** the total earnings of the employee, **(2)** the number of *withholding allowances* claimed by the employee, **(3)** the marital status of the employee, and **(4)** the length of the employee's pay period.

Each federal income taxpayer is entitled to one exemption for himself or for herself and one each for certain other qualified relatives whom he or she supports. The law specifies the relationship that must exist, the extent of support required, and how much the *dependent* may earn in order that an exemption may be claimed. As of 1972, each single taxpayer, or each married taxpayer whose spouse is not also employed, has become entitled to one *special withholding allowance*. A taxpayer and spouse each get an extra exemption for age over 65 years and still another exemption for blindness.

An employed taxpayer must furnish his employer with an Employee's Withholding Allowance Certificate, Form W-4, showing the number of allowances, if any, claimed. The allowance certificate completed by Ronald Marlin Lee is shown on the next page.

Employees with large itemized deductions are permitted to claim *additional withholding allowances*. Each additional withholding allowance will give the taxpayer an additional income tax deduction.

Form **W-4**	**Employee's Withholding Allowance Certificate**	
Department of the Treasury Internal Revenue Service	(This certificate is for income tax withholding purposes only; it will remain in effect until you change it.)	

Type or print your full name	Your social security number
Ronald Marlin Lee	474-52-4829

Home address (Number and street or rural route)	Marital status
502 Kingsland Avenue	☐ Single ☒ Married

City or town, State and ZIP code	(If married but legally separated, or spouse is a nonresident alien, check the single block.)
St. Louis, MO 63130	

1 Total number of allowances you are claiming 4

2 Additional amount, if any, you want deducted from each pay (if your employer agrees) . . . . $ -0-

I certify that to the best of my knowledge and belief, the number of withholding allowances claimed on this certificate does not exceed the number to which I am entitled.

Signature ▶ *Ronald Marlin Lee*   Date ▶ January 2,   , 19 77

16—83587-1

Completed Withholding Allowance Certificate (Form W-4)

Any employee desiring to claim one or more additional withholding allowances must estimate his expected total earnings and itemized deductions for the coming year. Generally, the amount of these itemized deductions cannot exceed the amount of itemized deductions (or standard deduction) claimed on the income tax return filed for the preceding year.

The instructions provided for completing Form W-4 include a table, illustrated at the top of the next page, from which the taxpayer can determine the number of additional withholding allowances to which he may be entitled. As shown on Line 1 of the W-4 illustrated above, Mr. Lee claimed four withholding allowances. This was because his estimated earnings and estimated itemized deductions did not qualify him for any additional withholding allowances. (Mr. Lee is married and has two minor children. However, since his wife is also employed, he would not be entitled to a so-called *special* withholding allowance. A special withholding allowance is *one* additional allowance granted to a taxpayer with only one job whose wife or husband does not also work.)

Most employers use the *wage-bracket method* of determining the amount of tax to be withheld. This method involves the use of income tax withholding tables provided by the Internal Revenue Service. Such tables cover monthly, semimonthly, biweekly, weekly, and daily or miscellaneous periods. There are two types of tables: **(1)** single persons and unmarried heads of households, and **(2)** married persons. Copies may be obtained from any local Internal Revenue Service office. A portion of a weekly income tax wage-bracket withholding table for married persons is illustrated on page 74. As an example of the use of this table, assume that Ronald M. Lee (who claims 4 allowances) had gross earnings of $335 for the week ending December 16, 1977. On the line showing the tax on wages

Form W-4　　　　　　　　　　　　　　　　　　　　　　　　　　　　　　　　　　　　Page **2**

Table for Determining Number of Withholding Allowances Based on Itemized Deductions

Estimated salaries and wages	Number of additional withholding allowances for the amount of itemized deductions shown in the appropriate column (See Line i on other side)						
	0 Under	**1** At least / But less than	**2** At least / But less than	**3** At least / But less than	**4** At least / But less than	**5** At least / But less than	**6*** At least / But less than
Part I Single Employees							
Under $10,000	$2,200	$2,200–$2,950	$2,950–$3,700	$3,700–$4,450	$4,450–$5,200	$5,200–$5,950	$5,950–$6,700
10,000–15,000	2,500	2,500–3,250	3,250–4,000	4,000–4,750	4,750–5,500	5,500–6,250	6,250–7,000
15,000–25,000	2,800	2,800–3,550	3,550–4,300	4,300–5,050	5,050–5,800	5,800–6,550	6,550–7,300
25,000–30,000	3,200	3,200–3,950	3,950–4,700	4,700–5,450	5,450–6,200	6,200–6,950	6,950–7,700
30,000–35,000	4,000	4,000–4,750	4,750–5,500	5,500–6,250	6,250–7,000	7,000–7,750	7,750–8,500
35,000–40,000	5,000	5,000–5,750	5,750–6,500	6,500–7,250	7,250–8,000	8,000–8,750	8,750–9,500
40,000–45,000	6,500	6,500–7,250	7,250–8,000	8,000–8,750	8,750–9,500	9,500–10,250	10,250–11,000
45,000–50,000**	8,000	8,000–8,750	8,750–9,500	9,500–10,250	10,250–11,000	11,000–11,750	11,750–12,500
Part II Married Employees (When Spouse Is Not Employed)							
Under $15,000	2,900	2,900–3,650	3,650–4,400	4,400–5,150	5,150–5,900	5,900–6,650	6,650–7,400
15,000–35,000	3,400	3,400–4,150	4,150–4,900	4,900–5,650	5,650–6,400	6,400–7,150	7,150–7,900
35,000–40,000	3,700	3,700–4,450	4,450–5,200	5,200–5,950	5,950–6,700	6,700–7,450	7,450–8,200
40,000–45,000	4,300	4,300–5,050	5,050–5,800	5,800–6,550	6,550–7,300	7,300–8,050	8,050–8,800
45,000–50,000**	5,200	5,200–5,950	5,950–6,700	6,700–7,450	7,450–8,200	8,200–8,950	8,950–9,700
Part III Married Employees (When Both Spouses Are Employed), and other employees who are holding more than one job							
Under $10,000	3,200	3,200–3,950	3,950–4,700	4,700–5,450	5,450–6,200	6,200–6,950	6,950–7,700
10,000–12,000	3,700	3,700–4,450	4,450–5,200	5,200–5,950	5,950–6,700	6,700–7,450	7,450–8,200
12,000–15,000	4,200	4,200–4,950	4,950–5,700	5,700–6,450	6,450–7,200	7,200–7,950	7,950–8,700
15,000–20,000	5,000	5,000–5,750	5,750–6,500	6,500–7,250	7,250–8,000	8,000–8,750	8,750–9,500
20,000–25,000	5,600	5,600–6,350	6,350–7,100	7,100–7,850	7,850–8,600	8,600–9,350	9,350–10,100
25,000–30,000	6,200	6,200–6,950	6,950–7,700	7,700–8,450	8,450–9,200	9,200–9,950	9,950–10,700
30,000–35,000	7,100	7,100–7,850	7,850–8,600	8,600–9,350	9,350–10,100	10,100–10,850	10,850–11,600
35,000–40,000	7,900	7,900–8,650	8,650–9,400	9,400–10,150	10,150–10,900	10,900–11,650	11,650–12,400
40,000–45,000	8,900	8,900–9,650	9,650–10,400	10,400–11,150	11,150–11,900	11,900–12,650	12,650–13,400
45,000–50,000**	10,200	10,200–10,950	10,950–11,700	11,700–12,450	12,450–13,200	13,200–13,950	13,950–14,700

*7 or More Allowances: If your itemized deductions exceed the amount shown in Column 6 (above), you may claim 6 allowances plus one more for each $750 or fraction thereof of itemized deductions in excess of the amounts shown in Column 6 for your salary and wage bracket.

**When annual salary or wage exceeds $50,000, "0" column amounts may be determined as follows: for single employees (Part I)—22% of their annual salary; for married employees whose spouse is not employed (Part II)—15% of their annual salary; and for married employees when both spouses are employed and other employees who are holding more than one job (Part III)—24% of their combined annual salary. An additional withholding allowance may be claimed for each $750 or fraction thereof by which itemized deductions exceed the "0" column amount determined in this manner.

Completed Withholding Allowance Certificate Form W-4 (Back)

of "at least $330, but less than $340," in the column headed "4 withholding allowances," $49.30 is given as the amount to be withheld.

Whether the wage-bracket method or some other method is used in computing the amount of tax to be withheld, the employee is given full benefit for all allowances claimed plus a standard deduction of approximately 15 percent. In any event, the sum of the taxes withheld from an employee's wages only approximates the tax on his actual income derived solely from wages. An employee may be liable for a tax larger than the amount withheld. On the other hand, the amount of the taxes withheld by the employer may be greater than the employee's actual tax liability. In such an event, the employee will be entitled to a refund of the excess taxes withheld, or he may elect to apply the excess to his tax liability for the following year.

Several of the states have adopted state income tax withholding procedures. Some of these states supply employers with withholding allowance

WEEKLY Payroll Period — Employee MARRIED

And the wages are-		And the number of withholding allowances claimed is—										
At least	But less than	0	1	2	3	4	5	6	7	8	9	10 or more
		The amount of income tax to be withheld shall be—										
$100	$105	$14.10	$11.80	$9.50	$7.20	$4.90	$2.80	$.80	$0	$0	$0	$0
105	110	14.90	12.60	10.30	8.00	5.70	3.50	1.50	0	0	0	0
110	115	15.70	13.40	11.10	8.80	6.50	4.20	2.20	.10	0	0	0
115	120	16.50	14.20	11.90	9.60	7.30	5.00	2.90	.80	0	0	0
120	125	17.30	15.00	12.70	10.40	8.10	5.80	3.60	1.50	0	0	0
125	130	18.10	15.80	13.50	11.20	8.90	6.60	4.30	2.20	.20	0	0
130	135	18.90	16.60	14.30	12.00	9.70	7.40	5.10	2.90	.90	0	0
135	140	19.70	17.40	15.10	12.80	10.50	8.20	5.90	3.60	1.60	0	0
140	145	20.50	18.20	15.90	13.60	11.30	9.00	6.70	4.40	2.30	.30	0
145	150	21.30	19.00	16.70	14.40	12.10	9.80	7.50	5.20	3.00	1.00	0
150	160	22.50	20.20	17.90	15.60	13.30	11.00	8.70	6.40	4.10	2.00	0
160	170	24.10	21.80	19.50	17.20	14.90	12.60	10.30	8.00	5.70	3.40	1.40
170	180	26.00	23.40	21.10	18.80	16.50	14.20	11.90	9.60	7.30	5.00	2.80
180	190	28.00	25.20	22.70	20.40	18.10	15.80	13.50	11.20	8.90	6.60	4.30
190	200	30.00	27.20	24.30	22.00	19.70	17.40	15.10	12.80	10.50	8.20	5.90
200	210	32.00	29.20	26.30	23.60	21.30	19.00	16.70	14.40	12.10	9.80	7.50
210	220	34.40	31.20	28.30	25.40	22.90	20.60	18.30	16.00	13.70	11.40	9.10
220	230	36.80	33.30	30.30	27.40	24.50	22.20	19.90	17.60	15.30	13.00	10.70
230	240	39.20	35.70	32.30	29.40	26.50	23.80	21.50	19.20	16.90	14.60	12.30
240	250	41.60	38.10	34.60	31.40	28.50	25.60	23.10	20.80	18.50	16.20	13.90
250	260	44.00	40.50	37.00	33.60	30.50	27.60	24.70	22.40	20.10	17.80	15.50
260	270	46.40	42.90	39.40	36.00	32.50	29.60	26.70	24.00	21.70	19.40	17.10
270	280	48.80	45.30	41.80	38.40	34.90	31.60	28.70	25.80	23.30	21.00	18.70
280	290	51.20	47.70	44.20	40.80	37.30	33.90	30.70	27.80	25.00	22.60	20.30
290	300	53.60	50.10	46.60	43.20	39.70	36.30	32.80	29.80	27.00	24.20	21.90
300	310	56.00	52.50	49.00	45.60	42.10	38.70	35.20	31.80	29.00	26.10	23.50
310	320	58.40	54.90	51.40	48.00	44.50	41.10	37.60	34.10	31.00	28.10	25.20
320	330	60.80	57.30	53.80	50.40	46.90	43.50	40.00	36.50	33.10	30.10	27.20
330	340	63.60	59.70	56.20	52.80	49.30	45.90	42.40	38.90	35.50	32.10	29.20
340	350	66.40	62.40	58.60	55.20	51.70	48.30	44.80	41.30	37.90	34.40	31.20

*As of the date of printing, the above Weekly Federal Income Tax Withholding Table is the most current available.

Portion of Weekly Federal Income Tax Withholding Table for Married Persons

certificate forms and income tax withholding tables that are similar in appearance to those used by the federal Internal Revenue Service. Note, however, that each state that has an income tax law uses the specific tax rates and dollar amounts for allowances as required by its law. Some states determine the amount to be withheld merely by applying a fixed percentage to the federal withholding amount.

Employees' FICA tax withheld

Payroll taxes are imposed on almost all employers and employees for old-age, survivors, and disability insurance (OASDI) benefits and health insurance benefits for the aged (HIP) — both under the Federal Insurance Contributions Act (FICA). The base of the tax and the tax rate have been changed several times since the law was first enacted and are subject to change by Congress at any time in the future. For purposes of this chapter, the rate is assumed to be 4.8 percent of the taxable wages paid during the calendar year for OASDI and 1.2 percent for HIP. It is also assumed that the first $15,000 of the wages paid to each employee in any calendar year is taxable. Any amount of compensation paid in excess of $15,000 is assumed to be exempt from the tax. The employees' portion of the FICA tax must be withheld from their wages by the employer. Although it is true that the base and rate of the tax may be changed at the pleasure of Congress, the accounting principles or methods of recording payroll transactions are not affected.

A few states require employers to withhold a percentage of the employees' wages for unemployment compensation benefits or for disability benefits. In some states and cities, employers are required to withhold a percentage of the employees' wages for other types of payroll taxes. The withholding of income taxes at the state and city level has already been mentioned. Despite the number of withholdings required, each employer must comply with the proper laws in withholding any taxes based on payrolls and in keeping his payroll accounting records.

Payroll records

The needs of management and the requirements of various federal and state laws make it necessary for employers to keep records that will provide the following information:

    (a) The name, address, and social security number of each employee.
    (b) The gross amount of each employee's earnings, the date of payment, and the period of employment covered by each payroll.
    (c) The total amount of gross earnings accumulated since the first of the year.
    (d) The amount of any taxes or other items withheld from each employee's earnings.

Regardless of the number of employees or type of business, three types of payroll records usually need to be prepared for or by the employer. They are: **(1)** the payroll register or payroll journal; **(2)** the payroll check with earnings statement attached; and **(3)** the earnings record of the individual employee (on a weekly, monthly, quarterly, or annual basis). These records can be prepared either by *manual* or by *automated* methods.

Payroll Register. A manually prepared payroll register used by Central States Diversified, Inc., for the payroll period ended December 16, 1977, is illustrated on pages 76 and 77. The usual source of information for preparing a payroll register is a time memorandum book, the batch of time clock cards, or a computer print-out. Central States Diversified, Inc., has eight employees, as the illustration shows. Michelle Coxx and Wayne Thomas each claim only one allowance because each has two jobs. Stephen Akos and James Paynter each claim only two withholding allowances because their wives also work. Ole Brandal, John MacArthur and

James O'Donnell each get the special withholding allowance, but none as yet has any children. Regular deductions are made from the earnings of employees for FICA tax, federal income tax, and city earnings tax. In addition, for the pay period ending nearest to the middle of the month, deductions are made for life insurance, private hospital insurance, the company credit union, and (if desired) for the purchase of United States savings bonds.

Ole L. Brandal and Ronald M. Lee have each authorized Central States Diversified, Inc., to withhold $15 on the payday nearest to the middle of each month for United States savings bonds. When the amount withheld reaches the sum of $75, a $100 Series E, United States savings bond is purchased at the bank for each employee and delivered to him.

Only the first $15,000 of earnings received in any calendar year is subject to FICA tax. Mr. Lee's earnings for the week ending December 16 are exempt from the FICA tax because he has already been taxed on earnings totaling $15,000.

After the payroll register has been completed, the amount columns should be footed and the footings proved as follows:

Regular earnings...................................		$1,635.00
Overtime earnings.................................		205.00
Gross earnings....................................		$1,840.00
Deductions:		
FICA tax.....................................	$ 69.90	
Federal income tax...........................	268.60	
City earnings tax............................	36.80	
Life insurance premiums......................	31.00	
Private hospital insurance premiums..........	18.00	
Credit union................................	20.00	
United States savings bonds..................	30.00	474.30
Net amount of payroll..............................		$1,365.70

PAYROLL REGISTER

	NAME	EMPLOYEE NO.	NO. OF ALLOW.	MARITAL STATUS	EARNINGS REGULAR	EARNINGS OVER-TIME	EARNINGS TOTAL	EARNINGS CUMULATIVE TOTAL	TAXABLE EARNINGS UNEM-PLOY. COMP.	TAXABLE EARNINGS FICA	
1	Akos, Stephen W.	1	2	M	180 00		180 00	9,250 00		180 00	1
2	Brandal, Ole L.	2	3	M	275 00	65 00	340 00	16,250 00			2
3	Cody, Michelle R.	3	1	S	150 00		150 00	7,600 00		150 00	3
4	Lee, Ronald M.	4	4	M	275 00	60 00	335 00	16,500 00			4
5	MacArthur, John D.	5	3	M	240 00	50 00	290 00	13,750 00		290 00	5
6	O'Donnell, James V.	6	3	M	175 00		175 00	9,000 00		175 00	6
7	Paynter, James R.	7	2	M	180 00	30 00	210 00	10,000 00		210 00	7
8	Thomas, Wayne D.	8	1	S	160 00		160 00	8,050 00		160 00	8
9					1,635 00	205 00	1,840 00	90,400 00		1,165 00	9
					1,635 00	205 00	1,840 00	90,400 00		1,165 00	

Payroll Register — Manually Prepared (Left Page)

After proving the footings, the totals should be entered in ink and the record should be ruled with single and double lines as shown in the illustration. Employees may be paid in cash or by check. Many businesses prepare a check for the net amount of the payroll and deposit it in a special payroll bank account. Individual paychecks are then drawn on that account for the amount due each employee. The employer usually furnishes a statement of payroll deductions to the employee along with each wage payment. Paychecks with detachable stubs, like the one for Ronald M. Lee, illustrated on pages 78 and 79, are widely used. The stub should be detached before the check is cashed, and the stub should be retained by the employee as a permanent record of his earnings and payroll deductions.

Employee's Earnings Record. An auxiliary record of each employee's earnings usually is kept in order to provide the information needed in preparing the various federal, state, and local reports required of employers. A manually prepared employee's earnings record used by Central States Diversified, Inc., for Ronald M. Lee, during the last two quarters of the current calendar year is illustrated on pages 80 and 81. This record may be kept on separate sheets or on cards, which may be filed alphabetically or numerically for ready reference. The information recorded on this form is taken from the payroll register.

Ronald Lee's earnings for the last half of the year up to December 16 are shown on this form. The entry for the pay period ended December 16 is posted from the payroll register illustrated on page 76 and below. It can be seen from Mr. Lee's earnings record that his cumulative earnings passed the $15,000 mark during the week ended November 18. Although his

FOR PERIOD ENDED *December 16*   19 77

			DEDUCTIONS						
FICA TAX	FEDERAL INC. TAX	CITY TAX	LIFE INS.	PRIV. HOSP. INS.	CREDIT UNION	OTHER	TOTAL	NET PAY	CK. NO.
10 80	22 70	3 60	6 00		4 00		47 10	132 90	301
	55 20	6 80			4 00	Sav. Bonds 15 00	81 00	259 00	302
9 00	24 50	3 00		4 00			40 50	109 50	303
	49 30	6 70	7 50	5 00	4 00	Sav. Bonds 15 00	87 50	247 50	304
17 40	43 20	5 80	7 50	5 00	4 00		82 90	207 10	305
10 50	18 80	3 50	5 00				37 80	137 20	306
12 60	28 30	4 20			4 00		49 10	160 90	307
9 60	26 60	3 20	5 00	4 00			48 40	111 60	308
69 90	268 60	36 80	31 00	18 00	20 00	30 00	474 30	1,365 70	
69 90	268 60	36 80	31 00	18 00	20 00	30 00	474 30	1,365 70	

Payroll Register — Manually Prepared (Right Page)

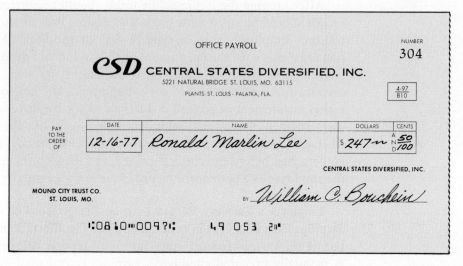

OFFICE PAYROLL

CSD CENTRAL STATES DIVERSIFIED, INC.

5221 NATURAL BRIDGE ST. LOUIS, MO. 63115

PLANTS: ST. LOUIS - PALATKA, FLA.

NUMBER
304

4-97
810

PAY TO THE ORDER OF	DATE	NAME	DOLLARS	CENTS
	12-16-77	Ronald Marlin Lee	$ 247	A N D 50/100

CENTRAL STATES DIVERSIFIED, INC.

MOUND CITY TRUST CO.
ST. LOUIS, MO.

BY *William C. Bouchein*

⑆0810⑈0097⑆   49 053 2⑈

Completed Paycheck — Manually Prepared

total earnings for that week amounted to $330, only $40 of such wages was subject to the combined FICA tax of 6 percent, hence only $2.40 was withheld from his wages for that week. For the remainder of the current calendar year, his entire earnings will be exempt from further FICA tax withholding.

The payroll register is a summary of the earnings of all employees for each pay period, while the earnings record is a summary of the annual earnings of each employee. The earnings record illustrated on pages 80 and 81 is designed so that a record of the earnings of the employee for the first half of the year may be kept on one side of the form and a record of the earnings for the last half of the year may be kept on the reverse side of the form. Thus, at the end of the year, the form provides a complete record of the earnings of the employee for the year. It also provides a record of the employee's earnings for each calendar quarter needed by the employer in the preparation of his quarterly returns. These returns will be discussed later in this chapter.

Automated payroll systems

Automated payroll systems may involve the use of small-capacity bookkeeping machines, large-capacity (often electronic) bookkeeping machines, or computer equipment. Both bookkeeping machine payroll systems and computerized payroll systems make it possible to prepare a payroll check with deduction stub, an earnings record, and a payroll register simultaneously. This is an application of the *write-it-once principle*, which recog-

CENTRAL STATES DIVERSIFIED, INC.
ST. LOUIS, MO.

STATEMENT OF EARNINGS

MISC.	HOSPITAL	BONDS	INSURANCE	CR. UNION	PARK	CHARITY	CHECK NO.	DATE
	5.00	15.00	7.50	4.00			304	12-16-77

REGULAR	O'TIME	OTHER	WH. TAX	FICA	CITY	STATE	TOTAL DEDUCTIONS	NET PAY
275.00	60.00		49.30		6.70		87.50	247.50
	EARNINGS			TAXES				

NON-NEGOTIABLE

and Deduction Stub

nizes that each time the same information is recopied there is another chance for an error.

Automation Companies and Payroll Accounting. The development of automated accounting methods and computer equipment have led to the establishment of a large number of *automation companies.* Automation companies are business organizations engaged in data processing on a contract basis for other businesses of small and medium size. They either are independently operated or are owned and operated by the major business machine manufacturers, banks, or other financial institutions. Their employees are trained in accounting and information systems work and can set up and operate effective payroll systems for customers.

When payroll accounting is done for a business by an automation company, the preliminary work that the business needs to do usually is quite limited. One or more cards are punched for each employee for each payroll period, with the aid of a keypunch machine and these cards contain necessary information such as:

(a) Employee name
(b) Employee address
(c) Employee social security number
(d) Regular earnings
(e) Overtime earnings
(f) Federal income tax withheld
(g) FICA (OASDI and HIP) tax withheld
(h) Other deductions

EMPLOYEE'S EARNINGS RECORD

	1977 PERIOD ENDING	EARNINGS REGULAR	OVER-TIME	TOTAL	CUMULATIVE TOTAL	TAXABLE EARNINGS UNEMPLOY. COMP.	FICA	DEDUCTIONS FICA TAX	FEDERAL INC. TAX	
1	7/8	275 00		275 00	9,555 00		275 00	16 50	34 90	1
2	7/15	275 00	55 00	330 00	9,885 00		330 00	19 80	49 30	2
3	7/22	275 00		275 00	10,160 00		275 00	16 50	34 90	3
4	7/29	275 00	65 00	340 00	10,500 00		340 00	20 40	51 70	4
5	8/5	275 00		275 00	10,775 00		275 00	16 50	34 90	5
6	8/12	275 00		275 00	11,050 00		275 00	16 50	34 90	6
7	8/19	275 00	60 00	335 00	11,385 00		335 00	20 10	49 30	7
8	8/26	275 00		275 00	11,660 00		275 00	16 50	34 90	8
9	9/2	275 00		275 00	11,935 00		275 00	16 50	34 90	9
10	9/9	275 00	55 00	330 00	12,265 00		330 00	19 80	49 30	10
11	9/16	275 00		275 00	12,540 00		275 00	16 50	34 90	11
12	9/23	275 00	60 00	335 00	12,875 00		335 00	20 10	49 30	12
13	9/30	275 00		275 00	13,150 00		275 00	16 50	34 90	13
	THIRD QUARTER	3,575 00	295 00	3,870 00			3,870 00	232 20	528 10	
1	10/7	275 00		275 00	13,425 00		275 00	16 50	34 90	1
2	10/14	275 00	60 00	335 00	13,760 00		335 00	20 10	49 30	2
3	10/21	275 00	50 00	325 00	14,085 00		325 00	19 50	46 90	3
4	10/28	275 00		275 00	14,360 00		275 00	16 50	34 90	4
5	11/4	275 00		275 00	14,635 00		275 00	16 50	34 90	5
6	11/11	275 00	50 00	325 00	14,960 00		325 00	19 50	46 90	6
7	11/18	275 00	55 00	330 00	15,290 00		40 00	2 40	49 30	7
8	11/25	275 00	50 00	325 00	15,615 00				46 90	8
9	12/2	275 00		275 00	15,890 00				34 90	9
10	12/9	275 00		275 00	16,165 00				34 90	10
11	12/16	275 00	60 00	335 00	16,500 00				49 30	11
12										12
13										13
	FOURTH QUARTER									
	YEARLY TOTAL									

SEX	DEPARTMENT	OCCUPATION	SOCIAL SECURITY NO.	MARITAL STATUS	ALLOW-ANCES
M ✓ F	Maintenance	Service	474-52-4829	M	4

Employee's Earnings Record — Manually Prepared (Left Page)

FOR PERIOD ENDED *December 31* 19 77

	CITY TAX	LIFE INS.	PRIVATE HOSP. INS.	CREDIT UNION	OTHER		TOTAL	NET PAY	CK. NO.	
1	5 50						56 90	218 10	120	1
2	6 60	7 50	5 00	4 00	Sav. Bonds	15 00	107 20	222 80	128	2
3	5 50						56 90	218 10	136	3
4	6 80						78 90	261 10	144	4
5	5 50						56 90	218 10	152	5
6	5 50						56 90	218 10	160	6
7	6 70	7 50	5 00	4 00	Sav. Bonds	15 00	107 60	227 40	168	7
8	5 50						56 90	218 10	176	8
9	5 50						56 90	218 10	184	9
10	6 60						75 70	254 30	192	10
11	5 50	7 50	5 00	4 00	Sav. Bonds	15 00	88 40	186 60	200	11
12	6 70						76 10	258 90	208	12
13	5 50						56 90	218 10	216	13
	77 40	22 50	15 00	12 00		45 00	932 20	2,937 80		
1	5 50						56 90	218 10	224	1
2	6 70	7 50	5 00	4 00	Sav. Bonds	15 00	107 60	227 40	232	2
3	6 50						72 90	252 10	240	3
4	5 50						56 90	218 10	248	4
5	5 50						56 90	218 10	256	5
6	6 50						72 90	252 10	264	6
7	6 60	7 50	5 00	4 00	Sav. Bonds	15 00	89 80	240 20	272	7
8	6 50						53 40	271 60	280	8
9	5 50						40 40	234 60	288	9
10	5 50						40 40	234 60	296	10
11	6 70	7 50	5 00	4 00	Sav. Bonds	15 00	87 50	247 50	304	11
12										12
13										13

PAY RATE	DATE OF BIRTH	DATE EMPLOYED	NAME - LAST	FIRST	MIDDLE	EMP. NO.
#275/wk.	7-30-48	1-3-77	Lee,	Ronald	Marlin	4

Employee's Earnings Record — Manually Prepared (Right Page)

PAYROLL

NAME	EMPLOYEE NUMBER	NUMBER OF ALLOW.	MARITAL STATUS	EARNINGS				TAXABLE EARNINGS	
				REGULAR	OVERTIME	TOTAL	CUMULATIVE TOTAL	UNEMPLOYMENT COMP.	FICA
Akos, Stephen W.	1	2	M	180.00		180.00	9,250.00		180.00
Brandal, Ole L.	2	3	M	275.00	65.00	340.00	16,250.00		
Coxx, Michelle R.	3	1	S	150.00		150.00	7,600.00		150.00
Lee, Ronald Marlin	4	4	M	275.00	60.00	335.00	16,500.00		
MacArthur, John D.	5	3	M	240.00	50.00	290.00	13,750.00		290.00
O'Donnell, James V.	6	3	M	175.00		175.00	9,000.00		175.00
Paynter, James R.	7	2	M	180.00	30.00	210.00	10,000.00		210.00
Thomas, Wayne D.	8	1	S	160.00		160.00	8,050.00		160.00
				1,635.00	205.00	1,840.00	90,400.00		1,165.00

Payroll Register — Machine Prepared (Left Page)

These punched cards are picked up by the automation company at regular intervals, and the payroll records desired by the business customer are prepared.

A recent development in payroll accounting is the use of *time sharing*. Several small- to medium-sized businesses may own or rent time on a computer jointly. These businesses contact the computer by telephone over leased lines and carry on their payroll accounting through a typewriter-printer console.

In a manual payroll system, the payroll register normally is prepared first and serves as a journal. The employees earnings records, checks, and stubs are then prepared from the payroll register information. However, in an automated payroll system all three records are prepared simultaneously. Because of this, the order of their preparation is not of any concern to the accountant.

Employer-Operated Payroll Systems. A payroll check with deduction stub, earnings record, and payroll register entry prepared simultaneously on a bookkeeping machine are illustrated above and on the following pages. Assume that these records were prepared by Central States Diversified, Inc., for its employee, Ronald M. Lee, for the same pay period as the manual records previously illustrated on pages 76 to 81, inclusive. Contrast the two types of payroll systems. The primary advantage of the machine system is the saving of time and labor.

REGISTER

		DEDUCTIONS								
FICA TAX	FEDERAL INC. TAX	CITY TAX	LIFE INS.	PRIVATE HOSP. INS.	CREDIT UNION	U.S. SAVINGS BONDS	TOTAL	DATE	NET PAY	CK. NO.
10.80	22.70	3.60	6.00		4.00		47.10	Dec. 16, '77	132.90	301
	55.20	6.80			4.00	15.00	81.00	Dec. 16, '77	259.00	302
9.00	24.50	3.00		4.00			40.50	Dec. 16, '77	109.50	303
	49.30	6.70	7.50	5.00	4.00	15.00	87.50	Dec. 16, '77	247.50	304
17.40	43.20	5.80	7.50	5.00	4.00		82.90	Dec. 16, '77	207.10	305
10.50	18.80	3.50	5.00				37.80	Dec. 16, '77	137.20	306
12.60	28.30	4.20			4.00		49.10	Dec. 16, '77	160.90	307
9.60	26.60	3.20	5.00	4.00			48.40	Dec. 16, '77	111.60	308
69.90	268.60	36.80	31.00	18.00	20.00	30.00	474.30		1,365.70	

Payroll Register — Machine Prepared (Right Page)

In addition to the *write-it-once* features of modern bookkeeping machines, computer-based payroll systems can also provide speed and storage as well as needed adding and multiplying ability. Through the use of computerized equipment, adding and multiplying of payrolls can be speeded up, and information such as wage rates and withholding table amounts can be stored inside the equipment. As one would expect, the cost of computerized payroll equipment is noticeably higher than the cost of more conventional bookkeeping machines. The type of computer-based accounting system well suited to payroll accounting, among other things, is described and illustrated in the appendix to this textbook.

Much of the work usually required to figure employees' gross earnings, deductions, and net pay may be eliminated if the equipment provides sufficient automation, storage capacity, and electronic calculation capability. When conventional electric bookkeeping machines are used, gross earnings are often computed separately on a calculator, and withholding and other tax amounts are either read from tables or worked out manually.

A computer-based payroll accounting system completes all of the major payroll records at once, just as do modern electronic bookkeeping machines. Also, a computer-based payroll accounting system determines automatically:

(a) The presence of the proper earnings record.
(b) The next available posting line.
(c) Whether overtime earnings are due.

EMPLOYEE'S

NAME	RONALD MARLIN LEE
ADDRESS	502 KINGSLAND AVENUE
CITY	ST. LOUIS, MISSOURI 63130

SEX	Male	NUMBER OF ALLOWANCES
MARITAL STATUS	Married	4

EARNINGS				TAXABLE EARNINGS	
REGULAR	OVERTIME	TOTAL	CUMULATIVE TOTAL	UNEMPLOY-MENT COMP.	FICA
275.00		275.00	9,555.00		275.00
275.00	55.00	330.00	9,885.00		330.00
275.00		275.00	10,160.00		275.00
275.00	65.00	340.00	10,500.00		340.00
275.00		275.00	10,775.00		275.00
275.00		275.00	11,050.00		275.00
275.00	60.00	335.00	11,385.00		335.00
275.00		275.00	11,660.00		275.00
275.00		275.00	11,935.00		275.00
275.00	55.00	330.00	12,265.00		330.00
275.00		275.00	12,540.00		275.00
275.00	60.00	335.00	12,875.00		335.00
275.00		275.00	13,150.00		275.00
THIRD QUARTER					
3,575.00	295.00	3,870.00			3,870.00
275.00		275.00	13,425.00		275.00
275.00	60.00	335.00	13,760.00		335.00
275.00	50.00	325.00	14,085.00		325.00
275.00		275.00	14,360.00		275.00
275.00		275.00	14,635.00		275.00
275.00	50.00	325.00	14,960.00		325.00
275.00	55.00	330.00	15,290.00		40.00
275.00	50.00	325.00	15,615.00		
275.00		275.00	15,890.00		
275.00		275.00	16,165.00		
275.00	60.00	335.00	16,500.00		
FOURTH QUARTER					
YEARLY TOTAL					

Employee's Earnings Record — Machine Prepared (Left Page)

(d) Whether there are other earnings.
(e) Whether the FICA limit has been reached.
(f) What tax deductions should be made.
(g) Whether insurance premiums should be deducted.
(h) Whether there are any other deductions to be made.
(i) Whether there are any delinquent deductions to be made.
(j) Whether there is anything else to be done.

EARNINGS RECORD

DEPARTMENT	Maintenance	SOCIAL SECURITY NUMBER	474-52-4829
OCCUPATION	Service	DATE OF BIRTH	July 30, 1948
PAY RATE	$275 Weekly	DATE EMPLOYED	January 3, 1977
EMPLOYEE NO.	4	DATE EMPLOYMENT TERMINATED	

FICA TAX	FEDERAL INC. TAX	CITY TAX	LIFE INS.	PRIVATE HOSP. INS.	CREDIT UNION	U.S. SAVINGS BONDS	TOTAL	DATE	NET PAY	CK. NO.
16.50	34.90	5.50					56.90	July 8, '77	218.10	120
19.80	49.30	6.60	7.50	5.00	4.00	15.00	107.20	July 15, '77	222.80	128
16.50	34.90	5.50					56.90	July 22, '77	218.10	136
20.40	51.70	6.80					78.90	July 29, '77	261.10	144
16.50	34.90	5.50					56.90	Aug. 5, '77	218.10	152
16.50	34.90	5.50					56.90	Aug. 12, '77	218.10	160
20.10	49.30	6.70	7.50	5.00	4.00	15.00	107.60	Aug. 19, '77	227.40	168
16.50	34.90	5.50					56.90	Aug. 26, '77	218.10	176
16.50	34.90	5.50					56.90	Sept. 2, '77	218.10	184
19.80	49.30	6.60					75.70	Sept. 9, '77	254.30	192
16.50	34.90	5.50	7.50	5.00	4.00	15.00	88.40	Sept. 16, '77	186.60	200
20.10	49.30	6.70					76.10	Sept. 23, '77	258.90	208
16.50	34.90	5.50					56.90	Sept. 30, '77	218.10	216
232.20	528.10	77.40	22.50	15.00	12.00	45.00	932.20		2,937.80	
16.50	34.90	5.50					56.90	Oct. 7, '77	218.10	224
20.10	49.30	6.70	7.50	5.00	4.00	15.00	107.60	Oct. 14, '77	227.40	232
19.50	46.90	6.50					72.90	Oct. 21, '77	252.10	240
16.50	34.90	5.50					56.90	Oct. 28, '77	218.10	248
16.50	34.90	5.50					56.90	Nov. 4, '77	218.10	256
19.50	46.90	6.50					72.90	Nov. 11, '77	252.10	264
2.40	49.30	6.60	7.50	5.00	4.00	15.00	89.80	Nov. 18, '77	240.20	272
	46.90	6.50					53.40	Nov. 25, '77	271.60	280
	34.90	5.50					40.40	Dec. 2, '77	234.60	288
	34.90	5.50					40.40	Dec. 9, '77	234.60	296
	49.30	6.70	7.50	5.00	4.00	15.00	87.50	Dec. 16, '77	247.50	304

Employee's Earnings Record — Machine Prepared (Right Page)

Once this system is properly set up, the operator is relieved of manual figuring and of looking up amounts in tables. The primary job is one of feeding in blank payroll accounting record forms and getting these forms back as completed payroll accounting records. (For a further discussion of computer-based accounting systems and procedures, see Appendix, page A-1.)

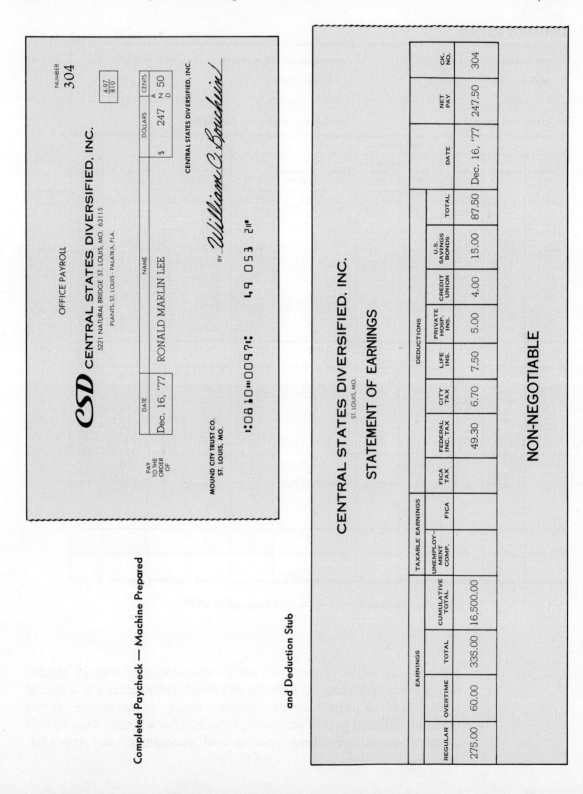

Completed Paycheck — Machine Prepared and Deduction Stub

OFFICE PAYROLL

NUMBER
304

4-97
810

CSD **CENTRAL STATES DIVERSIFIED, INC.**
5221 NATURAL BRIDGE ST. LOUIS, MO. 63115
PLANTS: ST. LOUIS - PALATKA, FLA.

DATE		DOLLARS	CENTS
Dec. 16, '77	NAME	$ 247	A N 50 D

RONALD MARLIN LEE

CENTRAL STATES DIVERSIFIED, INC.

PAY TO THE ORDER OF

MOUND CITY TRUST CO.
ST. LOUIS, MO.

BY *William C. Bouchein*

⑈081⑈0009⑈: 49 053 2⑈

CENTRAL STATES DIVERSIFIED, INC.
ST. LOUIS, MO.

STATEMENT OF EARNINGS

EARNINGS			TAXABLE EARNINGS		DEDUCTIONS										CK. NO.
REGULAR	OVERTIME	TOTAL	CUMULATIVE TOTAL	UNEMPLOY-MENT COMP.	FICA	FICA TAX	FEDERAL INC. TAX	CITY TAX	LIFE INS.	PRIVATE HOSP. INS.	CREDIT UNION	U.S. SAVINGS BONDS	TOTAL	DATE	NET PAY	
275.00	60.00	335.00	16,500.00				49.30	6.70	7.50	5.00	4.00	15.00	87.50	Dec. 16, '77	247.50	304

NON-NEGOTIABLE

Wage and tax statement

Not later than January 31 of each year the law requires employers to furnish each employee from whom income taxes have been withheld the Wage and Tax Statement, Form W-2, showing the total amount of wages paid and the amount of such tax withheld during the preceding calendar year. This statement should be issued 30 days after the last wage payment to a terminating employee. If the employee's wages were subject to FICA tax as well as federal, state, or local income tax, the employer must report total wages paid and the amounts deducted both for income tax and for FICA tax. Information for this purpose should be provided by the employee's earnings record. A completed form W-2 is illustrated below.

		Wage and Tax Statement **1975**	
43-0211630 CENTRAL STATES DIVERSIFIED, INC. 5221 Natural Bridge St. Louis, MO 63115	Type or print EMPLOYER'S name, address, ZIP code and Federal identifying number.	Copy C For employee's records	
		Employer's State Identifying number 21-686001	
Employee's social security number	1 Federal Income tax withheld	2 Wages, tips, and other compensation	3 FICA employee tax withheld	4 Total FICA wages
474-52-4829	$2,132.60	$17,050.00	$900.00	$15,000.00
Type or print Employee's name, address, and ZIP code below.	5 Was employee covered by a qualified pension plan, etc.?	6	7
Ronald M. Lee 502 Kingsland Avenue St. Louis, MO 63130	8 State or local tax withheld	9 State or local wages	10 State or locality
	11 State or local tax withheld	12 State or local wages	13 State or locality
Form W-2 This information is being furnished to the Internal Revenue Service.		Department of the Treasury—Internal Revenue Service	

Completed Wage and Tax Statement (Form W-2)

The number appearing on the Wage and Tax Statement above the name and address of the employer is an *identification number* assigned to the employer by the Social Security Administration. Every employer of even one person receiving taxable wages must get an identification number within a week of the beginning of such employment. This number must be shown on all reports required of Central States Diversified, Inc., under the Federal Insurance Contributions Act.

Wage and Tax Statements must be prepared in quadruplicate (four copies). Copy A goes to the Internal Revenue Service Center with the employer's return of taxes withheld for the fourth quarter of the calendar year. Copies B and C are furnished to the employee, so that he can send Copy B in with his federal income tax return as required and keep Copy C for his files. Copy D is kept by the employer for his records. In states or cities which have state or city income tax withholding laws, two more copies are furnished. One copy is sent in by the employer to the appropriate state or city tax department, and the other is sent in by the employee with his state or city income tax return.

Accounting for wages and wage deductions

In accounting for wages and wage deductions it is desirable to keep separate accounts for **(1)** wages earned and **(2)** wage deductions. Various account titles are used in recording wages, such as Payroll Expense, Salaries Expense, and Salaries and Commissions Expense. The accounts needed in recording wage deductions depend upon what deductions are involved. A separate account should be kept for recording the liability incurred for each type of deduction, such as FICA tax, employees income tax, and savings bond deductions.

Payroll Expense. This is an expense account which should be debited for the total amount of the gross earnings of all employees for each pay period. Sometimes separate

PAYROLL EXPENSE	
Debit	
to record gross earnings of employees for each pay period.	

payroll accounts are kept for the employees of different departments. Thus, separate accounts might be kept for Office Salaries Expense, Sales Salaries Expense, and Factory Payroll Expense.

FICA Tax Payable. This is a liability account which should be credited for **(1)** the FICA tax withheld from employees' wages and **(2)** the FICA tax imposed on the employer. The account should be debited for amounts paid to apply on

FICA TAX PAYABLE	
Debit	Credit
to record payment of FICA tax.	to record FICA taxes (a) withheld from employees' wages and (b) imposed on the employer.

such taxes. When all of the FICA taxes have been paid, the account should be in balance.

Employees Income Tax Payable. This is a liability account which should be credited for the total income tax withheld from employees' wages. The account should be

EMPLOYEES INCOME TAX PAYABLE	
Debit	Credit
to record payment of income tax withheld.	to record income tax withheld from employees' wages.

debited for amounts paid to apply on such taxes. When all of the income taxes withheld have been paid, the account will be in balance. A city or state earnings tax payable account is used in a similar manner.

Life Insurance Premiums Payable. This is a liability account which should be credited with amounts withheld from employees' wages for the future payment of life insurance premiums. The account should be debited for the subsequent payment

LIFE INSURANCE PREMIUMS PAYABLE	
Debit	Credit
to record the payment of life insurance premiums withheld.	to record amounts withheld for the future payment of life insurance premiums.

of these premiums to the life insurance company. Accounts for private hospital insurance premiums payable, credit union contributions payable, and savings bond deductions payable are similarly used.

Journalizing Payroll Transactions. The payroll register should provide the information needed in recording wages paid. The payroll register illustrated on pages 82 and 83 provided the information needed in drafting the following general journal entry to record the wages paid on December 16:

```
Dec. 16.  Payroll Expense...............................  1,840.00
            FICA Tax Payable............................              69.90
            Employees Income Tax Payable................             268.60
            City Earnings Tax Payable...................              36.80
            Life Insurance Premiums Payable.............              31.00
            Private Hospital Insurance Premiums Payable....           18.00
            Credit Union Contributions Payable..........              20.00
            Savings Bond Deductions Payable.............              30.00
            Cash........................................           1,365.70
            Payroll for week ended December 16.
```

It will be noted that the above journal entry involves one debit and eight credits. Regardless of the number of debits and credits needed to record a transaction, the total amount debited must be equal to the total amount credited.

Report **No. 4-1**	Complete Report No. 4-1 in the study assignments and submit your working papers to the instructor for approval. After completing the report, continue with the following textbook discussion until the next report is required.

PAYROLL TAXES IMPOSED ON THE EMPLOYER

The employer is liable to the government for the taxes which are required by law to be withheld from the wages of employees. These taxes include the federal income tax and the FICA tax which must be withheld from wages paid to employees. Such taxes are not an expense of the employer; nevertheless, the employer is required by law to collect the taxes and he is liable for the taxes until payment is made.

Certain taxes are also imposed on the employer for various purposes, such as old-age, survivors, and disability insurance benefits; hospital insurance benefits for the aged; and unemployment, relief, and welfare. Most employers are subject to payroll taxes imposed under the Federal

Insurance Contributions Act (FICA) and the Federal Unemployment Tax Act (FUTA). An employer may also be subject to the payroll tax imposed under the unemployment compensation laws of one or more states. These commonly are called "State Unemployment Tax."

Payroll taxes expense

All of the payroll taxes imposed on an employer under federal and state social security laws are an expense of the employer. In accounting for such taxes at least one expense account should be maintained. This account may be entitled Payroll Taxes Expense. It is an expense account which should be debited for all taxes imposed on the employer under federal and state social security laws. Sometimes separate expense accounts are kept for **(1)** FICA Tax Expense, **(2)** FUTA Tax Expense, and **(3)** State Unemployment Tax Expense. In small business enterprises it is usually considered satisfactory to keep a single expense account for all federal and state social security taxes imposed on the employer.

PAYROLL TAXES EXPENSE	
Debit to record FICA, FUTA, and State Unemployment Taxes imposed on the employer.	

Employer's FICA tax

The taxes imposed under the Federal Insurance Contributions Act apply equally to employers and to employees. As explained on page 75, both the rate and base of the tax may be changed by Congress at any time. In this discussion it is assumed that the combined rate is 6 percent which applies both to the employer and to his employees (a total of 12 percent) with respect to taxable wages. Only the first $15,000 of the wages paid to each employee in any calendar year constitutes taxable wages. Any amount of wages paid to an employee during a year in excess of $15,000 is exempt from FICA tax. While the employer is liable to the government both for the tax withheld from his employees' wages and for the tax imposed on the business, only the latter constitutes an expense of the business.

Employer's FUTA tax

Under the Federal Unemployment Tax Act, a payroll tax is levied on employers for the purpose of implementing more uniform administration of the various state unemployment compensation laws. Employers who employ one or more individuals for at least 20 calendar weeks in the calendar year, *or* who pay wages of $1,500 or more in any calendar quarter, are subject to this tax. The federal law imposes a specific rate of tax but allows a substantial credit against this levy if the state in which the employer is located has an unemployment compensation law that meets certain requirements. Since all states have such laws, the rate actually paid by most employers is much less than the maximum legal rate. As in the case of the FICA tax, Congress can and does change the rate from time to time. For the purpose of this discussion, a rate of 3.2 percent with a credit of 2.7 percent available to most employers is used. The difference, 0.5 percent $(3.2 - 2.7)$ is, then, the effective rate. This is applied to the first $4,200 of compensation paid to each employee during the calendar year. It is important to note this limitation in contrast to the $15,000 limit in the case of the FICA tax. It is also important to note that all of the payroll taxes relate to gross wages paid — not to wages earned. Sometimes wages are earned in one quarter or year, but not paid until the following period.

FUTA tax payable

In recording the federal unemployment tax, it is customary to keep a separate liability account entitled FUTA Tax Payable. This is a liability account which should be credited for the tax imposed on employers under the Federal Unemployment Tax Act. The account should be debited for amounts paid to apply on such taxes. When all of the FUTA taxes have been paid, the account should be in balance.

FUTA Tax Payable	
Debit	Credit
to record payment of FUTA tax.	to record FUTA tax imposed on the employer with respect to wages paid.

State unemployment tax

All of the states and the District of Columbia have enacted unemployment compensation laws providing for the payment of benefits to qualified unemployed workers. The cost of administering the state unemployment compensation laws is borne by the federal government. Under the federal law an appropriation is made for each year by the Congress from which grants are made to the states to meet the proper administrative costs of their unemployment compensation laws. As a result of this provision, the entire amount paid into the state funds may be used for the payment of benefits to qualified workers. While in general there is considerable uniformity in the provisions of the state laws, there are many variations in coverage, rates of tax imposed, and benefits payable to qualified workers. The date of payment of unemployment taxes also varies from state to state, and a penalty generally is imposed on the employer for late payment. Not all employers covered by the Federal Unemployment Tax

Act are covered by the unemployment compensation laws of the states in which they have employees. But most employers of one or more individuals are covered by the federal law.

The minimum number of employees specified under state laws varies from 1 to 4. However, in many of the states an employer who is covered by the federal law and has one or more individuals employed within the state is also covered by the state law. Furthermore, under the laws of most states an employer who is covered by the federal law may elect voluntary coverage in states where he has one or more employees, even though he may have less than the number of employees specified by the law in that particular state. In any event, it is necessary for each employer to be familiar with the unemployment compensation laws of all the states in which he has one or more employees, and if such employees are covered, he must keep such records and pay such taxes for unemployment compensation purposes as are prescribed by those laws.

In most states the unemployment benefit plan is financed entirely by taxes imposed on employers. However, in a few states employees are also required to contribute, and the amount of the tax imposed on the employees must be withheld from their wages.

In most states the maximum tax imposed upon employers is 2.7 percent of the first $4,200 of wages paid to each employee in any calendar year. However, under the laws of most states there is a *merit-rating* system which provides a tax-saving incentive to employers to stabilize employment. Under this system an employer's rate may be considerably less than the maximum rate if he provides steady work for his employees.

There are frequent changes in the state laws with respect to coverage, rates of contributions required, eligibility to receive benefits, and amounts of benefits payable. In this discussion, it is assumed that the state tax rate is 2.7 percent of the first $4,200 of wages paid each employee each year.

State unemployment tax payable

In recording the tax imposed under state unemployment compensation laws, it is customary to keep a separate liability account entitled State Unemployment Tax Payable. This is a liability account which

STATE UNEMPLOYMENT TAX PAYABLE	
Debit	Credit
to record state unemployment tax paid.	to record liability for state unemployment tax required of employers.

should be credited for the tax imposed on employers under the state unemployment compensation laws. The account should be debited for the amount paid to apply on such taxes. When all of the state taxes have been paid, the account should be in balance. Some employers who are subject to taxes imposed under the laws of several states keep a separate liability account for the tax imposed by each state.

Journalizing employer's payroll taxes

The payroll taxes imposed on employers may be recorded periodically, such as monthly or quarterly. It is more common to record such taxes at the time that wages are paid so that the employer's liability for such taxes and related expenses may be recorded in the same period as the wages on which the taxes are based. The payroll register illustrated on pages 82 and 83 provides the information needed in recording the FICA tax imposed on Central States Diversified, Inc., with respect to wages paid on December 16. The FICA taxable earnings for the pay period involved amounted to $1,165.00. Assuming that the combined rate of the tax imposed on the employer was 6 percent, which is the same as the rate of the tax imposed on the employees, the tax would amount to $69.90. (This amount will not necessarily be the same as that calculated by multiplying the tax rate times total taxable earnings due to the rounding up of amounts in calculating the tax deduction for each employee.) If only $875.00 of the earnings for the period had been subject to unemployment taxes (none actually were), the federal and state taxes would have been computed as follows:

State unemployment tax, 2.7% of $875.00	$23.63
FUTA tax, 0.5% of $875.00	4.38
Total unemployment taxes	$28.01

The following general journal entry may be made to record the payroll taxes imposed on the employer with respect to the wages paid on December 16:

Dec. 16. Payroll Taxes Expense	97.91	
FICA Tax Payable		69.90
FUTA Tax Payable		4.38
State Unemployment Tax Payable		23.63
Payroll taxes imposed on employer with respect to wages paid December 16.		

Filing returns and paying the payroll taxes

When the cumulative amount withheld from employees' wages for income tax and FICA tax purposes plus the amount of the FICA tax imposed on the employer during the first or second month of any quarter is more than $200, the total must be deposited at a District Federal Reserve Bank or some other United States depositary by the 15th of the following month. If at the end of a quarter the total amount of undeposited taxes is $200 or more, the total amount must be deposited in a federal depositary or Federal Reserve bank on or before the last day of the first month after the end of the quarter. If at the end of a quarter the total amount of undeposited taxes is less than $200, a deposit is not necessary. The taxes may either be paid directly to the Internal Revenue Service along with Form 941 or a deposit may be made.

When the cumulative amount of income and FICA tax is over $200 but under $2,000, the total is required to be deposited by the 15th day of the next month. If this $200–$2,000 limitation is reached in the third month of any quarter, no deposit need be made until the last day of the month following the quarter.

When the cumulative amount is $2,000 or more by the 7th, 15th, 22d, or last day of any month, a deposit must be made within three banking days after that quarter-monthly period.

A completed copy of the Federal Tax Deposit — Withheld Income and FICA Taxes, Form 501, is shown below. The stub is detached by the bank on payment of the taxes due and is the employer's record of the deposit.

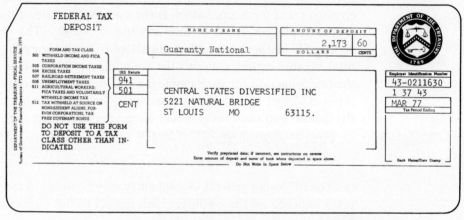

Completed Federal Tax Deposit Form (Form 501)

To illustrate the accounting procedure in recording the payment of employees' income tax and FICA tax withheld, it will be assumed that on February 3 Central States Diversified, Inc., issued a check in payment of the following taxes imposed with respect to wages paid during the month of January:

Employees' income tax withheld from wages...............		$1,274.40
FICA tax:		
Withheld from employees' wages.......................	$449.60	
Imposed on employer.................................	449.60	899.20
Amount of check.......................................		$2,173.60

A check for this amount accompanied by the Federal Tax Deposit form, Form 501, was sent to a bank that is qualified as a depositary for federal taxes. (All national banks are qualified.) This transaction may be recorded as indicated by the following general journal entry:

Feb. 3. FICA Tax Payable.............................	899.20	
Employees Income Tax Payable	1,274.40	
Cash.......................................		2,173.60
Remitted $2,173.60 in payment of taxes.		

Further assume that on March 3, $2,165.30 was deposited. This covered income tax withholdings of $1,268.80 during February and the employer's and employees' FICA tax of $896.50 for February. The proper entry was made to record the payment of $2,165.30. Also assume that during March, income tax withholdings amounted to $1,286.50 and FICA tax (employer's and employees'), $904.30 — a total of $2,190.80, which amount was deposited on April 4. The proper entry was made to record the payment of $2,190.80 to the Internal Revenue Service. Finally assume that on April 15, the quarterly return, Form 941, illustrated on page 96 was sent to the nearest Internal Revenue Service Center.

The amount on lines 11 and 13 of the quarterly tax return illustration, $3,829.70, is the sum of the employees' income tax withheld in January ($1,274.40), February ($1,268.80), and March ($1,286.50). The amount on line 14 of this return comes from the total of wages reported on line 8 (the total taxable FICA wages reported on Schedule A) times 12 percent (the combined FICA tax rate for employer and employee). The adjusted total of FICA tax on line 18 is added to the adjusted total of income tax withheld, line 13, to give the amount on line 19, which is the total income tax and FICA tax due to the federal government.

The amount on line 20 of the Form 941 illustration, $6,529.70, is the sum of the tax deposits for February 3 ($2,173.60), March 3 ($2,165.30), and $2,190.80, the balance due to the Internal Revenue Service for which a final deposit was made and listed in Schedule B (not illustrated).

The amount of the tax imposed on employers under the state unemployment compensation laws must be remitted to the proper state office during the month following the close of the calendar quarter. Each state provides an official form to be used in making a return of the taxes due. Assuming that a check for $494.91 was issued on April 30 in payment of state unemployment compensation tax on wages paid during the preceding quarter ended March 31, the transaction may be recorded as indicated by the following journal entry:

```
Apr. 30. State Unemployment Tax Payable....................   494.91
            Cash............................................            494.91
                Paid state unemployment tax.
```

Federal unemployment tax must be computed on a quarterly basis. If the amount of the employer's liability under the Federal Unemployment Tax Act during any quarter is more than $100, the total must be paid to the District Federal Reserve Bank or some other United States depositary on or before the last day of the first month following the close of the quarter. If the amount is $100 or less, no deposit is necessary, but this amount must be added to the amount subject to deposit for the next quarter.

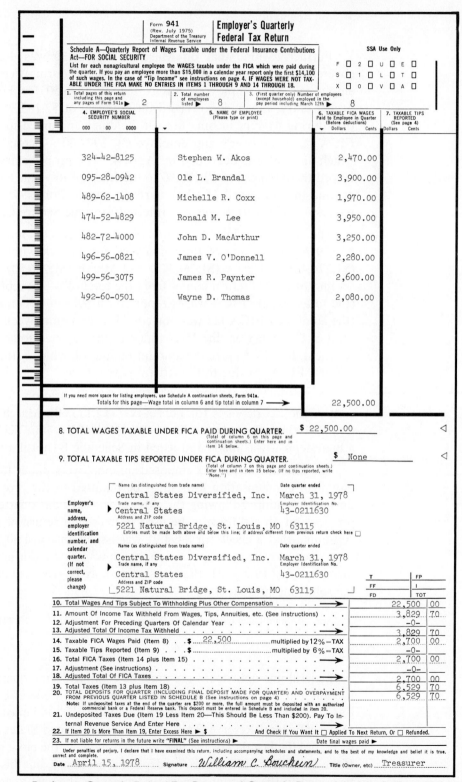

Form **941** (Rev. July 1975) Department of the Treasury Internal Revenue Service	**Employer's Quarterly Federal Tax Return**

Schedule A—Quarterly Report of Wages Taxable under the Federal Insurance Contributions Act—FOR SOCIAL SECURITY

List for each nonagricultural employee the WAGES taxable under the FICA which were paid during the quarter. If you pay an employee more than $15,000 in a calendar year report only the first $14,100 of such wages. In the case of "Tip Income" see instructions on page 4. IF WAGES WERE NOT TAXABLE UNDER THE FICA MAKE NO ENTRIES IN ITEMS 1 THROUGH 9 AND 14 THROUGH 18.

SSA Use Only

F ☐ 2 ☐ U ☐ E ☐
S ☐ 1 ☐ L ☐ T ☐
X ☐ 0 ☐ V ☐ A ☐

1. Total pages of this return including this page and any pages of Form 941a ▶ **2**	2. Total number of employees listed ▶ **8**	3. (First quarter only) Number of employees (except household) employed in the pay period including March 12th ▶ **8**

4. EMPLOYEE'S SOCIAL SECURITY NUMBER 000 00 0000	5. NAME OF EMPLOYEE (Please type or print)	6. TAXABLE FICA WAGES Paid to Employee in Quarter (Before deductions) Dollars / Cents	7. TAXABLE TIPS REPORTED (See page 4) Dollars / Cents
324-42-8125	Stephen W. Akos	2,470.00	
095-28-0942	Ole L. Brandal	3,900.00	
489-62-1408	Michelle R. Coxx	1,970.00	
474-52-4829	Ronald M. Lee	3,950.00	
482-72-4000	John D. MacArthur	3,250.00	
496-56-0821	James V. O'Donnell	2,280.00	
499-56-3075	James R. Paynter	2,600.00	
492-60-0501	Wayne D. Thomas	2,080.00	

If you need more space for listing employees, use Schedule A continuation sheets, Form 941a.

Totals for this page—Wage total in column 6 and tip total in column 7 ⟶ **22,500.00**

8. TOTAL WAGES TAXABLE UNDER FICA PAID DURING QUARTER. $ 22,500.00 ◁
(Total of column 6 on this page and continuation sheets.) Enter here and in item 14 below.

9. TOTAL TAXABLE TIPS REPORTED UNDER FICA DURING QUARTER. $ None ◁
(Total of column 7 on this page and continuation sheets.) Enter here and in item 15 below. (If no tips reported, write "None.")

Employer's name, address, employer identification number, and calendar quarter. (If not correct, please change)

Name (as distinguished from trade name)
Central States Diversified, Inc.   Date quarter ended March 31, 1978
Trade name, if any
▶ Central States   Employer Identification No. 43-0211630
Address and ZIP code
5221 Natural Bridge, St. Louis, MO 63115
Entries must be made both above and below this line; if address different from previous return check here ☐

Name (as distinguished from trade name)
Central States Diversified, Inc.   Date quarter ended March 31, 1978
Trade name, if any
Central States   Employer Identification No. 43-0211630
Address and ZIP code
5221 Natural Bridge, St. Louis, MO 63115

T		FP	
FF		I	
FD		TOT	

10. Total Wages And Tips Subject To Withholding Plus Other Compensation ⟶	22,500	00
11. Amount Of Income Tax Withheld From Wages, Tips, Annuities, etc. (See instructions)	3,829	70
12. Adjustment For Preceding Quarters Of Calendar Year	-0-	
13. Adjusted Total Of Income Tax Withheld	3,829	70
14. Taxable FICA Wages Paid (Item 8) . $ 22,500 .multiplied by 12%=TAX	2,700	00
15. Taxable Tips Reported (Item 9) . . $ ....multiplied by 6%=TAX	-0-	
16. Total FICA Taxes (Item 14 plus Item 15) ⟶	2,700	00
17. Adjustment (See instructions)	-0-	
18. Adjusted Total Of FICA Taxes ⟶	2,700	00
19. Total Taxes (Item 13 plus Item 18) ⟶	6,529	70
20. TOTAL DEPOSITS FOR QUARTER (INCLUDING FINAL DEPOSIT MADE FOR QUARTER) AND OVERPAYMENT FROM PREVIOUS QUARTER LISTED IN SCHEDULE B (See instructions on page 4)	6,529	70

Note: If undeposited taxes at the end of the quarter are $200 or more, the full amount must be deposited with an authorized commercial bank or a Federal Reserve bank. This deposit must be entered in Schedule B and included in item 20.

21. Undeposited Taxes Due (Item 19 Less Item 20—This Should Be Less Than $200). Pay To Internal Revenue Service And Enter Here . . . . ⟶

22. If Item 20 Is More Than Item 19, Enter Excess Here ▶ $ .... And Check If You Want It ☐ Applied To Next Return, Or ☐ Refunded.

23. If not liable for returns in the future write "FINAL" (See instructions) ▶ .... Date final wages paid ▶

Under penalties of perjury, I declare that I have examined this return, including accompanying schedules and statements, and to the best of my knowledge and belief it is true, correct and complete.

Date April 15, 1978   Signature *William C. Bouchein*   Title (Owner, etc) Treasurer

Employer's Quarterly Federal Tax Return and Quarterly Report, Schedule A (Form 941)

When paying FUTA tax, it is necessary to complete the Federal Tax Deposit form, Form 508, and to send or take it to the bank with the remittance. This form is not illustrated here, but it is similar in nature to Form 501, previously illustrated on page 94.

The amount of the tax on employers under the Federal Unemployment Tax Act for the entire year must be paid to the District Director of Internal Revenue by the end of the month following the close of the calendar year. An official form (Form 940) is provided to the employer for use in making a report of the taxes due. This form is not illustrated here.

Assuming that a check for $96.10 was issued on January 31 in payment of the tax imposed under the Federal Unemployment Tax Act with respect to wages paid during the preceding year ended December 31, the transaction may be recorded as indicated by the following journal entry:

```
Jan. 31.  FUTA Tax Payable.............................    96.10
              Cash.........................................          96.10
                  Paid federal unemployment tax.
```

**Report
No. 4-2**

Complete Report No. 4-2 in the study assignments and submit your working papers to the instructor for approval. After completing the report, you may continue with the textbook discussion in Chapter 5 until the next report is required.

Chapter 5

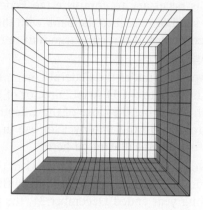

ACCOUNTING FOR A PERSONAL SERVICE ENTERPRISE

A personal service enterprise is one in which the principal source of revenue is compensation for personal services rendered. There are two types of personal service enterprises:

(a) Business enterprises
(b) Professional enterprises

Business enterprises of the personal service type include real estate, insurance, advertising, transportation, storage, entertainment, brokerage, and various others in which the revenue is derived chiefly from personal services rendered. Mercantile enterprises are not classified as personal service enterprises for the reason that their principal source of revenue is from the sale of merchandise rather than from compensation received for services provided.

Professional enterprises include law, medicine, dentistry, public accounting, management consulting, engineering, architecture, art, and education. The principal source of revenue for individuals engaged in such professions is usually the compensation received for the personal services rendered.

The cash basis of accounting for a personal service enterprise

Accounting for revenue on a cash basis means that, in most cases, no record of revenue is made in the accounts until cash is received for the services performed. This may mean that the services are rendered in one period, and the revenue is accounted for in the succeeding period. The business or professional man may well take the view that, in most cases, he has had no revenue until it is received in such form that it can be spent. He cannot "spend" the promise of a customer or client to pay him some money.

The cash basis of accounting for the revenue of a personal service enterprise is widely used. It is acceptable for federal and state income tax purposes. Not only is the receipt of cash accounted for as revenue under this basis; many other types of transactions are accounted for similarly. Any property or service that is accepted in place of cash for services is treated as revenue to the extent of its fair market value at the time received. Revenue is said to be *constructively received* if it is credited to a depositor's account or set apart so that it can be drawn upon. For example, when interest on a savings account is credited to the depositor's account, such interest is considered to be revenue to the depositor even though it is not actually received in cash or is not immediately withdrawn.

Accounting for expenses on the cash basis generally means that expenses are not recorded in the accounts until paid in cash. An expense may be incurred in one period and recorded in the accounts in the succeeding period. In the case of many expenses of a recurring nature, however, this set of circumstances is regarded as a minor objection. If, for example, twelve monthly telephone bills of about the same amount must be paid during each year, little importance is attached to the fact that the bill that is paid and recorded as an expense in January was really for service received in December.

An exception to the cash basis of accounting for expenses is made in connection with most long-lived assets. For example, it would be unreasonable to consider the entire cost of a building or of most equipment to be an expense of the period in which such assets were purchased. If it is expected that an asset will serve for a number of years, its cost (less expected scrap or salvage value, if any) is allocated over its estimated life. The share of cost assigned to each period is described as *depreciation expense*. Such expense cannot be calculated with precise accuracy. Still, an allocation that eventually turns out to have been somewhat in error results in a far more equitable periodic net income (profit) or loss measurement than one that simply considers the cost of such assets to be entirely an expense of the period in which they were purchased.

Another exception to the cash basis of accounting for expenses is sometimes made in connection with supplies purchased and used. If the amount of money involved is substantial and the end of the accounting period finds a considerable quantity of expensive supplies still on hand, an effort is made to determine the cost of those items which are on hand, so that only the cost of the supplies used will be treated as an expense of the period. If both the quantity and the cost of the items on hand at the end of a period are small, the usual practice is to ignore them and to consider the total cost of all items purchased during that accounting period to be an expense of that period.

ACCOUNTING PROCEDURE

As an aid in applying the principles involved in keeping the accounts of a personal service enterprise on the cash basis, a system of accounts for John H. Roberts, a management consultant, will be described. While certain distinctive problems may arise in keeping the accounts of any specific enterprise, it will be found that the principles are generally the same; hence, the system of accounts used by Mr. Roberts may readily be adapted to the needs of any personal service enterprise regardless of whether it is of a professional or a business nature.

Chart of accounts

Mr. Roberts' chart of accounts is reproduced on page 101. Note that all account numbers beginning with 1 relate to assets; 2, liabilities; 3, owner's equity; 4, revenue; and 5, expenses. Account numbers beginning with 0 represent *contra accounts* (meaning "opposite" or "offsetting" accounts) used to show the decrease in the related element. This system of account numbering permits the addition of new accounts as they may be needed without disturbing the numerical order of the existing accounts.

Most of the accounts in the foregoing list have been discussed and their use illustrated in the preceding chapters. Three notable exceptions are: Accumulated Depreciation — Office Equipment (No. 013), Depreciation Expense (No. 517), and Expense and Revenue Summary (No. 321). Each of these will be explained and its use illustrated as the need for the account arises in the narrative of transactions later in the chapter. Except for Depreciation Expense (No. 517), every debit to an expense account arises in connection with a cash disbursement. The cost of all forms and supplies purchased is debited (charged) to Account No. 515. The amount of any unused forms and supplies that may be on hand at the end of the year is ignored because such quantities normally are very small. (Note that there is no asset account for forms and supplies.) The car that Mr. Roberts uses for business purposes is leased. The monthly car rental and the cost

JOHN H. ROBERTS, MANAGEMENT CONSULTANT
CHART OF ACCOUNTS

*Assets**
  111 County National Bank
  112 Petty Cash Fund
  131 Office Equipment
  013 Accumulated Depreciation—
      Office Equipment

Liabilities
  211 Employees Income Tax Payable
  212 FICA Tax Payable

Owner's Equity
  311 John H. Roberts, Capital
  031 John H. Roberts, Drawing
  321 Expense and Revenue Summary

Revenue
  411 Professional Fees

Expenses
  511 Salary Expense
  512 Payroll Taxes Expense
  513 Rent Expense
  514 Telephone Expense
  515 Forms and Supplies Expense
  516 Automobile Expense
  517 Depreciation Expense
  518 Insurance Expense
  519 Travel and Entertainment Expense
  521 Charitable Contributions Expense
  522 Miscellaneous Expense

Words in italics represent headings and not account titles.

of gasoline, oil, lubrication, washing, and automobile insurance are charged to Automobile Expense, Account No. 516. The cost of all other types of insurance that relate to the enterprise, such as workmen's compensation, "errors and omissions" insurance (normally carried by management consultants), and fire insurance on the office equipment and contents, is charged to Insurance Expense, Account No. 518, when the premiums on the policies are paid.

Books of account

Mr. Roberts uses the following books of account:
  (a) General books
    (1) Combined cash journal
    (2) General ledger
  (b) Auxiliary records
    (1) Petty cash disbursements record
    (2) Employees' earnings records
    (3) Copies of statements rendered to clients (billings for fees) with collections noted thereon

Combined Cash Journal. The two-column journal could be used to record every transaction of a business enterprise. However, there are likely to be numerous similar transactions that involve the same account or accounts. Outstanding examples are receipts and disbursements of cash. Suppose that in a typical month there are 30 transactions that result in an increase in cash and 40 transactions that involve a decrease in cash. In a two-column journal, this would require writing the word "Cash" (or, perhaps, "County National Bank" if all receipts are deposited in that bank and all payments, except for petty cash, are made by check) 70 times — using a journal line each time. A considerable saving of time and space would result if two columns were added to the journal: one for debits to Cash (or Bank) and the other for credits to Cash (or Bank). The regular Debit and Credit columns in the journal could be used for amounts that go to other accounts. At the end of the month, the "special" columns would each be totaled. The total of the Cash Debit column would be posted as one amount to the debit side of the cash account; the total of the Cash Credit column would be posted as one amount to the credit side of the cash account. Thus, instead of receiving 70 postings, Cash would receive only two (one debit and one credit). Posting would require much less time and the danger of posting error would be reduced.

There is no reason to limit special journal columns to those for cash. If there are other accounts frequently used in the recording of transactions, special columns may be used to assemble all amounts that have the same effect on an account. More space and time may be saved. A journal with such special columns (and always containing a General Debit column and a General Credit column to take care of changes in accounts infrequently involved) is called a *combined cash journal.*

Mr. Roberts uses a combined cash journal as his only book of original entry. This journal, reproduced on pages 106–109, has eight amount columns, two at the left and six at the right of the Description column. The headings of the amount columns (as they read from left to right on the journal page) are as follows:

County National Bank
  Deposits 111 Dr.
  Checks 111 Cr.

General
  Debit
  Credit

Professional Fees 411 Cr.

Salary Expense 511 Dr.

Wage Deductions
  Employees Income Tax Payable 211 Cr.
  FICA Tax Payable 212 Cr.

The account numbers in the headings of the six special amount columns are an aid in completing the summary posting at the end of each month. Each of the six special columns is justified because there are enough transactions requiring entries in the accounts indicated by the column headings to warrant this arrangement which will save time and labor in the bookkeeping process. A narrative of transactions completed by Mr. Roberts during the month of December, 19--, is given on pages 103–110. These transactions are recorded in the combined cash journal on pages 106–109. Attention is called to the fact that before any transactions were recorded in this journal, a memo notation of the bank balance at the start of the month, $3,120.45, was entered in the Description column just above the words "Amounts Forwarded."

General Ledger. The standard form of account is used in the general ledger of Mr. Roberts' enterprise. The ledger is reproduced on pages 110–

113. In each instance, the balance of the account as of December 1 has been entered. Two accounts are omitted: Expense and Revenue Summary (No. 321) and Depreciation Expense (No. 517). They are not included because neither had a balance on December 1, and neither received any debits or credits as a result of the cash receipt and disbursement transactions in December. These accounts are not used until the end-of-year process of adjusting and closing the accounts takes place. This procedure will be explained and illustrated on pages 118–124.

Auxiliary Records. The auxiliary records included in Mr. Roberts' system of accounts are not reproduced in this chapter. The petty cash disbursements record that is used is almost identical in form to the one illustrated in Chapter 3 on pages 50 and 51. However, the combined cash journal entry to record the reimbursement of the petty cash fund at the end of December is shown (see the first entry of December 30 on pages 108 and 109). Mr. Roberts has two employees: Mr. Edward Hess, a full-time systems programmer, and Ms. Jeanne Haug, a part-time secretary. An employee's earnings record, similar to the one illustrated in Chapter 4 on pages 80 and 81, is maintained for each employee. Mr. Roberts keeps a file for each client which includes, among other things, a copy of the contract or agreement with the client. This agreement stipulates the fee for the assignment and the time of payment (or payments, if the fee is to be paid in installments — which is the usual case). A carbon copy of each statement or billing for fees earned is placed in each client's file. When money is received from a client, the date and amount are noted on the copy of the billing in addition to the formal record made in the combined cash journal.

JOHN H. ROBERTS, MANAGEMENT CONSULTANT

NARRATIVE OF TRANSACTIONS

Friday, December 2

Issued Check No. 211 for $278.10 to Edward Hess, systems programmer, in payment of his salary for week: $325 less income tax withholding, $46.90. (Note: Mr. Hess has been employed since the start of the year. His gross earnings reached $15,000 during the week ended November 26. Since that time, no FICA tax has been withheld.)

> Since individual posting of this entry was not required, a check mark was placed in the Posting Reference column of the combined cash journal at the time the transaction was recorded. This is a way of noting that there is nothing in the General Debit and Credit columns on that line.

Issued Check No. 212 for $95.20 to Jeanne Haug, secretary (part-time), in payment of her salary for week: $120 less income tax withholding, $17.60, and FICA tax withholding, $7.20.

Issued Check No. 213 for $300 to W. G. Chance for December office rent.

Monday, December 5

Received a check for $1,000 from J. E. Berra, a client.

Note that the client's name was written in the Description column and that a check mark was placed in the Posting Reference column.

Wednesday, December 7

Issued Check No. 214 for $43.60 to Edward O. Maes, an insurance agent, in payment of the one-year premium on a fire insurance policy covering Mr. Roberts' office equipment and contents.

Friday, December 9

Issued Check No. 215 for $278.10 to Edward Hess and Check No. 216 for $95.20 to Jeanne Haug in payment of salaries for the week. (See explanation relating to Checks Nos. 211 and 212 issued on December 2.)

END-OF-THE-WEEK WORK

(1) Proved the footings of the combined cash journal.

In order to be sure that the debits recorded in the journal are equal to the credits, the journal must be *proved*. Each amount column should be footed and the sum of the footings of the debit columns and the sum of the footings of the credit columns compared. The footings should be recorded in small pencil figures immediately below the last regular entry. If these sums are not the same, the journal entries must be checked to discover and correct any errors that are found. The footings should be proved frequently; when the transactions are numerous, it may be advisable to prove the footings daily. The footings must be proved when a page of the journal is filled to be sure that no error is carried forward to a new page. Proof of the footings is essential at the end of the month before the journal is ruled or any column totals are posted. Below is a proof of the footings of Mr. Roberts' combined cash journal. As is common practice, the footings were proved using an adding machine. The first set of amounts is the totals of the three debit columns, followed by a second set of amounts which is the totals of the four credit columns that had anything in them. (There was nothing in the General Credit column at this point.)

```
                        *
          1,000.00
            343.60
            890.00

          2,233.60*

                        *
          1,090.20
          1,000.00
            129.00
             14.40

          2,233.60*
```

(2) Deposited the $1,000 check from J. E. Berra in the bank, proved the bank balance ($3,030.25), and entered the new balance in the Description column following the second transaction of December 9. **(3)** Posted each entry individually from the General Debit column of the combined cash journal to the proper general ledger accounts. (Note that there were two such postings and that their respective account numbers, 513 and 518, were entered in the Posting Reference column.)

Monday, December 12

Issued Check No. 217 for $69.31 to UARCO Forms Co. in payment for supplies.

Received a check for $9.00 from Edward O. Maes, the insurance agent to whom Mr. Roberts had sent a check (No. 214) a few days earlier in the amount of $43.60 in payment of the premium on a fire insurance policy on his office equipment and contents. The check for $9.00 was accompanied by a letter from Mr. Maes explaining that a clerk in his office had made an error in preparing the invoice for the policy. The correct amount was $34.60 — not $43.60. Mr. Roberts' check for $43.60 had been deposited before the mistake was discovered. Accordingly, Mr. Maes sent his check for $9.00 as a refund of the excess premium.

> This insurance premium refund check was recorded in the combined cash journal by a debit to County National Bank, Account No. 111, and a credit to Insurance Expense, Account No. 518, in the amount of $9.00. Since the entry to record Check No. 214 had already been posted as a debit to Insurance Expense, this manner of handling was required. (The trouble resulted from the fact that the clerk in Mr. Maes' office had made a *transposition* error — a mistake well known to bookkeepers and accountants. The intention was to write or type "$34.60, but "$43.60" was written instead. The "3" and the "4" were placed in the wrong order — they were *transposed*.)

Tuesday, December 13

Received a check for $1,200 from G. L. Adams, a client.

Issued Check No. 218 for $315.60 to the County National Bank, a United States depositary, in payment of the following taxes:

Employees' income tax withheld during November..............		$258.00
FICA tax imposed —		
On employees (withheld during November)..................	$28.80	
On the employer......................................	28.80	57.60
Total...		$315.60

> This disbursement involved three factors (in addition to the decrease in the bank balance): **(1)** payment of the recorded liability, Employees Income Tax Payable, Account No. 211, of $258.00; **(2)** payment of the recorded liability, FICA Tax Payable, Account No. 212, of $28.80; and **(3)** payment of the unrecorded liability of $28.80, the employer's FICA tax relating to the taxable earnings paid in November. To record the transaction correctly, the first two amounts were debited to the proper liability accounts, and the third amount was debited to Payroll Taxes Expense, Account No. 512. Note that three lines were needed in the combined cash journal.
> (The checks from Mr. Adams and Mr. Maes were deposited in the bank, and the check for $315.60, together with a Tax Deposit Form, was presented at the bank

in payment of the taxes. The stub attached to the form was filled out and retained as a record of the deposit.)

Wednesday, December 14

Issued Check No. 219 for $1,500 to Mr. Roberts for personal use.

Thursday, December 15

Issued Check No. 220 for $87.60 to the Executive Auto Leasing Co. in payment of one month's rent of the leased automobile used by Mr. Roberts for business purposes.

This disbursement was recorded by a debit to Automobile Expense, Account No. 516.

PAGE *36*   COMBINED CASH JOURNAL

	COUNTY NATIONAL BANK		CK. NO.	DAY	DESCRIPTION	POST. REF.	
	DEPOSITS 111 DR.	CHECKS 111 CR.					
1					AMOUNTS FORWARDED *Balance 3,120.45*		1
2		278 10	211	2	Edward Hess	✓	2
3		95 20	212	2	Jeanne Haug	✓	3
4		300 00	213	2	Rent Expense	513	4
5	1000 00			5	J. E. Berra	✓	5
6		43 60	214	7	Insurance Expense	518	6
7		278 10	215	9	Edward Hess	✓	7
8	1000 00	95 20	216	9	Jeanne Haug	✓	8
9		69 31	217	12	Forms and Supplies Expense 3,030.25	515	9
10	9 00			12	Insurance Expense	518	10
11	1200 00			13	G. L. Adams	✓	11
12		315 60	218	13	Employees Income Tax Payable	211	12
13					FICA Tax Payable	212	13
14					Payroll Taxes Expense	512	14
15		1500 00	219	14	John H. Roberts, Drawing	031	15
16		87 60	220	15	Automobile Expense	516	16
17		278 10	221	16	Edward Hess	✓	17
18		95 20	222	16	Jeanne Haug	✓	18
19	2209 00	75 00	223	16	Charitable Contributions Expense	521	19
20		38 57	224	19	Automobile Expense 1,818.44	516	20
21		15 75	225	19	Miscellaneous Expense	522	21
22		38 65	226	20	Telephone Expense	514	22
23	150 00			21	Ms. Roberta McDougall	✓	23
24		78 12	227	22	Forms and Supplies Expense	515	24
25		278 10	228	23	Edward Hess	✓	25
26		95 20	229	23	Jeanne Haug	✓	26
27	3709 00	4055 40			Carried Forward 2,774.05		27

John H. Roberts, Management Consultant — Combined Cash Journal (Left Page)

Friday, December 16

Issued Check No. 221 for $278.10 to Edward Hess and Check No. 222 for $95.20 to Jeanne Haug in payment of salaries for week. (See explanation relating to Checks Nos. 211 and 212 issued on December 2.)

Issued Check No. 223 for $75 to American Red Cross.

END-OF-THE-WEEK WORK

(1) Proved the footings of the combined cash journal. **(2)** Proved the bank balance $1,818.44). **(3)** Posted each entry individually from the General Debit and General Credit columns of the combined cash journal to the proper general ledger accounts. When the entry of December 13

FOR MONTH OF *December*   19 - -   PAGE **36**

#	GENERAL DEBIT	GENERAL CREDIT	PROFESSIONAL FEES 411 CR.	SALARY EXPENSE 511 DR.	EMP. INC. TAX PAY. 211 CR.	FICA TAX PAY. 212 CR.
1						
2				325 00	46 90	
3				120 00	17 60	7 20
4	300 00					
5			1000 00			
6	43 60					
7				325 00	46 90	
8	343 60		1000 00	120 00	17 60	7 20
9	69 31			890 00	129 00	14 40
10		9 00				
11			1200 00			
12	258 00					
13	28 80					
14	28 80					
15	1500 00					
16	87 60					
17				325 00	46 90	
18				120 00	17 60	7 20
19	75 00					
20	239 17 38 57	9 00	2200 00	1335 00	193 50	21 60
21	15 75					
22	38 65					
23			1500 00			
24	78 12					
25				325 00	46 90	
26				120 00	17 60	7 20
27	2562 20 / 2562 20	9 00 / 9 00	3700 00 / 3700 00	1780 00 / 1780 00	258 00 / 258 00	28 80 / 28 80

John H. Roberts, Management Consultant — Combined Cash Journal (Right Page) relating to Check No. 218 was posted, debits were made to Employees Income Tax Payable, Account No. 211, and FICA Tax Payable, Account No. 212, which caused those accounts to be in balance. Each of those two accounts was ruled with a double line as illustrated on page 111.

Monday, December 19

Issued Check No. 224 for $38.57 to Wes's Service Station in payment of charges for gasoline, oil, and lubrication purchased on credit during the past month. (All of these purchases related to the leased car used for business purposes.)

Issued Check No. 225 for $15.75 to Apex Typewriter Service in payment of charges for cleaning and repairing office typewriter.

> The amount of this check was charged to Miscellaneous Expense, Account No. 522.

Tuesday, December 20

Issued Check No. 226 for $38.65 to Southwestern Bell Telephone Co. in payment of statement just received showing charges for local service and long distance calls, during the past month. (This telephone bill related exclusively to the phone in Mr. Roberts' office.)

Wednesday, December 21

Received a check for $1,500 from Ms. Roberta McDougall, a client.

PAGE *37*   COMBINED CASH JOURNAL

	COUNTY NATIONAL BANK		CK. NO.	DAY	DESCRIPTION	POST. REF.	
	DEPOSITS 111 DR.	CHECKS 111 CR.					
1	3 7 0 9 00	4 0 5 5 40		23	AMOUNTS FORWARDED *Balance 2,774.05*	✓	1
2		9 7 80	230	28	*Travel + Entertainment Expense*	519	2
3	9 0 0 00			29	*Frank Presker*	✓	3
4		6 6 83	231	30	*John H. Roberts, Drawing*	031	4
5					*Forms and Supplies Expense*	515	5
6					*Automobile Expense*	516	6
7					*Travel + Entertainment Expense*	519	7
8					*Charitable Contributions Expense*	521	8
9					*Miscellaneous Expense*	522	9
10		2 7 8 10	232	30	*Edward Hess*	✓	10
11		9 5 20	233	30	*Jeanne Haug*	✓	11
12	4 6 0 9 00 / 4 6 0 9 00	4 5 9 3 33 / 4 5 9 3 33			*3,136.12*		12
13	(111)	(111)					13

John H. Roberts, Management Consultant — Combined Cash Journal (Left Page) *(concluded)*

Thursday, December 22

Issued Check No. 227 for $78.12 to Systems Supply Co. in payment for supplies purchased.

Friday, December 23

Issued Check No. 228 for $278.10 to Edward Hess and Check No. 229 for $95.20 to Jeanne Haug in payment of salaries for week. (See explanation relating to Checks Nos. 211 and 212 issued on December 2.)

END-OF-THE-WEEK WORK

(1) Proved the footings of the combined cash journal. **(2)** Deposited the $1,500 check from Ms. McDougall and proved the bank balance ($2,774.05). **(3)** Posted each entry individually from the General Debit column of the combined cash journal.

> Because a page of the combined cash journal was filled after Check No. 229 was recorded, the footings of the columns were proved, these footings were recorded as totals on the last line of the page, and the words "Carried Forward" were written in the Description column. The totals were entered in the appropriate columns on the top line of the next page. The bank balance was entered in the Description column of the new page just above the words "Amounts Forwarded."

Wednesday, December 28

Issued Check No. 230 for $97.80 to Sunset Hills Country Club in payment of food and beverage charges for one month.

FOR MONTH OF *December*   19 – –   PAGE *37*

	GENERAL			PROFESSIONAL FEES 411 CR.	SALARY EXPENSE 511 DR.	WAGE DEDUCTIONS			
	DEBIT		CREDIT			EMP. INC. TAX PAY. 211 CR.		FICA TAX PAY. 212 CR.	
1	2 5 6 2 20		9 00	3 7 0 0 00	1 7 8 0 00	2 5 8 00		2 8 80	1
2	9 7 80								2
3				9 0 0 00					3
4	1 5 00								4
5	1 0 95								5
6	4 30								6
7	2 3 80								7
8	7 50								8
9	5 28								9
10					3 2 5 00	4 6 90			10
11					1 2 0 00	1 7 60		7 20	11
12	2 7 2 6 83		9 00	4 6 0 0 00	2 2 2 5 00	3 2 2 50		3 6 00	12
12	2 7 2 6 83		9 00	4 6 0 0 00	2 2 2 5 00	3 2 2 50		3 6 00	12
13	(✓)		(✓)	(411)	(511)	(211)		(212)	13

John H. Roberts, Management Consultant — Combined Cash Journal (Right Page) *(concluded)*

The amount of this check was charged to Travel and Entertainment Expense, Account No. 519. Mr. Roberts uses the facilities of the club to entertain prospective clients.

Thursday, December 29

Received a check for $900 from Frank Presker, a client.

Friday, December 30

Issued Check No. 231 for $66.83 to replenish the petty cash fund. Following is a summary of the petty cash disbursements for the month of December prepared from the Petty Cash Disbursements Record:

John H. Roberts, Drawing	$15.00
Forms and Supplies Expense	10.95
Automobile Expense	4.30
Travel and Entertainment Expense	23.80
Charitable Contributions Expense	7.50
Miscellaneous Expense	5.28
Total disbursements	$66.83

Issued Check No. 232 for $278.10 to Edward Hess and Check No. 233 for $95.20 to Jeanne Haug in payment of salaries for week. (See explanation relating to Checks Nos. 211 and 212 issued on December 2.)

ROUTINE END-OF-THE-MONTH WORK

(1) Proved the footings and entered the totals in the combined cash journal. **(2)** Deposited the $900 check from Mr. Presker and proved the bank balance ($3,136.12). **(3)** Completed the individual posting from the General Debit column of the combined cash journal. **(4)** Completed the summary posting of the six special-column totals of the combined cash journal and ruled the journal as illustrated on pages 108 and 109. (Note that the number of the account to which the total was posted was written in parentheses just below the total, and that check marks were placed below the General Debit and General Credit column totals in parentheses to indicate that these amounts were not posted.) **(5)** Footed the ledger accounts and noted the balances where necessary, as illustrated below and on pages 111–113. **(6)** Prepared a trial balance of the ledger accounts.

Usually a trial balance at the end of a month is prepared using two-column paper. However, because Mr. Roberts has chosen the calendar year for his fiscal year (a common, but by no means universal, practice), the trial balance at the end of December is put in the first two amount columns of a page known as a *work sheet*. The need for and preparation of a work sheet is explained and illustrated on pages 114–117.

ACCOUNT *County National Bank*   ACCOUNT NO. *111*

DATE	ITEM	POST. REF.	DEBIT	DATE	ITEM	POST. REF.	CREDIT
19-- Dec. 1	Balance	✓	3 120 45	19-- Dec. 30		CJ37	4 593 33
30		CJ37	4 609 00				
	3,136.12		7 729 45				

John H. Roberts, Management Consultant — General Ledger

ACCOUNT *Petty Cash Fund*   ACCOUNT NO. *112*

DATE	ITEM	POST. REF.	DEBIT	DATE	ITEM	POST. REF.	CREDIT
19-- Dec. 1	Balance	✓	10000				

ACCOUNT *Office Equipment*   ACCOUNT NO. *131*

DATE	ITEM	POST. REF.	DEBIT	DATE	ITEM	POST. REF.	CREDIT
19-- Dec. 1	Balance	✓	1057560				

ACCOUNT *Accumulated Depreciation – Office Equip.*   ACCOUNT NO. *013*

DATE	ITEM	POST. REF.	DEBIT	DATE	ITEM	POST. REF.	CREDIT
				19-- Dec. 1	Balance	✓	352167

ACCOUNT *Employees Income Tax Payable*   ACCOUNT NO. *211*

DATE	ITEM	POST. REF.	DEBIT	DATE	ITEM	POST. REF.	CREDIT
19-- Dec. 13		CJ36	25800	19-- Dec. 1	Balance	✓	25800
				Dec. 30		CJ37	32250

ACCOUNT *FICA Tax Payable*   ACCOUNT NO. *212*

DATE	ITEM	POST. REF.	DEBIT	DATE	ITEM	POST. REF.	CREDIT
19-- Dec. 13		CJ36	2880	19-- Dec. 1	Balance	✓	2880
				Dec. 30		CJ37	3600

ACCOUNT *John H. Roberts, Capital*   ACCOUNT NO. *311*

DATE	ITEM	POST. REF.	DEBIT	DATE	ITEM	POST. REF.	CREDIT
				19-- Dec. 1	Balance	✓	728550

ACCOUNT *John H. Roberts, Drawing*   ACCOUNT NO. *031*

DATE	ITEM	POST. REF.	DEBIT	DATE	ITEM	POST. REF.	CREDIT
19-- Dec. 1	Balance	✓	1875500				
14		CJ36	150000				
30		CJ37	1500				
			2027000				

John H. Roberts, Management Consultant — General Ledger (*continued*)

ACCOUNT *Professional Fees*   ACCOUNT NO. *411*

DATE	ITEM	POST. REF.	DEBIT	DATE	ITEM	POST. REF.	CREDIT
				19-- Dec. 1	Balance	✓	5276000
				30		CJ37	460000
							5736000

ACCOUNT *Salary Expense*   ACCOUNT NO. *511*

DATE	ITEM	POST. REF.	DEBIT	DATE	ITEM	POST. REF.	CREDIT
19-- Dec. 1	Balance	✓	2091500				
30		CJ37	222500				
			2314000				

ACCOUNT *Payroll Taxes Expense*   ACCOUNT NO. *512*

DATE	ITEM	POST. REF.	DEBIT	DATE	ITEM	POST. REF.	CREDIT
19-- Dec. 1	Balance	✓	177783				
13		CJ36	2880				
			180663				

ACCOUNT *Rent Expense*   ACCOUNT NO. *513*

DATE	ITEM	POST. REF.	DEBIT	DATE	ITEM	POST. REF.	CREDIT
19-- Dec. 1	Balance	✓	330000				
2		CJ36	30000				
			360000				

ACCOUNT *Telephone Expense*   ACCOUNT NO. *514*

DATE	ITEM	POST. REF.	DEBIT	DATE	ITEM	POST. REF.	CREDIT
19-- Dec. 1	Balance	✓	38560				
20		CJ36	3865				
			42425				

ACCOUNT *Forms and Supplies Expense*   ACCOUNT NO. *515*

DATE	ITEM	POST. REF.	DEBIT	DATE	ITEM	POST. REF.	CREDIT
19-- Dec. 1	Balance	✓	136108				
12		CJ36	6931				
22		CJ36	7812				
30		CJ37	1095				
			151946				

John H. Roberts, Management Consultant — General Ledger (*continued*)

ACCOUNT *Automobile Expense*   ACCOUNT NO. *516*

DATE	ITEM	POST. REF.	DEBIT	DATE	ITEM	POST. REF.	CREDIT
19-- Dec. 1	Balance	✓	1214 95				
15		CJ36	87 60				
19		CJ36	38 57				
30		CJ37	4 30				
			1345 42				

ACCOUNT *Insurance Expense*   ACCOUNT NO. *518*

DATE	ITEM	POST. REF.	DEBIT	DATE	ITEM	POST. REF.	CREDIT
19-- Dec. 1	Balance	✓	167 38	19-- Dec. 12		CJ36	9 00
7	*201.98*	CJ36	43 60				
			210 98				

ACCOUNT *Travel and Entertainment Expense*   ACCOUNT NO. *519*

DATE	ITEM	POST. REF.	DEBIT	DATE	ITEM	POST. REF.	CREDIT
19-- Dec. 1	Balance	✓	1653 26				
28		CJ37	97 80				
30		CJ37	23 80				
			1774 86				

ACCOUNT *Charitable Contributions Expense*   ACCOUNT NO. *521*

DATE	ITEM	POST. REF.	DEBIT	DATE	ITEM	POST. REF.	CREDIT
19-- Dec. 1	Balance	✓	385 00				
16		CJ36	75 00				
30		CJ37	7 50				
			467 50				

ACCOUNT *Miscellaneous Expense*   ACCOUNT NO. *522*

DATE	ITEM	POST. REF.	DEBIT	DATE	ITEM	POST. REF.	CREDIT
19-- Dec. 1	Balance	✓	142 82				
19		CJ36	15 75				
30		CJ37	5 28				
			163 85				

John H. Roberts, Management Consultant — General Ledger (*concluded*)

Work at close of the fiscal period

As soon as possible after the end of the fiscal period, the owner (or owners) of an enterprise wants to be provided with **(1)** an income statement covering the period just ended, and **(2)** a balance sheet as of the last day of the period. In order to provide these statements, the accountant must consider certain matters that will not have been recorded in routine fashion. (Depreciation of Office Equipment for the past year is the one such matter in the case of Mr. Roberts' enterprise.) Furthermore, the revenue accounts, the expense accounts, and the account showing the owner's withdrawals will have performed their function for the period just ended (in this case, the year) and need to be made ready to receive the entries of the new period. In the language of accountants and bookkeepers, "the books must be adjusted and closed." Actually, it is only the temporary owner's equity accounts — those for revenue, expense, and the owner's drawings — that are closed, but the remark quoted is widely used to describe what takes place at this time.

The End-of-Period Work Sheet. To facilitate **(1)** the preparing of the financial statements, **(2)** the making of needed adjustments in the accounts, and **(3)** the closing of the temporary owner's equity accounts, it is common practice to prepare what is known as a *work sheet*. Because that term is used to describe a variety of schedules and computations that accountants may prepare, the specific type to be discussed here is commonly called an *end-of-period work sheet*. Various forms of this device are used. Because of the nature of Mr. Roberts' enterprise, an eight-column work sheet is adequate. This form is illustrated on page 115. Note that the heading states that it is for the year ended December 31, 19--. The fact that December 30 was the last working day is not important. The income statement will relate to the full year, and the balance sheet will show the financial position as of the last day of the fiscal period.

The first pair of columns of the work sheet was used to show the trial balance taken after the routine posting for the month of December had been completed. Note that the account Depreciation Expense (No. 517) was included in the list of accounts and account numbers even though that account had no balance at this point. The second pair of columns, headed "Adjustments," was used to show the manner in which the expense of estimated depreciation of office equipment for the year affects the accounts. The trial balance shows that the account Office Equipment (No. 131) had a balance of $10,575.60, and that the balance of the account Accumulated Depreciation — Office Equipment (No. 013) was $3,521.67. No new equipment was purchased during the year and there were no sales or retirements of such property during the year. Accordingly, the balances of these two accounts had not changed during the year. The two accounts are closely related: the debit balance of the office equipment account indicates the cost of such assets, and the credit balance of the accumulated depreciation account indicates the amount of such cost that has been charged off as depreciation in past years — that is, to January 1 of the

John H. Roberts, Management Consultant
Work Sheet
For the Year Ended December 31, 19--

Account	Acct No.	Trial Balance Debit	Trial Balance Credit	Adjustments Debit	Adjustments Credit	Income Statement Debit	Income Statement Credit	Balance Sheet Debit	Balance Sheet Credit
1 Security National Bank	111	313612						313612	
2 Petty Cash Fund	112	10000						10000	
3 Office Equipment	131	1057560						1057560	
4 Accum. Depr.—Office Equip.	013		352167		105756				457923
5 Employees Income Tax Pay.	211		32250						32250
6 FICA Tax Payable	212		3600						3600
7 John H. Roberts, Capital	311		728550						728550
8 John H. Roberts, Drawing	031	2027000						2027000	
9 Professional Fees	411		5736000				5736000		
10 Salary Expense	511	2314000				2314000			
11 Payroll Taxes Expense	512	180163				180163			
12 Rent Expense	513	360000				360000			
13 Telephone Expense	514	42425				42425			
14 Forms & Supplies Expense	515	151946				151946			
15 Automobile Expense	516	134542				134542			
16 Depreciation Expense	517			105756		105756			
17 Insurance Expense	518	20198				20198			
18 Travel & Entertainment Exp.	519	177486				177486			
19 Charitable Contributions Exp.	521	46750				46750			
20 Miscellaneous Expense	522	16385				16385			
21		6852567	6852567	105756	105756	3550151	5736000	3408172	1222323
22 Net Income						2185849			2185849
23						5736000	5736000	3408172	3408172

John H. Roberts, Management Consultant — End-of-Period Work Sheet current year. The amount of the difference between the two balances, $7,053.93, is described as the *undepreciated cost* of the office equipment. The amount may also be called the *book value* of the equipment. A better description of the difference is "cost yet to be charged to expense."

Since the year had just ended, it was necessary to record as an expense the estimated depreciation for that year. Mr. Roberts estimates that the various items of office equipment have average useful lives of ten years and that any scrap or salvage value at the end of that time is likely to be so small that it can be ignored. Accordingly, estimated depreciation expense for the year was calculated to be $1,057.56 (10 percent of $10,575.60). This expense was due to be recorded in the ledger accounts, but that had to wait. The immediate need was to get the expense entered on the work sheet so that it would be considered when the financial statements were prepared. The record was made on the work sheet as follows: $1,057.56 was written in the Adjustments Debit column on the line for Depreciation Expense, and the same amount was written in the Adjustments Credit column on the line for Accumulated Depreciation — Office Equipment. The Adjustments Debit and Credit columns were totaled.

The next step was to combine each amount in the Trial Balance columns with the amount, if any, in the Adjustments columns and to extend the total into the Income Statement or Balance Sheet columns. Revenue and expense account balances are extended to the Income Statement columns and balance sheet account balances to the Balance Sheet columns. Note that the new amount for Accumulated Depreciation — Office Equipment, $4,579.23 ($3,521.67 + $1,057.56), appears in the Balance Sheet Credit column, and that the depreciation expense of $1,057.56 appears, along with all other expenses, in the Income Statement Debit column. The last four columns were totaled. The total of the Income Statement Credit column exceeded the total of the Income Statement Debit column by $21,858.49 — the calculated net income for the year. That amount, so designated, was placed in the Income Statement Debit column to bring the pair of Income Statement columns into balance. When the same amount ($21,858.49) was placed in the Balance Sheet Credit column, the last pair of columns was brought into balance. The final totals of the last four columns were recorded at the bottom of the work sheet.

The fact that adding the net income for the year, $21,858.49, to the Balance Sheet Credit column caused its total to equal the total of the Balance Sheet Debit column is explained as follows. The amounts for the assets and liabilities in the last pair of columns were up-to-date. The difference between total assets and total liabilities, $8,873.99, was Mr. Roberts' equity in the enterprise at the year's end. The balance of his capital account was $7,285.50 — the amount of his equity at the start of the year (since he had made no additional investments during the year).

His withdrawals during the year, according to the balance in the account John H. Roberts, Drawing, were $20,270.00. How could he start the year with an owner's equity of $7,285.50, make no additional investments, withdraw $20,270.00, and end the year with an owner's equity of $8,873.99? The explanation is that there had been profitable operations during the year that caused the owner's equity element to increase $21,858.49. This can be expressed in the form of the following equation:

OWNER'S EQUITY AT START OF PERIOD	+	NET INCOME FOR THE PERIOD	+	INVESTMENTS	−	WITHDRAWALS	=	OWNER'S EQUITY AT END OF PERIOD
$7,285.50	+	$21,858.49	+	0	−	$20,270.00	=	$8,873.99

Since the correct amounts for assets and liabilities and two of the three factors (owner's equity at start of period and withdrawals) needed to determine the correct amount of the owner's equity as of December 31 were already in the Balance Sheet columns, only the amount of the third factor — the net income for the year — had to be included in order that those columns would reflect the basic equation: Assets = Liabilities + Owner's Equity.

The Financial Statements. The work sheet supplied all of the information needed to prepare an income statement and a balance sheet. These statements for Mr. Roberts' enterprise are shown below and on page 118.

Three features of the balance sheet on page 118 should be noted: **(1)** It is in so-called *report form* — the liabilities and the owner's equity sections are shown below the assets section. An alternative is the so-called *account form* — the assets are at the left, and the liabilities and the owner's equity sections are at the right. (See the balance sheet of The Eason Employment

JOHN H. ROBERTS, MANAGEMENT CONSULTANT
Income Statement
For the Year Ended December 31, 19--

Professional fees...........................		$57,360.00
Professional expenses:		
Salary expense...........................	$23,140.00	
Payroll taxes expense....................	1,806.63	
Rent expense.............................	3,600.00	
Telephone expense........................	424.25	
Forms and supplies expense...............	1,519.46	
Automobile expense.......................	1,345.42	
Depreciation expense.....................	1,057.56	
Insurance expense........................	201.98	
Travel and entertainment expense.........	1,774.86	
Charitable contributions expense.........	467.50	
Miscellaneous expense....................	163.85	
Total professional expenses............		35,501.51
Net income...............................		$21,858.49

John H. Roberts, Management Consultant — Income Statement

Agency on pages 42 and 43.) **(2)** The assets are classified on the basis of whether they are *current* or *long-lived*. Current assets include cash and any other assets that will be converted into cash within the *normal operating cycle* of the business. This cycle is often a year in length. Mr. Roberts' enterprise does not take into account any current assets other than cash. (The amount shown includes both cash in bank and petty cash.) The long-lived assets are those which are expected to serve for many years. **(3)** All of the liabilities are classified as current, since they must be paid in the near future. Certain types of obligations are classified as long-term, but Mr. Roberts had no debts of this type.

```
              JOHN H. ROBERTS, MANAGEMENT CONSULTANT
                           Balance Sheet
                        December 31, 19--

                               Assets
Current assets:
  Cash...........................                          $3,236.12
Long-lived assets:
  Office equipment.................        $10,575.60
  Less accumulated depreciation....         4,579.23       5,996.37
Total assets......................                        $9,232.49

                            Liabilities
Current liabilities:
  Employees income tax payable......       $   322.50
  FICA tax payable.................             36.00
  Total current liabilities........                     $   358.50

                          Owner's Equity
John H. Roberts, capital:
  Capital, January 1, 19--.........        $ 7,285.50
  Net income for year..............  $21,858.49
  Less withdrawals.................   20,270.00  1,588.49
  Capital, December 31, 19--.......                        8,873.99
Total liabilities and owner's
  equity...........................                       $9,232.49
```

John H. Roberts, Management Consultant — Balance Sheet

Adjusting Entries for a Personal Service Enterprise. The financial statements must agree with the ledger accounts. To speed up the preparation of the statements, a work sheet was used with the one needed adjustment included. Subsequently this adjustment had to be formally recorded in the accounts. This was accomplished by posting the first journal entry at the top of page 119. The two accounts affected by the entry, Depreciation Expense (No. 517) and Accumulated Depreciation — Office Equipment

(No. 013) are reproduced at the top of page 120 as they appeared after the entry was posted. After this posting was completed, the balance of the depreciation expense account agreed with the amount shown in the income statement, and the balance of the accumulated depreciation account was the same as the amount shown in the balance sheet.

Closing Entries for a Personal Service Enterprise. The revenue and expense accounts and the account for John H. Roberts, Drawing (No. 031) had served their purpose for the year 19--, and the balance of each of these accounts needed to be reduced to zero in order to make the accounts ready for entries in the following year. Since the means of closing a ledger account under the double-entry procedure is to add the amount of the account's balance to the side of the account having the smaller total (so that

COMBINED CASH JOURNAL FOR MONTH OF *December* 19 - -   PAGE *38*

	DAY	DESCRIPTION	POST. REF.	GENERAL DEBIT	GENERAL CREDIT	
1		AMOUNTS FORWARDED				1
2	31	*Adjusting Entry*				2
3		Depreciation Expense	517	105756		3
4		Accumulated Deprec:--Office Equip.	013		105756	4
5						5
6	31	*Closing Entries*				6
7		Professional Fees	411	5736000		7
8		Expense and Revenue Summary	321		5736000	8
9		Expense and Revenue Summary	321	3550151		9
10		Salary Expense	511		2314000	10
11		Payroll Taxes Expense	512		180663	11
12		Rent Expense	513		360000	12
13		Telephone Expense	514		42425	13
14		Forms and Supplies Expense	515		151946	14
15		Automobile Expense	516		134542	15
16		Depreciation Expense	517		105756	16
17		Insurance Expense	518		20198	17
18		Travel + Entertainment Expense	519		177486	18
19		Charitable Contributions Expense	521		46750	19
20		Miscellaneous Expense	522		16385	20
21		Expense and Revenue Summary	321	2185849		21
22		John H. Roberts, Capital	311		2185849	22
23		John H. Roberts, Capital	311	2027000		23
24		John H. Roberts, Drawing	031		2027000	24
25				13604756	13604756	25
26						26

John H. Roberts, Management Consultant — Adjusting and Closing Entries

ACCOUNT *Depreciation Expense*   ACCOUNT NO. *517*

DATE	ITEM	POST. REF.	DEBIT	DATE	ITEM	POST. REF.	CREDIT
19-- Dec. 31		CJ38	1 057 56				

ACCOUNT *Accumulated Depreciation - Office Equip.*   ACCOUNT NO. *013*

DATE	ITEM	POST. REF.	DEBIT	DATE	ITEM	POST. REF.	CREDIT
				19-- Dec. 1	Balance	✓	3 521 67
				31		CJ38	1 057 56
							4 579 23

John H. Roberts, Management Consultant — Ledger Accounts After Posting Adjusting Entries

the account will have no balance), each of the temporary owner's equity accounts was closed in this way. The net effect was an increase in the credit balance of the account for John H. Roberts, Capital (No. 311) of $1,588.49 — the excess of his net income for the year, $21,858.49, over his withdrawals for the year, $20,270.00. However, this result was accomplished by means of four entries illustrated in the combined cash journal shown on page 119:

    (a) The $57,360 credit balance of Professional Fees, Account No. 411, was closed to (transferred to the credit side of) Expense and Revenue Summary, Account No. 321.

    (b) The debit balances of all eleven expense accounts (Nos. 511 through 519 and 521 and 522) which, in total, amounted to $35,501.51, were closed to (transferred to the debit side of) Expense and Revenue Summary (No. 321).

    (c) The result of entries **(a)** and **(b)** was a credit balance of $21,858.49 — the net income for the year — in Expense and Revenue Summary (No. 321). This was closed to John H. Roberts, Capital, Account No. 311.

    (d) The $20,270 debit balance of John H. Roberts, Drawing, Account No. 031, was closed to John H. Roberts, Capital (No. 311).

As in the case of the adjusting entry, these closing entries were made as of December 31. It should be noted that the work sheet provided all of the data needed to prepare the adjusting and closing entries. The purpose and use of Expense and Revenue Summary, Account No. 321, should be apparent from this illustration. As its name indicates, the account is used to summarize the amounts of expense and revenue which are *reasons* for changes in owner's equity that were *not* the result of investments and withdrawals by the owner.

Ruling the Closed Accounts. After posting the closing entries, all of the temporary owner's equity accounts were in balance (closed), and they were ruled in the manner illustrated below and on pages 122–124.

The following procedures were used:

(a) Where two or more amounts had been posted to either side of an account, the amount columns were footed to be sure that the total debits were equal to the total credits.

(b) A single line was ruled across the debit and credit amount columns immediately below the last amount on the side with the most entries.

(c) The totals of the debit and credit amount columns were entered on the next line in ink.

(d) Double lines were ruled just below the totals. These rulings extended through all but the Item columns.

ACCOUNT *John H. Roberts, Drawing*   ACCOUNT NO. *031*

DATE	ITEM	POST. REF.	DEBIT	DATE	ITEM	POST. REF.	CREDIT
19-- Dec. 1	Balance	✓	18 755 00	19-- Dec. 31		CJ38	20 270 00
14		CJ36	1 500 00				
30		CJ37	15 00				
			20 270 00				
			20 270 00				20 270 00

ACCOUNT *Expense and Revenue Summary*   ACCOUNT NO. *321*

DATE	ITEM	POST. REF.	DEBIT	DATE	ITEM	POST. REF.	CREDIT
19-- Dec. 31		CJ38	35 501 51	19-- Dec. 31		CJ38	57 360 00
31		CJ38	21 858 49				
			57 360 00				
			57 360 00				57 360 00

John H. Roberts, Management Consultant — Closed General Ledger Accounts

(continued on next page)

ACCOUNT *Professional Fees*   ACCOUNT NO. *411*

DATE	ITEM	POST. REF.	DEBIT	DATE	ITEM	POST. REF.	CREDIT
19-- Dec. 31		CJ38	5736000	19-- Dec. 1	Balance	✓	5276000
				30		CJ37	460000
							5736000
			5736000				5736000

ACCOUNT *Salary Expense*   ACCOUNT NO. *511*

DATE	ITEM	POST. REF.	DEBIT	DATE	ITEM	POST. REF.	CREDIT
19-- Dec. 1	Balance	✓	2091500	19-- Dec. 31		CJ38	2314000
30		CJ37	222500				
			2314000				
			2314000				2314000

ACCOUNT *Payroll Taxes Expense*   ACCOUNT NO. *512*

DATE	ITEM	POST. REF.	DEBIT	DATE	ITEM	POST. REF.	CREDIT
19-- Dec. 1	Balance	✓	177783	19-- Dec. 31		CJ38	180663
13		CJ36	2880				
			180663				
			180663				180663

ACCOUNT *Rent Expense*   ACCOUNT NO. *513*

DATE	ITEM	POST. REF.	DEBIT	DATE	ITEM	POST. REF.	CREDIT
19-- Dec. 1	Balance	✓	330000	19-- Dec. 31		CJ38	360000
2		CJ36	30000				
			360000				
			360000				360000

ACCOUNT *Telephone Expense*   ACCOUNT NO. *514*

DATE	ITEM	POST. REF.	DEBIT	DATE	ITEM	POST. REF.	CREDIT
19-- Dec. 1	Balance	✓	38560	19-- Dec. 31		CJ38	42425
20		CJ36	3865				
			42425				
			42425				42425

John H. Roberts, Management Consultant — Closed General Ledger Accounts (*continued*)

ACCOUNT *Forms and Supplies Expense*   ACCOUNT NO. *515*

DATE	ITEM	POST. REF.	DEBIT	DATE	ITEM	POST. REF.	CREDIT
19-- Dec. 1	Balance	✓	1361 08	19-- Dec. 31		CJ38	1519 46
12		CJ36	69 31				
22		CJ36	78 12				
30		CJ37	10 95				
			1519 46				
			1519 46				1519 46

ACCOUNT *Automobile Expense*   ACCOUNT NO. *516*

DATE	ITEM	POST. REF.	DEBIT	DATE	ITEM	POST. REF.	CREDIT
19-- Dec. 1	Balance	✓	1214 95	19-- Dec. 31		CJ38	1345 42
15		CJ36	87 60				
19		CJ36	38 57				
30		CJ37	4 30				
			1345 42				
			1345 42				1345 42

ACCOUNT *Depreciation Expense*   ACCOUNT NO. *517*

DATE	ITEM	POST. REF.	DEBIT	DATE	ITEM	POST. REF.	CREDIT
19-- Dec. 31		CJ38	1057 56	19-- Dec. 31		CJ38	1057 56

ACCOUNT *Insurance Expense*   ACCOUNT NO. *518*

DATE	ITEM	POST. REF.	DEBIT	DATE	ITEM	POST. REF.	CREDIT
19-- Dec. 1	Balance	✓	167 38	19-- Dec. 12		CJ36	9 00
7	201.98	CJ36	43 60	31		CJ38	201 98
			210 98				210 98
			210 98				210 98

ACCOUNT *Travel and Entertainment Expense*   ACCOUNT NO. *519*

DATE	ITEM	POST. REF.	DEBIT	DATE	ITEM	POST. REF.	CREDIT
19-- Dec. 1	Balance	✓	1653 26	19-- Dec. 31		CJ38	1774 86
28		CJ37	97 80				
30		CJ37	23 80				
			1774 86				
			1774 86				1774 86

John H. Roberts, Management Consultant — Closed General Ledger Accounts (*continued*)

ACCOUNT *Charitable Contributions Expense*   ACCOUNT NO. *521*

DATE	ITEM	POST. REF.	DEBIT	DATE	ITEM	POST. REF.	CREDIT
19-- Dec. 1	Balance	✓	38500	19-- Dec. 31		CJ38	46750
16		CJ36	7500				
30		CJ37	750				
			46750				
			46750				46750

ACCOUNT *Miscellaneous Expense*   ACCOUNT NO. *522*

DATE	ITEM	POST. REF.	DEBIT	DATE	ITEM	POST. REF.	CREDIT
19-- Dec. 1	Balance	✓	14282	19-- Dec. 31		CJ38	16385
19		CJ36	1575				
30		CJ37	528				
			16385				
			16385				16385

John H. Roberts, Management Consultant — Closed General Ledger Accounts (*concluded*)

If an account had only one item on each side, only the double ruling was made. (Note the ruling for Depreciation Expense, Account No. 517.) If an account page is not filled, it may be used for recording the transactions of the following period.

Balancing and Ruling Open Accounts. After the temporary owner's equity accounts were closed, the open accounts (those for assets, liabilities, and John H. Roberts, Capital) were balanced and ruled, where necessary, to prepare them to receive entries in the next fiscal period. Only two of Mr. Roberts' ledger accounts needed to be balanced and ruled: County National Bank, Account No. 111, and John H. Roberts, Capital, Account No. 311. These two accounts are shown on page 125. The procedure in each case was as follows:

  (a) The amount of the balance of the account was entered on the side having the smaller total to equalize total debits and total credits. The word "Balance" was written in the Item column.

  (b) The columns were footed to prove the equality of the debits and credits.

  (c) A single line was ruled across the debit and credit amount columns immediately below the line with the last amount. (This line would have been below the last amount on the side with the most entries, if the number of entries on each side had not been the same.)

  (d) The totals of the debit and credit amount columns were entered on the next line in ink.

  (e) Double lines were ruled just below the totals extending through all but the Item column.

  (f) An entry was made on the next line under date of January 1, with the amount of the balance — so labeled in the Item column — entered in the amount column on the proper side (the debit side for the asset account and the credit side for the owner's equity account). If the account page had been filled, the balance would have been entered at the top of a new account page.

No balancing and ruling was needed in the cases of Petty Cash Fund, Account No. 112, or Office Equipment, Account No. 131, since each of these accounts had only one entry. (These two accounts remained just as illustrated on page 111.) Accumulated Depreciation — Office Equipment, Account No. 013, needed no further attention since it had only two entries, both on the same side. (This account remains as illustrated on page 119.) The two liability accounts, Employees Income Tax Payable (No. 211) and FICA Tax Payable (No. 212) remain as illustrated on page 111, inasmuch as each has had only one entry since previously ruled.

ACCOUNT *County National Bank*   ACCOUNT NO. *111*

DATE	ITEM	POST. REF.	DEBIT	DATE	ITEM	POST. REF.	CREDIT
19-- Dec. 1	*Balance*	✓	3 1 2 0 45	19-- Dec. 30		CJ37	4 5 9 3 33
30	3,136.12	CJ37	4 6 0 9 00 / 7 7 2 9 45 / 7 7 2 9 45	31	*Balance*	✓	3 1 3 6 12 / 7 7 2 9 45 / 7 7 2 9 45
19-- Jan. 1	*Balance*	✓	3 1 3 6 12				

ACCOUNT *John H. Roberts, Capital*   ACCOUNT NO. *311*

DATE	ITEM	POST. REF.	DEBIT	DATE	ITEM	POST. REF.	CREDIT
19-- Dec. 31		CJ38	20 2 7 0 00	19-- Dec. 1	*Balance*	✓	7 2 8 5 50
31	*Balance*	✓	8 8 7 3 99 / 29 1 4 3 99 / 29 1 4 3 99	31		CJ38	21 8 5 8 49 / 29 1 4 3 99 / 29 1 4 3 99
				19-- Jan. 1	*Balance*	✓	8 8 7 3 99

John H. Roberts, Management Consultant — Balancing and Ruling Open Accounts

Post-Closing Trial Balance. After posting the closing entries, it is advisable to take a *post-closing trial balance* to prove the equality of the debit and credit balances in the general ledger accounts. The post-closing trial balance of Mr. Robert's ledger is shown at the top of page 126.

The accounting cycle

The steps involved in handling all of the transactions and events completed during an accounting period, beginning with recording in a book of original entry and ending with a post-closing trial balance, are referred to collectively as the *accounting cycle*. This chapter has illustrated a complete accounting cycle. A brief summary of the various steps follows:

(a) Journalizing the transactions.
(b) Posting to the ledger accounts.

John H. Roberts, Management Consultant
Post-Closing Trial Balance
December 31, 19--

Account	Acct. No.	Dr. Balance	Cr. Balance
County National Bank	111	3136 12	
Petty Cash Fund	112	100 00	
Office Equipment	131	10575 60	
Accumulated Depreciation--Office Equip.	013		4579 23
Employees Income Tax Payable	211		322 50
FICA Tax Payable	212		36 00
John H. Roberts, Capital	311		8873 99
		13811 72	13811 72

John H. Roberts, Management Consultant — Post-Closing Trial Balance

(c) Taking a trial balance.
(d) Determining the needed adjustments.
(e) Completing an end-of-period work sheet.
(f) Preparing an income statement and a balance sheet.
(g) Journalizing and posting the adjusting and closing entries.
(h) Ruling the closed accounts and balancing and ruling the open accounts.
(i) Taking a post-closing trial balance.

In visualizing the accounting cycle, it is important to realize that steps (c) through (i) in the foregoing list are performed *as of the last day of the accounting period.* This does not mean that they necessarily are done *on* the last day. The accountant or bookkeeper may not be able to do any of these things until the first few days (sometimes weeks) of the next period. Nevertheless, the work sheet, statements, and entries are prepared or recorded as of the closing date. While the journalizing of transactions in the new period proceeds in regular fashion, it is not usual to post to the general ledger any entries relating to the new period until the steps relating to the period just ended have been completed.

Report No. 5-1

Complete Report No. 5-1 in the study assignments and submit your working papers to the instructor for approval. After completing the report you will then be given instructions as to the work to be done next.

Chapters 1-5

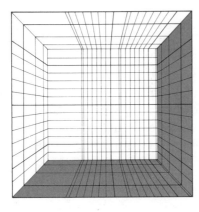

PRACTICAL ACCOUNTING PROBLEMS

The following problems supplement those in Reports 1-1 through 5-1 of the Part 1 Study Assignments. These problems are numbered to indicate the chapter of the textbook with which they correlate. For example, Problem 1-A and Problem 1-B correlate with Chapter 1. Loose-leaf stationery should be used in solving these problems. The paper required includes plain ruled paper, two-column journal paper, two-column and three-column statement paper, ledger paper, and work sheet paper.

Problem 1-A   T. B. Curtis is a practicing attorney. As of December 31 he owned the following property that related to his business: Cash, $1,521, office equipment, $2,540; and an automobile, $3,780. At the same time he owed business creditors $1,230.

REQUIRED: **(1)** On the basis of the above information, compute the amounts of the accounting elements and show them in equation form. **(2)** Assume that during the following year there is an increase in Mr. Curtis' business assets of $2,650 and a decrease in his business liabilities of $275. Indicate the changes in the accounting elements by showing them in equation form after the changes have occurred.

Problem 1-B   O. F. Otto, a CPA who has been employed by a large national firm of certified public accountants, decides to go into business for himself. His business transactions for the first month of operations were as follows:

   (a) Mr. Otto invested $15,000 cash in the business.
   (b) Paid office rent for one month, $250.
   (c) Purchased office equipment from the Von Brocken Office Equipment Co. (a supplier), $2,580 on account.

(d) Paid telephone bill, $27.

(e) Received $1,000 for services rendered to Public Finance Co.

(f) Paid $1,500 to the Von Brocken Office Equipment Co., on account.

(g) Received $750 for services rendered to the Kribs Garage.

(h) Paid $500 salary to office secretary.

REQUIRED: **(1)** On a plain sheet of paper rule eight "T" accounts and enter the following titles: Cash, Office Equipment, Accounts Payable, O. F. Otto, Capital, Professional Fees, Rent Expense, Telephone Expense, and Salary Expense. **(2)** Record the foregoing transactions directly in the accounts. **(3)** Foot the accounts and enter the balances where necessary. **(4)** Prepare a trial balance of the accounts, using a sheet of two-column journal paper.

Problem 2-A   Following is a narrative of the transactions completed by Ms. C. V. Little, management consultant, during the first month of her business operations:

Oct. 1. Ms. Little invested $10,000 cash in the business.

1. Paid office rent, $200.

3. Purchased office furniture for $1,675.

3. Paid $24.35 for installation of telephone and for one month's service.

4. Received $400 from The Premier Linen Service for consulting services rendered.

5. Purchased stationery and supplies on account from W. K. Woods Stationery Co., $262.49.

6. Paid $9 for subscription to a professional management magazine (Charge Miscellaneous Expense.)

8. Paid $65 to Dr. James Bynum, a dentist, for dental service performed for Ms. Little.
   (Note: This is equivalent to a withdrawal of $65 by Ms. Little for personal use. Charge to her drawing account.)

10. Received $150 from Tropicana Pools, Inc., for professional services rendered.

12. Paid $85.22 for an airplane ticket for a business trip.

14. Paid other traveling expenses, $72.40.

19. Received $450 from Wagner Electric Co. for professional services rendered.

20. Paid account of W. K. Woods Stationery Co. in full, $262.49.

31. Paid $500 monthly salary to secretary.

REQUIRED: Journalize the foregoing transactions, using a sheet of two-column journal paper. Number the pages and use both sides of the sheet, if necessary. Select the account titles from the chart of accounts on page 129.

After journalizing the transactions, prove the equality of the debits and credits by footing the amount columns. Enter the footings in pencil immediately under the line on which the last entry appears.

CHART OF ACCOUNTS

Assets
111 Cash
112 Stationery and Supplies
121 Office Furniture

Liabilities
211 Accounts Payable

Owner's Equity
311 C. V. Little, Capital
312 C. V. Little, Drawing

Revenue
411 Professional Fees

Expenses
511 Rent Expense
512 Telephone Expense
513 Traveling Expense
514 Salary Expense
515 Miscellaneous Expense

Problem 2-B   B. H. Sirkin is a certified data processor engaged in practice on his own account. Following is the trial balance of his business taken as of September 30, 19—.

B. H. SIRKIN, CERTIFIED DATA PROCESSOR
Trial Balance
September 30, 19—

Cash	111	2,073.08	
Office Equipment	121	1,155.00	
Automobile	122	4,840.00	
Accounts Payable	211		1,737.19
B. H. Sirkin, Capital	311		5,526.40
B. H. Sirkin, Drawing	312	3,960.00	
Professional Fees	411		8,800.00
Rent Expense	511	2,700.00	
Telephone Expense	512	193.05	
Electric Expense	513	132.00	
Automobile Expense	514	479.38	
Charitable Contributions Expense	515	352.00	
Miscellaneous Expense	516	179.08	
		16,063.59	16,063.59

A narrative of the transactions completed by Mr. Sirkin during the month of October follows below and on page 130.

NARRATIVE OF TRANSACTIONS FOR OCTOBER

Oct. 1. (Saturday) Paid one month's rent, $300.
3. Paid telephone bill, $19.20.
3. Paid electric bill, $15.12.
5. Received $400 from Associated Grocers for services rendered.
7. Paid a garage bill, $36.80.
10. Received $300 from the Breckenridge Hotels for services rendered.
12. Paid Venture Department Store, $42.30. (Charge to Mr. Sirkin's drawing account.)
15. Mr. Sirkin withdrew $400 for personal use.
17. Paid IBM, Inc., $250 on account.
19. Received $200 from IGA Food Stores for services rendered.
24. Gave the American Cancer Society $30.

Oct. 26. Paid the Data Processing Management Association $75 for annual membership dues and fees.

    29. Received $125 from Barford Motor Sales Co. for professional services.

    31. Mr. Sirkin withdrew $400 for personal use.

REQUIRED: **(1)** Journalize the October transactions, using a sheet of two-column journal paper. Number the pages and use both sides of the sheet, if necessary. Foot the amount columns. **(2)** Open the necessary accounts, using the standard account form of ledger paper. Allow one page for each account. Record the October 1 balances as shown in the September 30 trial balance and post the journal entries for October. **(3)** Foot the ledger accounts, enter the balances, and prove the balances by taking a trial balance as of October 31. Use a sheet of two-column journal paper for the trial balance.

Problem 2-C

THE R. E. BURLEW AGENCY

Trial Balance

March 31, 19—

Cash	111	6,372.10	
Stationery and Supplies	112	1,238.05	
Office Furniture	121	4,052.40	
Notes Payable	211		1,980.00
Accounts Payable	212		1,415.24
R. E. Burlew, Capital	311		7,737.12
R. E. Burlew, Drawing	312	1,386.88	
Professional Fees	411		3,711.84
Rent Expense	511	330.00	
Telephone Expense	512	47.52	
Salary Expense	513	616.00	
Traveling Expense	514	696.34	
Stationery and Supplies Expense	515	40.55	
Miscellaneous Expense	516	64.36	
		14,844.20	14,844.20

REQUIRED: **(1)** Prepare an income statement for The R. E. Burlew Agency showing the results of the first month of operations, March. **(2)** Prepare a balance sheet in account form showing the financial condition of the agency as of March 31. Use a sheet of two-column statement paper for the income statement. Two sheets of two-column statement paper may be used for the balance sheet. List the assets on one sheet and the liabilities and owner's equity on the other sheet.

Problem 3-A

Anne Pollack is an interior designer. The only book of original entry for her business is a two-column journal. She uses the standard form of account in the general ledger. Following is the trial balance of her business taken as of November 30:

ANNE POLLACK, INTERIOR DESIGNER

Trial Balance

November 30, 19—

Cash....................................	111	3,634.28	
Office Equipment........................	112	800.00	
Accounts Payable........................	211		191.45
Anne Pollack, Capital....................	311		7,371.93
Anne Pollack, Drawing...................	312	5,500.00	
Professional Fees.........................	411		11,990.00
Rent Expense............................	511	2,200.00	
Telephone Expense.......................	512	225.60	
Electric Expense..........................	513	143.70	
Salary Expense...........................	514	6,600.00	
Charitable Contributions Expense...........	515	325.00	
Miscellaneous Expense....................	516	124.80	
		19,553.38	19,553.38

NARRATIVE OF TRANSACTIONS FOR DECEMBER

Dec. 1. (Thursday) Paid December office rent in advance, $200.
      1. Paid electric bill, $12.67.
      2. Paid telephone bill, $16.85.
      2. Received a check from Wagner Electric Co. for $500 for services rendered.
      6. Received $400 from Wetterau Grocer Co. for services rendered.
      7. Donated $25 to the Heart Association.
      7. Paid $7.25 for cleaning office.
      8. Received check for $400 from Nooter Corporation for consulting services.
     12. Ms. Pollack withdrew $350 for personal use.
     15. Paid secretary's salary for the half month, $300.
     16. Purchased office furniture on credit from Union Furniture Co., $600.
     19. Paid $5 for having the office windows washed.
     20. Received $200 from Associated General Contractors for services rendered.
     22. Paid traveling expenses while on business, $32.25.
     23. Donated $30 to the United Fund.
     26. Paid Union Furniture Co. $200 on account.
     28. Ms. Pollack withdrew $150 for personal use.
     30. Paid secretary's salary for the half month, $300.

REQUIRED: **(1)** Journalize the December transactions. For the journal use two sheets of two-column journal paper and number the pages. **(2)** Open the necessary ledger accounts. Allow one page for each account and number the accounts. Record the December 1 balances and post the journal entries. Foot the journal. **(3)** Take a trial balance.

Problem 3-B   Gerald W. Renken, an electrician, completed the following transactions with the Merchants Trust and Savings Bank during the month of October:

Oct.	3. (Monday) Balance in bank per record kept on check stubs...........	$6,000.00	Oct.	11. Check No. 218..	180.00
				11. Check No. 219..	98.10
	3. Deposit........	4,000.00		13. Check No. 220..	859.50
	3. Check No. 208..	546.70		14. Check No. 221..	86.30
	3. Check No. 209..	50.00		14. Check No. 222..	446.49
	4. Check No. 210..	850.00		14. Deposit........	766.28
	4. Check No. 211..	230.00		17. Check No. 223..	250.00
	5. Check No. 212..	260.00		18. Check No. 224..	520.30
	6. Check No. 213..	170.00		21. Check No. 225..	149.90
	7. Check No. 214..	321.10		21. Deposit........	1,492.00
	7. Check No. 215..	100.00		24. Check No. 226..	264.82
	7. Check No. 216..	96.00		25. Check No. 227..	271.66
	7. Deposit........	569.30		27. Check No. 228..	545.95
	10. Check No. 217..	968.04		28. Check No. 229..	160.00
				31. Check No. 230..	1,269.50
				31. Deposit........	1,520.68

REQUIRED: **(1)** A record of the bank account as it would appear on the check stubs. **(2)** A reconciliation of the bank statement for October which indicated a balance of $7,442.87 on October 31, with Checks Nos. 216, 226, 229, and 230 outstanding, and a service charge of $1.35.

Problem 3-C   L. J. Sverdrup, a general contractor, had a balance of $150 in his petty cash fund as of June 1. During June the following petty cash transactions were completed:

June 2. (Thursday) $3.25 for typewriter repairs. Petty Cash Voucher No. 32.

      6. Paid for long-distance telephone call, $3.75. Petty Cash Voucher No. 33.

      8. Gave $20 to the United Fund. Petty Cash Voucher No. 34.

      9. Paid garage for washing car, $2.50. Petty Cash Voucher No. 35.

    12. Gave Mr. Sverdrup's son $5 (Charge L. J. Sverdrup, Drawing.) Petty Cash Voucher No. 36,

    14. Paid for postage stamps, $6, Petty Cash Voucher No. 37.

    17. Paid for newspaper for month, $2.75. Petty Cash Voucher No. 38.

    22. Paid for window washing, $3.75. Petty Cash Voucher No. 39.

    27. Paid $5 to the Parent-Teacher Organization for dues. (Charge L. J. Sverdrup, Drawing.) Petty Cash Voucher No. 40.

    28. Paid for car lubrication, $3.00. Petty Cash Voucher No. 41.

    29. Donated $25 to the American Red Cross. Petty Cash Voucher No. 42.

    30. Rendered report of petty cash expenditures for month and received the amount needed to replenish the petty cash fund.

REQUIRED: **(1)** Record the foregoing transactions in a petty cash disbursements record, distributing the expenditures as follows (a page of work sheet paper may be used):

L. J. Sverdrup, Drawing   Charitable Contributions Expense
Automobile Expense   Miscellaneous Expense
Telephone Expense

(2) Prove the petty cash disbursements record by footing the amount columns and proving the totals. Enter the totals and rule the amount columns with single and double lines. **(3)** Prepare a statement of the petty cash disbursements for June. **(4)** Bring down the balance in the petty cash fund below the ruling in the Description column. Enter the amount received to replenish the fund and record the total.

Problem 4-A   Following is a summary of the hours worked, rates of pay, and other relevant information concerning the employees of The Ozark Lead Co., N. C. Young, owner, for the week ended Saturday, November 5. Employees are paid at the rate of time and one half for all hours worked in excess of 8 in any day or 40 in any week.

No.	Name	Allowances Claimed	Hours Worked M T W T F S	Regular Hourly Rate	Cumulative Earnings Jan. 1–Oct. 29
1	Bono, Ben C.	3	8 8 8 8 8 6	$3.00	$7,212
2	Hauser, Lenore H.	4	8 9 8 8 8 4	3.25	$8,240
3	Messey, Robert J.	3	8 8 8 8 8 0	3.10	$8,135
4	Ring, John H.	1	8 8 8 9 8 4	2.90	$4,857
5	Sparks, Maralynn H.	2	8 8 8 8 8 4	3.15	$5,670
6	Wynn, W. T.	1	8 8 8 8 4 0	3.40	$6,400

Bono and Ring each have $4.00 withheld this payday for group life insurance. Hauser and Wynn each have $3.50 withheld this payday for private hospital insurance. Sparks has $10 withheld this payday as a contribution to the United Fund.

REQUIRED: **(1)** Using plain ruled paper size 8½″ by 11″, rule a payroll register form similar to that reproduced on pages 76 and 77 and insert the necessary columnar headings. Enter on this form the payroll for the week ended Saturday, November 5. Refer to the Weekly Income Tax Table on page 74 to determine the amounts to be withheld from the wages of each worker for income tax purposes. All of Young's employees are married. Six percent of the taxable wages of each employee should be withheld for FICA tax. Checks Nos. 611 through 616 were issued to the employees. Complete the payroll record by footing the amount columns, proving the footings, entering the totals, and ruling. **(2)** Assuming that the wages were paid on November 9, record the payment on a sheet of two-column journal paper.

Problem 4-B   The River Roads Store employs twelve people. They are paid by checks on the 15th and last day of each month. The entry to record each payroll includes the liabilities for the amounts withheld. The expense and liabilities arising from the employer's payroll taxes are recorded on each payday.

Following is a narrative of the transactions completed during the month of January that relate to payrolls and payroll taxes:

Jan. 15. Payroll for first half of month:

Total salaries.............................		$3,720.00
Less amounts withheld:		
FICA tax.............................	$223.20	
Employees' income tax...................	410.90	634.10
Net amount paid.........................		$3,085.90

15. Social security taxes imposed on employer:
FICA tax, 6%
State unemployment tax, 2%
FUTA tax, 0.5%

28. Paid $1,520.80 for December's payroll taxes:
FICA tax, $535.60.
Employees' income tax withheld, $985.20.

28. Paid State unemployment tax for quarter ended December 31, $329.40.

28. Paid balance due on FUTA tax for last half of year ended December 31, $150.68.

31. Payroll for last half of month:

Total salaries.............................		$3,800.00
Less amounts withheld:		
FICA tax.............................	$228.00	
Employees' income tax...................	440.30	668.30
Net amount paid.........................		$3,131.70

31. Social security taxes imposed on employer:
All salaries taxable; rates same as on January 15.

REQUIRED: **(1)** Journalize the foregoing transactions, using two-column general journal paper. **(2)** Foot the debit and credit amount columns as a means of proof.

Problem 5-A   Jean Gavin is a certified public accountant engaged in professional practice on her own account. Since her revenue consists entirely of compensation for personal services rendered, she keeps accounts on the cash basis. Her trial balance for the current year ending December 31 appears on page 135.

REQUIRED: **(1)** Prepare an eight-column work sheet making the necessary entries in the Adjustments columns to record the depreciation of the following assets:

Office equipment, 10%, $441.60
Automobiles, 25%, $2,093

(2) Prepare the following financial statements:

    (a) An income statement for the year ended December 31.

    (b) A balance sheet in report form as of December 31.

JEAN GAVIN, CPA

Trial Balance

December 31, 19—

Cash....................................	111	8,820.63	
Office Equipment.......................	131	4,416.00	
Accumulated Depreciation — Office Equipment.	013		441.60
Automobiles............................	141	8,372.00	
Accumulated Depreciation — Automobiles.....	014		2,093.00
Accounts Payable.......................	211		1,741.14
Employees Income Tax Payable............	212		180.60
FICA Tax Payable.......................	213		193.20
Jean Gavin, Capital.....................	311		13,081.89
Jean Gavin, Drawing....................	031	20,000.00	
Professional Fees........................	411		45,814.00
Rent Expense...........................	511	6,000.00	
Salary Expense.........................	512	12,880.00	
Automobile Expense....................	513	935.80	
Depreciation Expense...................	514		
Payroll Taxes Expense...................	515	862.50	
Charitable Contributions Expense...........	516	550.00	
Miscellaneous Expense..................	517	708.50	
		63,545.43	63,545.43

Problem 5-B   John Staples operates an airline charter service, specializing in all weather passenger and freight service. A trial balance of his general ledger accounts is reproduced on page 136.

REQUIRED: **(1)** Prepare an eight-column work sheet making the necessary adjustments to record the depreciation of long-lived assets as shown below.

PROPERTY	RATE OF DEPRECIATION	AMOUNT OF DEPRECIATION
Office equipment...............................	10%	$ 550
Air service equipment..........................	20%	49,660

(2) Prepare an income statement for the year ended December 31. **(3)** Prepare a balance sheet in report form as of December 31. **(4)** Using two-column journal paper, prepare the entries required:

    (a) To adjust the general ledger accounts so that they will be in agreement with the financial statements.

    (b) To close the temporary owner's equity accounts on December 31.

Foot the amount columns as a means of proof.

JOHN STAPLES AIR SERVICE
Trial Balance
December 31, 19—

Cash	111	28,939.29	
Office Equipment	131	5,500.00	
Accumulated Depreciation — Office Equipment	031		1,100.00
Air Service Equipment	141	248,300.00	
Accumulated Depr. — Air Service Equipment	014		99,320.00
Accounts Payable	211		12,862.00
Employees Income Tax Payable	212		600.00
FICA Tax Payable	213		575.00
John Staples, Capital	311		86,724.83
John Staples, Drawing	031	18,600.00	
Traffic Revenue	411		192,175.28
Rent Expense	511	14,400.00	
Salary Expense	512	36,000.00	
Office Expense	513	2,840.00	
Air Service Expense	514	35,687.12	
Depreciation Expense	515		
Payroll Taxes Expense	516	2,414.00	
Charitable Contributions Expense	517	500.00	
Miscellaneous Expense	518	176.70	
		393,357.11	393,357.11

Problem 5-C   Sue Taylor is the sole proprietor of a dry cleaning establishment called Taylor Cleaners. Since revenue consists of compensation for services rendered, she keeps her accounts on the cash basis. She does not extend credit to customers but operates on a cash-on-delivery basis. The Trial Balance columns of her work sheet for the current year ended December 31 are reproduced on the next page.

REQUIRED: **(1)** Complete the work sheet making the necessary adjusting entries to record the depreciation of long-lived assets as follows:

> Office equipment, 10% a year, $300
> Cleaning equipment, 8% a year, $688
> Delivery trucks, 30% a year, $1,158

(2) Prepare an income statement for the year ended December 31. **(3)** Prepare a balance sheet as of December 31 in report form. **(4)** Using two-column journal paper, prepare the entries required to adjust and close the ledger. Foot the amount columns as a means of proof.

TAYLOR CLEANERS
Work Sheet
For the Year Ended December 31, 19—

Account	Acct. No.	Trial Balance	
		Debit	Credit
Integrity National Bank..................	111	16,265.20	
Office Equipment.......................	131	3,000.00	
Accumulated Depreciation — Office Equip ...	013		300.00
Cleaning Equipment.....................	141	8,600.00	
Accumulated Depreciation — Cleaning Equip.	014		688.00
Delivery Trucks........................	151	3,860.00	
Accumulated Depreciation — Delivery Trucks.	015		1,158.00
Accounts Payable......................	211		864.61
Employees Income Tax Payable	212		513.90
FICA Tax Payable......................	213		275.16
Sue Taylor, Capital.....................	311		21,309.04
Sue Taylor, Drawing....................	031	15,600.00	
Dry Cleaning Revenue...................	411		42,820.60
Pressing Revenue......................	412		18,351.08
Rent Expense.........................	511	9,600.00	
Heat, Light, and Power Expense...........	512	5,641.28	
Salary Expense........................	513	19,640.00	
Delivery Expense......................	514	1,965.27	
Depreciation Expense...................	515		
Payroll Taxes Expense	516	1,321.51	
Miscellaneous Expense..................	517	787.13	
		86,280.39	86,280.39

Chapter 6

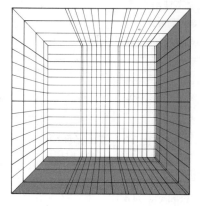

ACCOUNTING FOR MERCHANDISE

In the preceding chapter, accounting and bookkeeping practices suitable for a personal service enterprise were discussed and illustrated. The calculation of net income for the year was made on the so-called "cash basis" except for the matter of depreciation expense. Revenue was not recorded until money was received for the service performed, even though the service may have been performed in a prior period. Similarly, most expenses were not recorded until cash was disbursed for them, even though many of the payments were for things of value received and consumed in a prior period or for things to be received and consumed in a later period. An exception to this practice was made in the matter of depreciation, since it would be unrealistic to consider the entire cost of an asset such as an article of office equipment (expected to be used for many years) to be an expense only of the month or year of purchase. The cost of such long-lived assets is spread as expense over their expected useful lives.

The cash basis, even when slightly modified, is not technically perfect; but it has the virtues of simplicity and ease of understanding. This basis has proved to be quite satisfactory for most personal service enterprises. In the case of business enterprises whose major activity is the purchase and sale of merchandise, however, the cash basis of periodic income calculation usually does not give a meaningful or useful measure of net income or net loss. There are two reasons why this is true: **(1)** Merchandising businesses commonly purchase and often sell merchandise "on account" or "on credit" — meaning that payment is postponed a few days or weeks. The amount of cash paid or collected in any accounting period is almost never the same as the amount of purchases and sales of that period. **(2)** Merchandising businesses normally start and end each period with some goods on hand (commonly called *merchandise inventory*), but the dollar amount is not likely to be the same at both points of time. When either or both of these circumstances exist, the *accrual basis* of accounting must be used.

In the calculation of periodic income under the accrual basis, the focus of the effort is to try to match the *realized revenue* of a period against the expenses reasonably assignable to that period. ("Realized revenue" nearly always means the receipt of cash or a collectible claim to cash arising in return for something of value given up — commonly goods.) In the case of merchants, the process starts with the calculation of what is called *gross margin* (also known as *gross profit*). This is the difference between *net sales* and *cost of goods sold*. Net sales is simply the gross amount of revenue from sales less the sales price of any goods returned by customers because the merchandise has turned out to be unsatisfactory or unwanted for some reason. (Maybe the goods were found to be defective or the wrong color or size.) Sometimes a reduction in the price — an *allowance* — is given to the customer rather than having the goods returned. Cost of goods sold (really *expense* of goods sold) is most simply defined by the following formula:

$$\text{COST OF GOODS SOLD} = \text{MERCHANDISE INVENTORY, BEGINNING OF PERIOD} + \text{NET PURCHASES} - \text{MERCHANDISE INVENTORY, END OF PERIOD}$$

Net purchases is the difference between the cost of goods purchased and the total of **(1)** the cost of goods returned to suppliers and **(2)** the amount of any allowances made by suppliers. To illustrate, consider the following circumstances:

Cost of merchandise (goods) on hand, beginning of period............. $12,000

Cost of merchandise purchased during the period...................... 74,000

Cost of goods returned to the supplier for some reason (not ordered, unsatisfactory for some reason, etc.).................................... 2,000

Cash disbursements during the period for goods purchased both in prior periods and the current period...................................... 66,000

Sale price of all goods sold and delivered to customers during the current period.. 95,000

Sale price of goods returned by customers........................... 4,000

Cash received from customers during the period in payment for sales both of prior periods and the current period................................. 78,000

Cost of merchandise (goods) on hand, end of period.................. 15,000

If the *relevant* information in the foregoing array of data is assembled in the proper fashion, the gross margin for the period is calculated to be

$22,000. The conventional means of exhibiting the pertinent amounts is as follows:

Sales...		$95,000
Less sales returns and allowances...................		4,000
Net sales...		$91,000
Cost of goods sold:		
Merchandise inventory, beginning of period........	$12,000	
Add: Purchases................................ $74,000		
Less purchases returns and allowances 2,000		
Net purchases.................................	72,000	
Merchandise available for sale....................	$84,000	
Less merchandise inventory, end of period.........	15,000	
Cost of goods sold.............................		69,000
Gross margin on sales.............................		$22,000

Note that the movement of cash in both directions (to suppliers and from customers) has been ignored as being irrelevant. (It should be mentioned that the manner of accounting for depreciation illustrated in the last chapter was in accordance with the accrual basis of accounting.) Because accrual accounting is widely used, and because one of its major applications relates to the accounting for merchandise transactions, this subject will be examined in some detail.

In recording transactions concerned with merchandising, it is desirable to keep at least the following accounts:

(a) Purchases
(b) Purchases Returns and Allowances
(c) Sales
(d) Sales Returns and Allowances
(e) Merchandise Inventory

PURCHASES AND THE PURCHASES JOURNAL

The word *purchase* can refer to the act of buying almost anything or, if used as a noun, to the thing that is bought. In connection with the accounting for a merchandising business, however, the term usually refers to merchandise. A reference to "purchases for the year," unless qualified in some way, would relate to the merchandise (*stock in trade*) that had been bought.

Purchases account

The purchases account is a temporary owner's equity account in which the cost of merchandise purchased is recorded. The account should be debited for the cost of all merchandise purchased during the accounting period. If the purchase was for cash, the cash account should be credited; if on account, Accounts Payable should be credited. The purchases account may also be debited for any transportation charges, such as freight, express, and parcel post charges, that increase the cost of the merchandise purchased.

PURCHASES	
Debit to record the cost of merchandise pur- chased.	

Purchases returns and allowances account

This account is a temporary owner's equity account in which purchases returns and allowances are recorded. The account should be credited for the cost of any merchandise returned to creditors or suppliers and for any allowances received from creditors that decrease the cost of the merchandise purchased. The offsetting debit is to Accounts Payable if the goods were purchased on account, or to Cash if a refund is received because the purchase was originally for cash. Allowances may be received from creditors

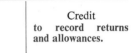

PURCHASES RETURNS AND ALLOWANCES	
	Credit to record returns and allowances.

for merchandise delivered in poor condition or for merchandise that does not meet specifications as to quality, weight, size, color, grade, or style.

Although purchases returns and allowances might be credited directly to Purchases, it is better to credit Purchases Returns and Allowances. The accounts will then show both the amount of gross purchases and the amount of returns and allowances. If returns and allowances are large in proportion to gross purchases, a weakness in the purchasing operations is indicated. It may be that better sources of supply should be sought or that purchase specifications should be stated more clearly.

Purchase invoice

A document received by the buyer from the seller that provides information for recording a purchase transaction is known as a *purchase invoice*. An invoice includes the supplier's invoice number, the purchaser's order number, the dates of shipment and billing, the terms of sale, a description of the goods, the quantities shipped, the unit prices, and the total amount of the purchase. A variety of forms and sizes of purchase invoices is in common use.

When both the goods and the invoice have been received, it is customary for the purchaser to assign the incoming invoice a number. (Note that the invoice on page 142 was marked "#37.") Someone must check to see that the invoice is correct as to quantities and unit prices, and that the extensions and total are correct. ("Extensions" are the amounts resulting from multiplying the quantity times the price of each item purchased.) It is common practice for the purchaser to imprint a form on the face of the invoice by means of a rubber stamp. This form provides spaces for the initials of the persons who have verified that the goods were received, and that the prices, extensions, and total are correct. Sometimes there is space to show the number of the account to be debited — Purchases, if the invoice relates to merchandise bought for resale. If everything is found to be in order, the invoice will be paid at the proper time.

Below is a reproduction of a purchase invoice as it would appear after the various aspects of the transaction have been verified and approved.

FINNEY FURNITURE COMPANY		#37 INVOICE

GRAND RAPIDS, MICHIGAN 49501	DATE May 2, 1977

SOLD TO W. F. BROWN 5401 MADISON ROAD CINCINNATI, OH 45227	INVOICE NO. 8712
	CUST. ORDER NO. 196
	SHIPPED VIA C & O RR

TERMS 30 days	DATE SHIPPED May 2, 1977

QUANTITY		DESCRIPTION	UNIT PRICE	AMOUNT
ORDERED	SHIPPED			
3	3	4119 End Table	26.40	79.20
1	1	662 Dropleaf Table	92.00	92.00
2	2	635 Mhg. Table	58.50	117.00
4	4	2630 Night Stand	27.10	108.40
2	2	2317 Coffee Table	39.80	79.60
				476.20

Date received . 5/5
Received by ... R.B.
Items o.k. .... R.B.
Prices o.k. ... W.H.
Ex. & tot. o.k. W.H.
Acct. no. 511
Appr. for pymt. B.R.

Purchase Invoice

Merchandise may be bought for cash or on account. When merchandise is bought for cash, the transaction results in an increase in purchases and a decrease in the asset cash; hence, it should be recorded by debiting Purchases and by crediting Cash. When merchandise is bought on account, the transaction results in an increase in purchases with a corresponding increase in the liability accounts payable; hence, it should be recorded by debiting Purchases and by crediting Accounts Payable.

Accounts payable

In order that the owner or manager may know the total amount owed to his suppliers (sometimes referred to as "creditors"), it is advisable to keep a summary ledger account for Accounts Payable. This is a liability account. The credit balance of the account at the beginning of the period represents the total amount owed to suppliers. During the period, the account should be credited for the amount of any transactions involving increases and should be debited for the amount of any transactions involving decreases in the amount owed to suppliers. At the end of the period, the credit balance of the account again represents the total amount owed to suppliers.

It is also necessary to keep some record of the transactions completed with each supplier in order that information may be readily available at all times as to the amount owed to each supplier and as to when each invoice should be paid. The following methods of accounting for purchases on account are widely used:

The Invoice Method. Under this method it is customary to keep a chronological record of the purchase invoices received and to file them systematically. All other vouchers or documents representing transactions completed with suppliers should be filed with the purchase invoices. Special filing equipment facilitates the use of this method.

The Ledger Account Method. Under this method it is also customary to keep a chronological record of the purchase invoices received; in addition, an individual ledger account with each supplier is kept. Special equipment may be used in maintaining a permanent file of the invoices and other vouchers or documents supporting the records.

Purchases journal

All of the transactions of a merchandising business can be recorded in an ordinary two-column general journal or in a combined cash journal. However, in many such enterprises purchase transactions occur frequently. If most of the purchases are made on account, such transactions may be recorded advantageously in a special journal called a *purchases journal*. One form of a purchases journal is illustrated on page 144.

It will be noted that in recording each purchase, the following information is entered in the purchases journal:

    (a) Date on which the invoice is received
    (b) Number of the invoice (i.e., the number assigned by the buyer)
    (c) From whom purchased (the supplier)
    (d) Amount of the invoice

When the invoice method of accounting is used for purchases on account, it is not necessary to record the address of the supplier in the purchases journal; neither is it necessary to record the terms in the purchases

PURCHASES JOURNAL   PAGE *9*

	DATE	INVOICE NO.	FROM WHOM PURCHASED	POST. REF.	AMOUNT	
1	*1977* May 5	37	Finney Furniture Company	✓	476 20	1
2	6	38	L. J. Carter Company	✓	891 63	2
3	12	39	Mathews Manufacturing Co.	✓	1527 90	3
4	27	40	Monroe Brothers	✓	1762 11	4
5	31		Purchases Dr.- Accounts Payable Cr.	511/231	4657 84	5

Model Purchases Journal

journal. With this form of purchases journal, each transaction can be recorded on one horizontal line.

If an individual ledger account is not kept with each supplier, the purchase invoices should be filed immediately after they have been recorded in the purchases journal. It is preferable that they be filed according to due date in an unpaid invoice file.

If a partial payment is made on an invoice, a notation of the payment should be made on the invoice, and it should be retained in the unpaid invoice file until it is paid in full. It is generally considered a better policy to pay each invoice in full. Paying specific invoices in full simplifies record keeping for both the buyer and the seller. If credit is received because of returns or allowances, a notation of the amount of the credit should also be made on the invoice so that the balance due will be indicated.

When an invoice is paid in full, the payment should be noted on the invoice, which should be transferred from the unpaid invoice file to a paid invoice file.

The unpaid invoice file is usually arranged with a division for each month with folders numbered 1 to 31 in each division. This makes it possible to file the unpaid invoices according to the date they will become due, which facilitates payment of the invoices on or before their due dates. Since certain invoices may be subject to discounts if paid within a specified time, it is important that they be handled in such a manner that payment in time to get the benefit of the discounts will not be overlooked.

The folders in the paid invoice file are usually arranged in alphabetic order, according to the names of suppliers. This facilitates the filing of all paid invoices, and all other vouchers or documents representing transactions with suppliers, in such a manner that a complete history of the business done with each supplier is maintained.

Posting from the Purchases Journal. Under the invoice method of accounting for purchases on account, individual posting from the purchases journal is not required. When this plan is followed, it is customary to place a check mark in the Posting Reference column of the purchases journal at the time of entering each invoice.

At the end of the month the Amount column of the purchases journal should be totaled and the ruling completed as illustrated. The total of the purchases on account for the month should then be posted as a debit to Purchases and as a credit to Accounts Payable. A proper cross-reference should be provided by entering the page of the purchases journal preceded by the initial "P" in the Posting Reference column of the ledger and by entering the account number in the Posting Reference column of the purchases journal. The titles of both accounts and the posting references may be entered on one horizontal line of the purchases journal as shown in the illustration. Posting the total in this manner usually is referred to as *summary posting*.

Regardless of whether the cash basis or the accrual basis of accounting is used, a special account form, called a *balance-column account* form, is widely used. While the standard two-column account form illustrated to this point is still favored by some, the four-column form of balance-column account, illustrated below, has the advantage of providing a place to note the balance of the account. This may be determined and recorded after each transaction, or only at the end of the month. (There is also a three-column form of balance-column account which will be used in subsequent chapters for accounts with individual customers and suppliers.)

The summary posting from W. F. Brown's purchases journal on May 31 is illustrated below:

ACCOUNT *Accounts Payable*   ACCOUNT NO. *231*

DATE	ITEM	POST. REF.	DEBIT	CREDIT	BALANCE DEBIT	BALANCE CREDIT
1977 May 31		P9		4657 84		4657 84

ACCOUNT *Purchases*   ACCOUNT NO. *511*

DATE	ITEM	POST. REF.	DEBIT	CREDIT	BALANCE DEBIT	BALANCE CREDIT
1977 May 31		P9	4657 84		4657 84	

General Ledger Accounts After Posting from Purchases Journal

The Ledger Account Method. If an individual ledger account is kept for each supplier, all transactions representing either increases or decreases in the amount owed to each supplier should be posted individually to the proper account. The posting may be done by hand, or posting machines may be used. If the posting is done by hand, it may be completed either directly from the purchase invoices and other vouchers or documents representing the transactions, or it may be completed from the books of original entry. If the posting is done with the aid of posting machines, it will usually be completed directly from the purchase invoices and other vouchers or documents. The ledger account method of accounting for accounts payable is explained in detail in Chapter 8.

<table>
<tr><td>

Report
No. 6-1

</td><td>

Refer to the study assignments and complete Report No. 6-1. After completing the report, continue with the textbook discussion until the next report is required.

</td></tr>
</table>

SALES AND THE SALES JOURNAL

On page 140 reference was made to the fact that in recording transactions arising from merchandising activities it is desirable to keep certain accounts, including accounts for sales and for sales returns and allowances. A discussion of these accounts, together with a discussion of the sales journal, follows.

Sales account   The sales account is a temporary owner's equity account in which the revenue resulting from sales of merchandise is recorded. The account should be credited for the selling price of all merchandise sold during the accounting period. If sales are for cash, the credit to Sales is offset by a debit to Cash; if the sales are on account, the debit is made to an asset account, Accounts Receivable.

SALES	
	Credit to record the selling price of merchandise sold.

Sales returns and allowances account   This account is a temporary owner's equity account in which sales returns and allowances are recorded. The account should be debited for the selling price of any merchandise returned by customers or for any allowances made to customers that decrease the selling price of the merchandise sold. The offsetting credit is to Accounts Receivable if the goods were sold on account, or to Cash if a refund was made because the sale was originally for cash. Such allow-

SALES RETURNS AND ALLOWANCES	
Debit to record returns and allowances.	

ances may be granted to customers for merchandise delivered in poor condition or for merchandise that does not meet specifications as to quality, weight, size, color, grade, or style.

While sales returns and allowances could be debited directly to Sales, it is better to debit Sales Returns and Allowances. The accounts will then show both the amount of gross sales and the amount of returns and allowances. If returns and allowances are large in proportion to gross sales, a weakness in the merchandising operations is indicated; and the trouble should be determined and corrected.

Retail sales tax

A tax imposed upon the sale of tangible personal property at retail is known as a *retail sales tax*. The tax is usually measured by the gross sales price or the gross receipts from sales. Retail sales taxes are imposed by most states and by many cities. Retail sales taxes may also include taxes imposed upon persons engaged in furnishing services at retail, in which case they are measured by the gross receipts for furnishing such services. The rates of the tax vary considerably but usually range from 1 percent to 6 percent. In most states the tax is a general sales tax. However, in some states the tax is imposed only on specific items, such as automobiles, cosmetics, radio and television sets, and playing cards.

To avoid fractions of cents and to simplify the determination of the tax, it is customary to use a sales tax table or schedule. For example, where the rate is 5 percent the tax may be calculated as shown in the following schedule:

AMOUNT OF SALE	AMOUNT OF TAX
1¢ to 10¢	None
11¢ to 27¢	1¢
28¢ to 47¢	2¢
48¢ to 68¢	3¢
69¢ to 89¢	4¢
90¢ to $1.09	5¢

and so on

The amount of the tax imposed under the schedule approximates the legal rate. Retail sales tax reports accompanied by remittances for the amounts due must be filed periodically, usually monthly or quarterly, depending upon the law of the state or city in which the business is located.

In the case of a retail store operated in a city or state where a sales tax is imposed on merchandise sold for cash or on account, it is advisable to keep an account for Sales Tax Payable. This is a liability account which should be credited for the

SALES TAX PAYABLE

Debit	Credit
to record payment of tax to the proper taxing authority or for tax on merchandise returned by customers.	to record tax imposed on sales.

amount of the tax collected or imposed on sales. The account should be debited for the amount of the tax paid to the proper taxing authority. A credit balance in the account at any time indicates the amount of the liability to the taxing authority for taxes collected or imposed.

Sales tax accounting may be complicated by such factors as **(1)** sales returns and allowances and **(2)** exempt sales. If the tax is recorded at the time the sale is recorded, it will be necessary to adjust for the tax when recording sales returns and allowances. If some sales are exempt from the tax, it will be necessary to distinguish between the taxable and the nontaxable sales. A common example of nontaxable sales is sales to out-of-state customers.

Sales ticket

The first written record of a sales transaction is called a *sales ticket*. Whether merchandise is sold for cash or on account, a sales ticket should be prepared. When the sale is for cash, the ticket may be printed by the cash register at the time that the sale is rung up. However, some stores prefer to use handwritten sales tickets no matter whether the sale is for cash or on account. Regardless of the method used in recording cash sales, it is necessary to prepare a handwritten sales ticket or charge slip for every sale on account. Such sales tickets are usually prepared in duplicate or in triplicate. The original copy is for the bookkeeping department. A carbon copy is given to the customer. Where more than one salesperson is employed, each is usually provided with a separate pad of sales tickets. Each pad bears a different number that identifies the clerk. The individual sales tickets are also numbered consecutively. This facilitates sorting the tickets by clerks if it is desired to compute the amount of goods sold by each clerk. Reference to the sales ticket illustrated here will show the type of information usually recorded.

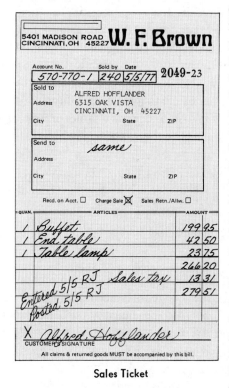

Sales Ticket

When merchandise is sold for cash in a state or a city which has a retail sales tax, the transaction results in an increase in the asset cash offset by an increase in sales revenue and an increase in the liability sales tax payable. Such transactions should be recorded by debiting Cash for the amount received and by crediting Sales for the sales price of the merchandise and crediting Sales Tax Payable for the amount of the tax collected. When merchandise is sold on account in such a state or city, the transaction results in an increase in the asset accounts receivable offset by an increase in sales revenue and an increase in the liability sales tax payable. Such transactions should be recorded by debiting Accounts Receivable for the total amount charged to the customer and by crediting Sales for the amount of the sale and crediting Sales Tax Payable for the amount of the tax imposed.

An alternative procedure that is permissible under some sales tax laws is to credit the total of both the sales and the tax to the sales account in the first place. Periodically — usually at the end of each month — a calculation is made to determine how much of the balance of the sales account is presumed to be tax, and an entry is made to remove this amount from the sales account and to transfer it to the sales tax payable account. Suppose, for example, that the tax rate is 5 percent, and that the sales account includes the tax collected or charged, along with the amount of the sales. In this event, 100/105 of the balance of the account is presumed to be the amount of the sales, and 5/105 of the balance is the amount of the tax. If the sales account had a balance of $10,500, the tax portion would be $500 (5/105 of $10,500). A debit to Sales of $500 would remove this tax portion; the credit would be to Sales Tax Payable.

Bank credit card sales

The use of bank credit cards in connection with the retail sales of certain types of goods and service is a common practice. The two most widely used credit cards of this type in the United States are the "Bank-Americard" and the "Master Charge" card. The former was started by the Bank of America in California. That bank now franchises numerous banks in other localities to offer the program. Likewise, several thousand banks participate in the Master Charge program. The two systems have much in common.

Participating banks encourage their depositors and other customers to obtain the cards by supplying the necessary information to establish their credit reliability. When this has been accomplished, a small (approximately 2″ x 3″) plastic card containing (in raised characters so that the card may be used for imprinting) the cardholder's name and an identifying number is issued to the applicant.

Merchants and other businesses are invited to participate in the program. If certain conditions are met, the bank will accept for deposit completed copies of the prescribed form of sales invoices (also sometimes called "tickets," "drafts," or "vouchers") for goods sold or services rendered to cardholders and evidenced by the invoices bearing the card imprints and the buyers' signatures. The bank, in effect, either "buys" the tickets at a discount (commonly 3 percent, though it may be more or less depending upon various factors) immediately, or gives the merchant immediate credit for the full face amount of the tickets, and, once a month, charges the merchant's account with the total amount of the discount at the agreed rate. (The latter practice is more usual.)

For the merchant, bank credit card sales are nearly the equivalent of cash sales. The service is performed or the goods are sold; and the money is secured. It is then up to the bank to collect from the buyer or to bear the loss, if the account proves to be uncollectible.

In most respects, the accounting for bank credit card sales is very much the same as the accounting for regular cash sales. Very often a regular sales ticket is prepared as well as the credit card form of invoice. Usually the transactions are accounted for as sales for the full price with the amount of the discount being treated as an expense when the bank makes the monthly charge.

It will be apparent that bank credit card sales are similar in many respects to the sales made by certain types of businesses that use other forms of retail credit cards — notably those of petroleum companies, and businesses participating in the "Diners Club," "Carte Blanche," and American Express programs.

Accounts receivable

In order that the owner or manager of an enterprise may know the total amount due from charge customers at any time, it is advisable to keep a summary ledger account with Accounts Receivable. This is an asset account. The debit balance of the account at the beginning of the period represents the total amount due from customers. During the period, the account should be debited for the amount of any transactions involving increases and should be credited for the amount of any transactions involving decreases in the amount due from customers. At the end of the period, the debit balance of the account again represents the total amount due from charge customers.

It is also necessary to keep some record of the transactions completed with each customer in order that information may be readily available at all times as to the amount due from each customer. The following methods of accounting for charge sales are widely used:

The Sales Ticket Method. Under this method it is customary to file the charge sales tickets systematically. All other related vouchers or documents representing transactions with customers should be filed with the appropriate sales tickets. Special filing equipment facilitates the use of this method. In some cases a chronological record of the charge sales tickets is kept as a means of control.

The Ledger Account Method. Under this method it is customary to keep a chronological record of the charge sales tickets. An individual ledger account with each customer is also kept. Special equipment may be used in maintaining a permanent file of the charge sales tickets and other vouchers or documents supporting the records.

Under either of these methods of accounting for transactions with charge customers, it is necessary that a sales ticket or charge slip be made for each sale on account. In making a charge sales ticket the date, the name and address of the customer, the quantity, a description of the items sold, the unit prices, the total amount of the sale, and the amount of the sales tax should be recorded.

Sales journal

Transactions involving the sale of merchandise on account can be recorded in an ordinary two-column general journal or in a combined cash journal. However, in many merchandising businesses sales transactions occur frequently, and if it is the policy to sell merchandise on account, such transactions may be recorded advantageously in a special journal. If the business is operated in an area where no sales taxes are imposed, all sales on account can be recorded in a *sales journal* with only one amount column as illustrated below.

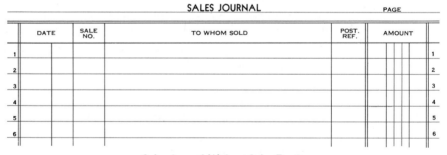

Sales Journal Without Sales Taxes

At the end of the month, the total of the amount column should be posted as a debit to Accounts Receivable and as a credit to Sales.

The second model sales journal illustrated on page 152 provides three amount columns. This format is most appropriate for use in an area where a sales tax is imposed. The transactions recorded in the journal were completed by W. F. Brown, a retail merchant, during the month of May. His store is located in a state that imposes a tax of 5 percent on the retail sale of all merchandise whether sold for cash or on account.

SALES JOURNAL   PAGE 14

	DATE	SALE NO.	TO WHOM SOLD	POST REF.	ACCOUNTS RECEIVABLE DR.	SALES CR.	SALES TAX PAYABLE CR.	
1	1977 May 5	240	Alfred Hofflander	✓	279 51	266 20	13 31	1
2	5	241	Louise C. Case	✓	1825 34	1738 42	86 92	2
3	11	242	Elanore S. Buffa	✓	609 95	580 90	29 05	3
4	16	243	C. H. Mason	✓	1544 34	1470 80	73 54	4
5	23	244	C. M. Williams	✓	989 36	942 25	47 11	5
6	26	245	Edward Sedgwick	✓	1517 46	1445 20	72 26	6
7	27	246	E. M. Keithley	✓	639 98	609 50	30 48	7
8					7405 94	7053 27	352 67	8
					7405 94	7053 27	352 67	
9					(121)	(411)	(241)	9

Sales Journal With Sales Taxes

It will be noted that the following information regarding each charge sales ticket is recorded in the sales journal:

(a) Date
(b) Number of the sales ticket
(c) To whom sold (the customer)
(d) Amount charged to customer
(e) Amount of sale
(f) Amount of sales tax

With this form of sales journal, each transaction can be recorded on one horizontal line. The sales ticket should provide all the information needed in recording each sale.

If an individual ledger account is not kept with each customer, the charge sales tickets should be filed immediately after they have been recorded in the sales journal. They are usually filed under the name of the customer. There are numerous types of trays, cabinets, and files on the market that are designed to facilitate the filing of charge sales tickets by customer name. Such devices are designed to save time, to promote accuracy, and to provide a safe means of keeping a record of the transactions with each charge customer.

When a customer makes a partial payment on an account, the amount of the payment should be noted on the most recent charge sales ticket and the new balance should be indicated. Sales tickets paid in full should be receipted and may either be given to the customer or may be transferred to another file for future reference. If a customer is given credit for merchandise returned or because of allowances, a notation of the amount of credit should be made on the most recent charge sales ticket and the new balance should be indicated. If a credit memorandum is issued to a customer, it should be prepared in duplicate and the carbon copy should be attached to the sales ticket on which the amount is noted.

Posting from the Sales Journal. Under the sales ticket method of accounting for sales on account, individual posting from the sales journal is not required. When this plan is followed, it is customary to place a check mark in the Posting Reference column of the sales journal at the time of entering each sale.

At the end of the month the amount columns of the sales journal should be footed in small figures. On a separate sheet of paper the total of the credit columns should then be added. The sum of the totals of the credit columns should equal the total of the debit column. If it does, the totals should be entered in ink and the ruling completed as illustrated. The totals should be posted to the general ledger accounts indicated in the column headings. This summary posting should be completed in the following order:

(a) Post the total of the Accounts Receivable Dr. column to the debit of Accounts Receivable.

(b) Post the total of the Sales Cr. column to the credit of Sales.

(c) Post the total of the Sales Tax Payable Cr. column to the credit of Sales Tax Payable.

A proper cross-reference should be provided by entering the page of the sales journal preceded by the initial "S" in the Posting Reference column of the ledger and by entering the account number immediately below the column total of the sales journal. The proper method of completing the summary posting from W. F. Brown's sales journal on May 31 is shown in the accounts affected as illustrated below.

ACCOUNT *Accounts Receivable*   ACCOUNT NO. *121*

DATE	ITEM	POST. REF.	DEBIT	CREDIT	BALANCE DEBIT	BALANCE CREDIT
1977 May 31		S14	7405 94		7405 94	

ACCOUNT *Sales Tax Payable*   ACCOUNT NO. *241*

DATE	ITEM	POST. REF.	DEBIT	CREDIT	BALANCE DEBIT	BALANCE CREDIT
1977 May 31		S14		352 67		352 67

ACCOUNT *Sales*   ACCOUNT NO. *411*

DATE	ITEM	POST. REF.	DEBIT	CREDIT	BALANCE DEBIT	BALANCE CREDIT
1977 May 31		S14		7053 27		7053 27

General Ledger Accounts After Posting from Sales Journal

The Ledger Account Method. If an individual ledger account is kept for each customer, all transactions representing either increases or decreases in the amount due from each customer should be posted individually to the proper account. The posting may be done by hand or posting machines may be used. If the posting is done by hand, it may be completed either directly from the charge sales tickets and other vouchers or documents representing the transactions, or it may be completed from the books of original entry. If the posting is done with posting machines, it will usually be completed directly from the charge sales tickets and other vouchers or documents.

<table>
<tr>
<td>

**Report
No. 6-2**

</td>
<td>

Refer to the study assignments and complete Report No. 6-2. After completing the report, continue with the textbook discussion until the next report is required.

</td>
</tr>
</table>

ACCOUNTING PROCEDURE

The accounting procedure in recording the transactions of a merchandising business is, in general, the same as that involved in recording the transactions of any other enterprise. In a small merchandising business where the number of transactions is not large and all the bookkeeping may be done by one person, a standard two-column general journal or a combined cash journal may be used as the only book of original entry. However, if desired, a purchases journal and a sales journal may be used also. The purchases journal may be used for keeping a chronological record of purchases of merchandise on account, and the sales journal may be used for keeping a chronological record of sales of merchandise on account. All of the accounts may be kept in one general ledger, which may be either a bound book, a loose-leaf book, or a card file. The posting from a two-column journal or from the "General" columns of a combined cash journal may be completed daily or periodically; summary posting from the purchases and sales journals and from the special columns of a combined cash journal is done at the end of the month.

A trial balance should be taken at the end of each month as a means of proving the equality of the debit and credit account balances. The balance of the summary account for Accounts Receivable should be proved periodically, or at least at the end of each month. This may be done by determining the total of the unpaid sales tickets or charge slips that are kept in a customer's file. Likewise, the balance of the summary account for Accounts Payable should be proved periodically, or at least at the end of each month. This may be done by determining the total of the unpaid invoices that are kept in an unpaid invoice file.

This procedure will be illustrated by **(1)** recording a narrative of certain transactions for one month in a purchases journal, a sales journal, and a combined cash journal, **(2)** by posting to the ledger accounts, **(3)** by preparing a schedule of accounts receivable to reconcile the balance of the summary account for Accounts Receivable, and **(4)** by preparing a schedule of accounts payable to reconcile the balance of the summary account for Accounts Payable. (The end-of-month trial balance is not shown since the illustration does not involve all of the accounts in the general ledger.)

Dallas Hubbard is the owner of a small retail business operated under the name of "The Hubbard Store." A purchases journal, a sales journal, and a combined cash journal are used as books of original entry. All of the accounts are kept in a general ledger. Individual ledger accounts with customers and suppliers are not kept; instead, the purchase invoices and the charge sales tickets are filed in the manner previously described. All sales are subject to a retail sales tax of 5 percent, whether for cash or on account. All sales on account are payable by the tenth of the following month unless otherwise agreed. A partial chart of accounts is reproduced below. It includes only the accounts needed to record certain transactions completed during March, 1977, the first month that Mr. Hubbard has owned and operated the business.

THE HUBBARD STORE

PARTIAL CHART OF ACCOUNTS

*Assets**	*Revenue from Sales*
111 Cash	411 Sales
121 Accounts Receivable	041 Sales Returns and Allowances
181 Store Equipment	
Liabilities	*Cost of Goods Sold*
231 Accounts Payable	511 Purchases
241 Sales Tax Payable	051 Purchases Returns and Allowances

Words in italics represent headings and not account titles.

THE HUBBARD STORE

PARTIAL NARRATIVE OF TRANSACTIONS

Thursday, March 3

Purchased store equipment on account from the Metro Store Equipment Co., 1500 Main Street, Lafayette, IN 47901, $1,624.90.

> Since this transaction involved a purchase of store equipment, it was recorded in the combined cash journal. (The purchases journal is used only for recording purchases of merchandise on account.)

Friday, March 4

Received invoice dated March 1 from Norton's, 469 Meridian, Indianapolis, IN 47906, for merchandise purchased, $215.30. Terms, 30 days net. (Assigned number "1" to this invoice.)

Saturday, March 5

Sold merchandise on account to Elaine C. Peters, 2402 Northwestern, Lafayette, IN 47906, $34.60, tax $1.73. Sale No. 1-1.

Sundry cash sales per cash register tape, $61, tax $3.05. This amount includes sales made to customers who used their BankAmericards. The special vouchers (tickets, slips) prepared are treated the same as checks received for cash sales. Periodically, these vouchers, along with checks and probably some currency and coin, are deposited in the bank. (Early in the following month, and each month thereafter, the bank will charge The Hubbard Store with the agreed percentage of the total amount of the vouchers.)

> Each Saturday the store's total cash sales for the week and related tax are recorded, using the cash register tape as the source of the amounts. This transaction was recorded in the combined cash journal by debiting Cash for the total amount received and by crediting Sales for the selling price of the merchandise and crediting Sales Tax Payable for the amount of the tax imposed on cash sales. This was recorded in the combined cash journal since only sales on account are entered in the sales journal. A check mark was entered in the Posting Reference column to indicate that no individual posting is required.

Monday, March 7

Purchased merchandise from Parks Company, Kokomo, IN 46901, for cash, $96. Check No. 4.

> This transaction was recorded in the combined cash journal since only purchases of merchandise on account are recorded in the purchases journal.

Tuesday, March 8

Sold merchandise on account to W. A. Adams, 908 Oak St., Lafayette, IN 47905, $41, tax $2.05. Sale No. 1-2.

Wednesday, March 9

Gave W. A. Adams credit for merchandise returned, $12, tax 60 cents.

> This transaction increased sales returns and allowances and decreased sales tax payable and accounts receivable. It was recorded in the combined cash journal by debiting Sales Returns and Allowances for the amount of the merchandise returned, by debiting Sales Tax Payable for the amount of the sales tax, and by crediting Accounts Receivable for the total amount of the credit allowed Mr. Adams.

Thursday, March 10

Received invoice (No. 2) dated March 9 from Norton's for merchandise purchased, $385. Terms, 30 days net.

Friday, March 11

Sold merchandise on account to Joseph F. Charles, 13 Bexley Rd., Lafayette, IN 47906, $21.80, tax $1.09. Sale No. 2-1.

Saturday, March 12

Sundry cash sales for week, $215.40, tax $10.77.

Received a check for $36.33 from Elaine C. Peters for merchandise sold to her March 5.

Monday, March 14

Received credit for $25.60 from Norton's for merchandise returned by agreement.

> The credit applies to Invoice No. 2, dated March 9. This transaction had the effect of increasing purchases returns and allowances and decreasing accounts payable. It was recorded in the combined cash journal by debiting Accounts Payable and by crediting Purchases Returns and Allowances for the amount of the credit received from Norton's.

Tuesday, March 15

Paid Transit, Inc., freight and drayage on merchandise purchased, $20.50. Check No. 5.

> In the simple set of accounts maintained for The Hubbard Store, no separate account is used to record the cost of freight on merchandise purchases. Instead, the amount is debited to the purchases account. This treatment is acceptable since freight on purchases is really a part of the cost of goods purchased.

Wednesday, March 16

Received invoice (No. 3) dated March 14 from C. E. Arthur & Son, Frankfort, IN 46041, for merchandise purchased, $51. Terms, 30 days net.

Thursday, March 17

Paid Norton's $215.30 in settlement of Invoice No. 1 dated March 1. Check No. 6.

Friday, March 18

Received $30.45 from W. A. Adams for merchandise sold March 8 less merchandise returned March 9.

Saturday, March 19

Sundry cash sales for week, $104.05, tax $5.20.

Monday, March 21

Paid Metro Store Equipment Co. $800 on account. Check No. 7.

Tuesday, March 22

Sold merchandise on account to Joseph F. Charles, $41, tax $2.05. Sale No. 1-3.

Wednesday, March 23

Received invoice (No. 4) dated March 21 from C. E. Arthur & Son for merchandise purchased, $81.20. Terms, 30 days net.

Thursday, March 24

Sold merchandise on account to Elaine C. Peters, $47, tax $2.35. Sale No. 2-2.

Saturday, March 26

Sundry cash sales for week, $103.80, tax $5.19.

Monday, March 28

Sold merchandise on account to W. A. Adams, $34.20, tax $1.71. Sale No. 2-3.

Thursday, March 31

Sundry cash sales, $61.95, tax $3.10.

Since this is the last day of the month, the amount of cash sales since March 26, including tax, was recorded.

Journalizing   The transactions completed by The Hubbard Store during the month of March were recorded in the combined cash journal reproduced on pages 160 and 161, the purchases journal reproduced on page 159, and the sales journal reproduced on page 159. (The footings of the combined cash journal reflect the amounts of more transactions than are actually recorded. The footings of the purchases journal and of the sales journal reflect only the amounts of the transactions recorded.)

Posting   The accounts affected by the transactions narrated are reproduced on pages 161 and 162. The posting was completed from the books of original entry in the following order; first, the combined cash journal; second, the purchases journal; and third, the sales journal. After the columns of the combined cash journal were footed and the footings were proved, the totals were entered and the rulings were made as illustrated. Each entry in the General Debit and General Credit columns was posted individually to the proper account. The total of each of the six special columns was posted to the account indicated by the column heading. The number of the account to which the posting was made was written below the total. Since the totals of the General Debit and General Credit columns were not posted, a check mark ($\sqrt{}$) was made under each of these columns to so indicate. The total of the single column in the purchases journal was posted as a debit to Purchases and also as a credit to Accounts Payable. The number of each of these accounts was noted in the Posting Reference column beside the total of the Amount column. After the three amount columns of the sales journal were footed and the footings were proved, the totals were entered and the rulings were made as illustrated. Each total was posted to the account indicated by the column heading, and the account number was shown below that total.

PURCHASES JOURNAL   PAGE 1

	DATE	INVOICE NO.	FROM WHOM PURCHASED	POST. REF.	AMOUNT	
1	1977 Mar. 4	1	Norton's	✓	215 30	1
2	10	2	Norton's	✓	385 00	2
3	16	3	C. E. Arthur + Son	✓	51 00	3
4	23	4	C. E. Arthur + Son	✓	81 20	4
5	31		Purchases Dr.-Accounts Payable Cr.	511/231	732 50	5
6						6
7						7
8						8

The Hubbard Store — Purchases Journal

SALES JOURNAL   PAGE 1

	DATE	SALE NO.	TO WHOM SOLD	POST REF.	ACCOUNTS RECEIVABLE DR.	SALES CR.	SALES TAX PAYABLE CR.	
1	1977 Mar. 5	1-1	Elaine C. Peters	✓	36 33	34 60	1 73	1
2	8	1-2	W. A. Adams	✓	43 05	41 00	2 05	2
3	11	2-1	Joseph F. Charles	✓	22 89	21 80	1 09	3
4	22	1-3	Joseph F. Charles	✓	43 05	41 00	2 05	4
5	24	2-2	Elaine C. Peters	✓	49 35	47 00	2 35	5
6	28	2-3	W. A. Adams	✓	35 91	34 20	1 71	6
7					230 58 / 230 58	219 60 / 219 60	10 98 / 10 98	7
8					(121)	(411)	(241)	8
9								9
10								10

The Hubbard Store — Sales Journal

When more than one book of original entry is used, it is advisable to identify each book by means of an initial (or initials) preceding the page

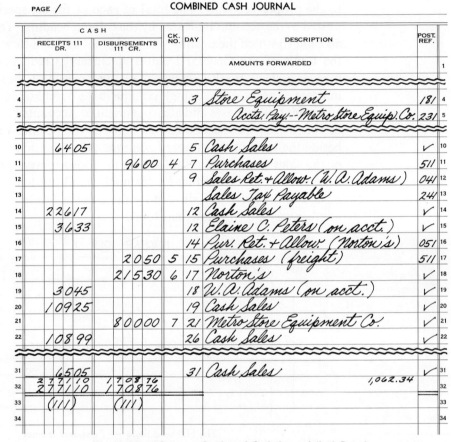

The Hubbard Store — Combined Cash Journal (Left Page)

number. The following code was used in conjunction with the page number to indicate the source of each entry in the ledger accounts:

CJ = Combined cash journal
P = Purchases journal
S = Sales journal

Trial balance

After completing the posting to the accounts in the general ledger, the balance of each account was extended to the proper debit or credit balance column. Usually a trial balance then would be prepared to prove the equality of the debit and credit account balances. However, since the illustration did not involve all of the general ledger accounts nor all of the transactions for the month, a trial balance of the general ledger of The Hubbard Store as of March 31, 1977, is not reproduced.

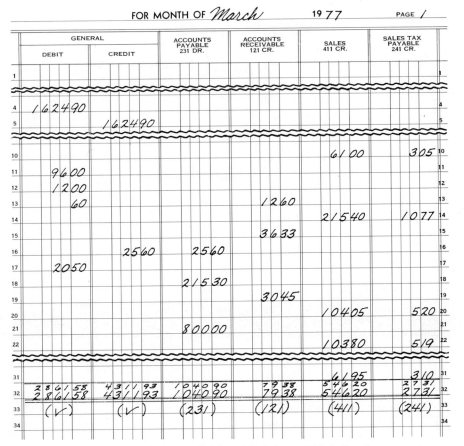

FOR MONTH OF *March*   19 77   PAGE *1*

	GENERAL		ACCOUNTS PAYABLE 231 DR.	ACCOUNTS RECEIVABLE 121 CR.	SALES 411 CR.	SALES TAX PAYABLE 241 CR.	
	DEBIT	CREDIT					
1							1
4	1 6 2 4 90						4
5		1 6 2 4 90					5
10					6 1 00	3 05	10
11	96 00						11
12	12 00						12
13		60		12 60			13
14					2 15 40	10 77	14
15				36 33			15
16		25 60	25 60				16
17	20 50						17
18			2 15 30				18
19				30 45			19
20					1 04 05	5 20	20
21			8 00 00				21
22					1 03 80	5 19	22
31					61 95	3 10	31
32	2 86 58	4 31 1 93	1 0 40 90	79 38	5 46 20	27 31	32
32	2 86 58	4 31 1 93	1 0 40 90	79 38	5 46 20	27 31	32
33	(✓)	(✓)	(231)	(121)	(411)	(241)	33
34							34

The Hubbard Store — Combined Cash Journal (Right Page)

ACCOUNT *Cash*   ACCOUNT NO. *111*

DATE	ITEM	POST. REF.	DEBIT	CREDIT	BALANCE DEBIT	BALANCE CREDIT
1977 Mar. 31		CJ1	2 77 1 10			
31		CJ1		1 70 8 76	1 06 2 34	

ACCOUNT *Accounts Receivable*   ACCOUNT NO. *121*

DATE	ITEM	POST. REF.	DEBIT	CREDIT	BALANCE DEBIT	BALANCE CREDIT
1977 Mar. 31		S1	2 30 58			
31		CJ1		79 38	1 51 20	

ACCOUNT *Store Equipment*   ACCOUNT NO. *181*

DATE	ITEM	POST. REF.	DEBIT	CREDIT	BALANCE DEBIT	BALANCE CREDIT
1977 Mar. 3		CJ1	1 62 4 90		1 62 4 90	

The Hubbard Store — General Ledger Accounts

ACCOUNT *Accounts Payable*   ACCOUNT NO. *231*

DATE		ITEM	POST. REF.	DEBIT	CREDIT	BALANCE DEBIT	BALANCE CREDIT
1977 Mar.	3		CJ1		1 624 90		
	31		P1		732 50		
	31		CJ1	1 040 90			1 316 50

ACCOUNT *Sales Tax Payable*   ACCOUNT NO. *241*

DATE		ITEM	POST. REF.	DEBIT	CREDIT	BALANCE DEBIT	BALANCE CREDIT
1977 Mar.	9		CJ1	60			
	31		CJ1		27 31		
	31		S1		10 98		37 69

ACCOUNT *Sales*   ACCOUNT NO. *411*

DATE		ITEM	POST. REF.	DEBIT	CREDIT	BALANCE DEBIT	BALANCE CREDIT
1977 Mar.	31		CJ1		546 20		
	31		S1		219 60		765 80

ACCOUNT *Sales Returns and Allowances*   ACCOUNT NO. *041*

DATE		ITEM	POST. REF.	DEBIT	CREDIT	BALANCE DEBIT	BALANCE CREDIT
1977 Mar.	9		CJ1	12 00		12 00	

ACCOUNT *Purchases*   ACCOUNT NO. *511*

DATE		ITEM	POST. REF.	DEBIT	CREDIT	BALANCE DEBIT	BALANCE CREDIT
1977 Mar.	7		CJ1	96 00			
	15		CJ1	20 50			
	31		P1	732 50		849 00	

ACCOUNT *Purchases Returns and Allowances*   ACCOUNT NO. *051*

DATE		ITEM	POST. REF.	DEBIT	CREDIT	BALANCE DEBIT	BALANCE CREDIT
1977 Mar.	14		CJ1		25 60		25 60

The Hubbard Store — General Ledger Accounts (*concluded*)

Schedule of accounts receivable

A list of customers showing the amount due from each one as of a specified date is known as a *schedule of accounts receivable.* It is usually advisable to prepare such a schedule at the end of each month. An example for The Hubbard Store as of March 31, 1977, is provided below. Such a schedule can be prepared easily by going through the customers' file and listing the names of the customers and the amount due from each. Should the total not be in agreement with the balance of the summary accounts receivable account, the error may be in either the file or the ledger account. The file may be incorrect in that either one or more sales tickets on which collection has been made have not been removed or that one or more uncollected ones are missing. Another possibility is that a memorandum of a partial collection was overlooked in preparing the list. The accounts receivable account could be incorrect, also, because of an error in posting or because of an error in a journal from which the totals were posted. In any event, the postings, journals, and sales tickets must be checked until the reason for the discrepancy is found so that the necessary correction can be made.

The Hubbard Store	
Schedule of Accounts Receivable	
March 31, 1977	
W. A. Adams	35 91
Joseph F. Charles	65 94
Elaine C. Peters	49 35
	151 20

The Hubbard Store — Schedule of Accounts Receivable

Schedule of accounts payable

A list of suppliers showing the amount due to each one as of a specified date is known as a *schedule of accounts payable.* It is usually advisable to prepare such a schedule at the end of each month. An example for The Hubbard Store as of March 31, 1977, is provided on the next page. Such a schedule can be prepared easily by going through the unpaid invoice file and listing the names of the suppliers and the amount due to each. Should the total of the schedule not be in agreement with the balance of the summary accounts payable account, the error may be in either the file or the ledger account. The file may be incorrect in that either one or more paid invoices have not been removed or in that one or more unpaid ones are missing. Another possibility is that a memorandum of a partial payment was overlooked in preparing the list. The accounts payable account could be incorrect, also, because of an error in posting or because of an error in a journal from which the total purchases was posted. In any event, the postings, journals, and invoices must be checked until the reason for the discrepancy is found so that the necessary correction can be made.

The Hubbard Store		
Schedule of Accounts Payable		
March 31, 1977		
C. E. Arthur & Son		132 20
Metro Store Equipment Co.		824 90
Norton's		359 40
		1316 50

The Hubbard Store — Schedule of Accounts Payable

Merchandise inventory

Apart from the fact that the foregoing illustration did not include any transactions or information about various operating expenses, Mr. Hubbard could not calculate his net income or net loss for the month because the amount of the merchandise inventory at March 31 was not determined. Lacking this information, cost of goods sold could not be calculated. Since there was no inventory at the first of the month, the amount of the month's purchases of merchandise, $849, less the amount of purchases returns and allowances, $25.60, is the cost of the goods that were *available* for sale, $823.40. To calculate the cost of the goods *sold*, however, the cost of the goods that remained on hand on March 31 would have to be deducted. The first step would have been to count the items of merchandise in the store at the end of that day. Next, these goods would have to have been assigned a reasonable share of the total purchases cost. Since Mr. Hubbard does not expect to calculate monthly net income (or net loss), he will not "take inventory" until the end of the year. This may be December 31, if he plans to keep his records on a calendar-year basis, or it might be February 28 (or 29), if he wants to use a fiscal year that ends on the last day of February. Whatever the period chosen, a crucial step in the calculation of the periodic net income (or net loss) of a merchandising business under the accrual basis of accounting is the determination of the merchandise inventory at the end of the fiscal period — a point in time that is also the beginning of the next fiscal period.

When the end of the fiscal period does arrive and the cost to be assigned to the merchandise then on hand is calculated, the amount of this calculation will have to be recorded in an asset account. The title of the account usually used is "Merchandise Inventory." This account will be debited; the related credit is made to an account with the title "Expense and Revenue Summary" — a temporary owner's equity account used in summarizing the accounts whose balances enter into the determination of the net income (or loss) for a period. The manner of using the expense and revenue summary account in the end-of-period process of adjusting and closing the books of a retail merchandising business will be explained and illustrated in Chapters 9 and 10.

**Report
No. 6-3**

> Refer to the study assignments and complete Report No. 6-3. After completing the report, you may proceed with the textbook discussion in Chapter 7 until the next report is required.

Chapter 7

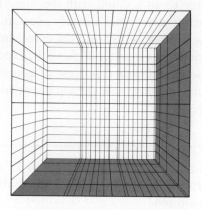

ACCOUNTING FOR NOTES AND INTEREST

A major characteristic of modern business is the extensive use of credit. Each day hundreds of millions of transactions occur that involve the sale of goods or services in return for promises to pay at a later date for what has been received. Sales of this type are said to be "on credit" or "on account"; they are often described as "charge sales." To facilitate such transactions, the use of *credit cards* has become commonplace. The majority of credit transactions do not involve a written promise to pay a specified amount of money. Often the buyer signs a sales slip or sales ticket, but this is done as an acknowledgment of the receipt of the merchandise or service. When "opening an account" the prospective customer may sign a form or document that obligates him to pay for all purchases that he (and, often, members of his family) may make, but this is a general promise to pay if and when something is purchased.

While not nearly so commonplace as transactions that involve "open account" credit, or the use of bank credit cards, *promissory notes* (usually just called *notes*) are sometimes involved. A promise to repay a loan of money nearly always takes the form of a note. The extension of credit for periods of more than 60 days, or when large amounts of money are involved, may entail the use of notes. Such notes nearly always have certain legal characteristics that cause them to be *negotiable instruments*. In order to be considered a negotiable instrument, a promissory note must evidence the following:

(a) Be in writing and signed by the person or persons agreeing to make payment;

(b) Be an unconditional promise to pay a certain amount of money;

(c) Be payable either on demand or at a definite time;

(d) Be payable to the order of a specified person or firm, or to bearer.

A promissory note is illustrated below. It will be observed that this note has all of the characteristics listed on page 166. It should also be understood that to Paul Clark it is a *note payable*, while to Alice Thompson it is a *note receivable*. Paul Clark is known as the *maker* of the note because he is the one who promises to pay. Alice Thompson is called the *payee* of the note because she is the one who is to receive the specified amount of money.

The note illustrated is interest bearing. This is often, though not always, the case. Sometimes no rate of interest is specified, but it is likely that a transaction in which a nominally non-interest-bearing note is involved will entail some interest. For example, a borrower might give a $1,000 note payable in 60 days to a bank in return for a loan of $985. The $15 difference between the amount received and the amount that must be repaid when the note matures will become, in reality, interest expense at maturity. Such a difference is described as *prepaid interest* until the date that the note matures. When a bank is involved in such a transaction, the difference between the amount received and the amount to be repaid may be referred to as *bank discount*.

$ 1,542.50	May 5	19 77

Ninety days *after date* I *promise to pay to the order of* Alice Thompson

One thousand five hundred forty-two 50/100----- *Dollars*

Payable at Citizens Savings Bank

Value received with interest at the rate of 8% per annum from date

No. 5   *Due* Aug. 3, 1977   Paul Clark

Model Filled-In Promissory Note

Calculating interest

In calculating interest on notes, it is necessary to take the following factors into consideration:

(a) The principal of the note
(b) The rate of interest
(c) The period of time involved

The principal is the face amount of the note — the amount that the maker promises to pay at maturity, apart from any specified interest. The principal is the base on which the interest is calculated.

The rate of interest is usually expressed in the form of a percentage, such as 7 percent or 9 percent. Ordinarily the rate is an annual percentage rate, but in some cases the rate is quoted on a monthly basis, such as 1½ percent a month. A rate of 1½ percent a month is equivalent to a rate of 18 percent a year payable monthly. When a note is interest bearing but the rate is not specified on the face of the note, it is subject to the legal rate, which varies under the laws of the different states.

The days or months from the date of issue of a note to the date of its maturity (or the interest payment date) is the time for which the interest is to be computed. Thus, if a note is payable in 60 days with interest, each and every day is considered in determining the date due, and the exact number of days is used in calculating interest.

When the time in a note is specified in months, the interest should be calculated on the basis of months rather than days. For example, if a note is payable 3 months from date, the interest should be calculated on the basis of 3 months or ¼ of a year. However, when the due date is specified in a note, the time should be computed by figuring the exact number of days that will elapse from the date of the note to the date of its maturity. The interest should then be computed on the basis of this number of days. For example, if a note is dated March 1 and the due date is specified as June 1, the time should be computed in the manner shown at the right.

Days in March	31
Date of note, March	1
Days remaining in March .	30
Days in April	30
Days in May	31
Note matures on June . . .	1
Total time in days	92

Notice that in this computation the date of maturity was counted but the date of the note was not counted. If the note had specified "3 months after date" instead of June 1, the interest should be computed on the basis of 90 days instead of 92 days.

In the case of long-term notes, the interest may be payable periodically, such as semiannually or annually.

In computing interest it is customary to consider 360 days as a year. Most banks and business firms follow this practice, though some banks and government agencies use 365 days as the base in computing daily interest. In any case, the formula for computing interest is:

$$\text{PRINCIPAL} \times \text{RATE} \times \text{TIME (usually a fraction of a 360-day year)} = \text{AMOUNT OF INTEREST}$$

The 60-Day, 6 Percent Method. There are short cuts that may be used in computing interest on the basis of a 360-day year. The interest on any amount for 60 days at 6 percent can be determined simply by moving the decimal point in the amount two places to the left. The reason for this is that 60 days is ⅙ of a year and the interest on any amount at 6 percent for $\frac{1}{6}$ of a year is the same as the interest at 1 percent for a full year. Thus, the interest on $550 for 60 days at 6 percent is $5.50.

The 60-day, 6 percent method may be used to advantage in many cases even though the actual time may be other than 60 days and the actual rate other than 6 percent. The following examples will serve to illustrate this fact (both involve rates of interest greater than 6 percent, but the same technique would be used for rates less than 6 percent):

FACTORS

(a) Principal of note, $1,000
(b) Time, 30 days
(c) Rate of interest, 8%

FACTORS

(a) Principal of note, $3,000
(b) Time, 120 days
(c) Rate of interest, 9%

CALCULATION

Interest at 6% for 60 days = $10
Interest at 6% for 30 days = $5
Interest at 8% = 1⅓ times $5 or $6.67

CALCULATION

Interest at 6% for 60 days = $30
Interest at 6% for 120 days = $60
Interest at 9% = 1½ times $60 or $90

Sometimes it is helpful to determine the interest for 6 days at 6 percent and to use the result as the basis for calculating the actual interest. The interest on any sum for 6 days at 6 percent may be determined simply by moving the decimal point three places to the left. For example, the interest on $1,000 at 6 percent for 6 days is $1. If the actual time were 18 days instead of 6 days, the interest would be three times $1 or $3. This method differs from the 60-day, 6 percent method only in that 6 days is used in the basic computation instead of 60 days.

Published tables are available for reference use in determining the amount of interest on stated sums at different rates for any length of time. Such tables are widely used by financial institutions and may also be used by other firms.

Accounting for notes receivable

Businesses other than lending institutions (such as commercial banks and savings and loan companies) sometimes have the following types of transactions involving notes receivable:

(a) Note received from customer in return for an extension of time for payment of his obligation
(b) Note collected at maturity
(c) Note renewed at maturity
(d) Note dishonored

Note Received from Customer to Obtain an Extension of Time for Payment. When a customer wishes to obtain an extension of time for the payment of his account, he may be willing to issue a note for all or part of the amount due. A merchant may be willing to accept a note in such a case because the note will be a written acknowledgment of the debt and undoubtedly will bear interest.

Lawrence Moore owes the Ridley Hardware Co. $816.32 on open account. The account is past due and Mr. Ridley insists upon a settlement. Mr. Moore offers to give his 60-day, 8 percent note. Mr. Ridley accepts Mr. Moore's offer; the note is dated April 14. It is recorded in the books of the Ridley Hardware Co. as indicated by the following general journal entry:

```
April 14.  Notes Receivable.................................   816.32
             Accounts Receivable............................            816.32
               Received note from Lawrence Moore.
```

If, instead of giving a note for the full amount, Mr. Moore gave a check for $16.32 and a note for the balance, the transaction would have been recorded in Mr. Ridley's books as indicated by the following general journal entry:

```
April 14.  Cash............................................    16.32
           Notes Receivable.................................   800.00
             Accounts Receivable............................            816.32
               Received check and note from Lawrence Moore.
```

(While the foregoing entry is shown in two-column journal form, it actually would be recorded in the combined cash journal or other appropriate book of original entry being used. This observation applies to all illustrations of entries involving the receipt and disbursement of cash.)

Note Collected at Maturity. When a note receivable matures, it may be collected by the holder or it may be left at the bank for collection. If the maker of the note resides in another locality, the note may be forwarded to a bank in that locality for collection. It is customary for banks to charge a fee for making such collections. When the bank makes the collection, it notifies the holder on a form similar to the credit advice shown below, that

ADVICE OF CREDIT	First National Bank	
	UNIONTOWN	KANSAS

To Ridley Hardware Co.

Account No. 315-39995   June 13   19 77

WE CREDIT YOUR ACCOUNT AS FOLLOWS:		
Lawrence Moore's note	$816.32	
Interest for 60 days @ 8%	10.88	
	$827.20	$ 817.20
Less collection charge	10.00	

OFFSETTING DR.   APPROVED *C. Valentine*

Credit Advice

the net amount has been credited to his account. Usually the maker is notified a few days before the maturity of a note so that he may know the due date and the amount that must be paid.

Suppose Mr. Ridley left Lawrence Moore's note for $816.32 at the First National Bank for collection and on June 13 received the notice of collection reproduced on the opposite page.

The transaction should be recorded as indicated by the following general journal entry:

```
June 13. Cash....................................................   817.20
         Collection Expense.................................    10.00
             Notes Receivable...................................            816.32
             Interest Earned....................................             10.88
                 Received credit for the proceeds of Lawrence Moore's
                 note collected by the bank.
```

Note Renewed at Maturity. If the maker of a note is unable to pay the amount due at maturity, he may be permitted to renew all or part of the note. If, instead of paying his note for $816.32 at maturity, Lawrence Moore was permitted to pay the interest and give another note for 60 days at the same rate of interest, the transaction should be recorded in the books of the Ridley Hardware Co. as indicated by the following general journal entry:

```
June 13. Notes Receivable (new note).........................   816.32
         Cash..............................................    10.88
             Notes Receivable (old note).......................            816.32
             Interest Earned...................................             10.88
                 Received a new note for $816.32 from Lawrence
                 Moore in renewal of his note due today and $10.88
                 in cash in payment of the interest on the old note.
```

Note Dishonored. If the maker of a note refuses or is unable to pay or renew it at maturity, the note is said to be *dishonored*. It thereby loses the quality of negotiability which, in effect, means that it loses its legal status as a note receivable. Usually, the amount is transferred from the notes receivable account to the accounts receivable account pending final disposition of the obligation involved. Suppose, for example, that Mr. Ridley was unable to collect a non-interest-bearing note for $400 received a few weeks before from Roger Jones, a customer. (Because of special circumstances, Mr. Ridley had accepted a non-interest-bearing note.) The following entry should be made in the books of the Ridley Hardware Co.:

```
July 18. Accounts Receivable................................   400.00
             Notes Receivable..................................            400.00
                 Roger Jones' note dishonored.
```

If the claim against Mr. Jones should turn out to be completely worthless, the $400 will have to be removed from the accounts receivable account and recognized as an uncollectible account loss. The manner of accounting for this type of transaction will be discussed in the next chapter.

**Notes
receivable
register**

When many notes are received in the usual course of business, it may be advisable to keep an auxiliary record of such notes that will provide more detailed information than a ledger account. Such an auxiliary record is usually known as a *notes receivable register*. One form of a notes receivable register is reproduced below and on the following page. The notes recorded in the illustration were those received by the L. H. Freeman Co. during the period indicated by the record.

The information recorded in the register is obtained directly from the notes received. The notes are numbered consecutively as they are entered in the register. (This number should not be confused with the maker's number.) The due date of each note is calculated and entered in the proper When Due column. The interest to maturity is calculated and entered in the Interest Amount column. When a remittance is received in settlement of a note, the date is entered in the Date Paid column.

**Notes
receivable
account**

The information recorded in the notes receivable account should agree with that entered in the notes receivable register. The account shown on the next page contains a record of the notes that were entered in the notes receivable register of the L. H. Freeman Co. Notice that each note is identified by the number assigned to the note. If the notes are not numbered, each note should be identified by writing the name of the maker in the Item column of the account.

PAGE *2*   **NOTES RECEIVABLE REGISTER**

	DATE RECEIVED	No.	BY WHOM PAYABLE	WHERE PAYABLE		DATE MADE		
				BANK OR FIRM	ADDRESS	Mo.	Day	Year
1	*1977* Mar. 7	1	S. J. Olson	First State Bank	Modesto	Mar. 7	'77	1
2	24	2	C. F. Purdy	County National Bank	Denison	Mar. 24	'77	2
3	Apr. 4	3	John A. Beal	City Savings Bank	Westridge	Apr. 4	'77	3
4	21	4	Mrs. C. M. Hollis	Central Trust	Modesto	Apr. 21	'77	4
5	May 23	5	C. F. Purdy	County National Bank	Denison	May 23	'77	5
6								6
7								7

Notes Receivable Register (Left Page)

**Proving the
notes
receivable
account**

Periodically (usually at the end of each month) the notes receivable account should be proved by comparing the balance of the account with the total of the notes owned as shown by the notes receivable register. A schedule of the notes owned on May 31 is given on page 173.

Notice that the total of this schedule is the same as the balance of the notes receivable account illustrated below.

SCHEDULE OF NOTES OWNED

No. 4......................	$510.00
No. 5......................	350.00
	$860.00

ACCOUNT *Notes Receivable*   ACCOUNT NO. *122*

DATE	ITEM	POST. REF.	DEBIT	CREDIT	BALANCE DEBIT	BALANCE CREDIT
1977 Mar. 7	No. 1	CJ3	398 16			
24	No. 2	CJ3	450 00		848 16	
Apr. 4	No. 3	CJ4	692 50			
21	No. 4	CJ4	510 00		2050 66	
May 4	No. 3	CJ5		692 50		
6	No. 1	CJ5		398 16		
23	No. 2	CJ5		450 00		
23	No. 5	CJ5	350 00		860 00	

Indorsement of notes

A promissory note is usually made payable to a specified person or firm, though some notes are made payable to "Bearer." If the note is payable to the order of a specified party, he must *indorse* the note to transfer the promise to pay to another party. The two major types of indorsements are **(1)** the *blank indorsement* and **(2)** the *special indorsement*. When the payee signs only his name on the left end of the back of the note, he is indorsing

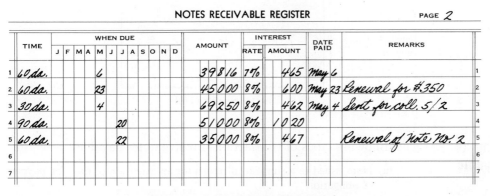

NOTES RECEIVABLE REGISTER   PAGE *2*

	TIME	WHEN DUE J	F	M	A	M	J	J	A	S	O	N	D	AMOUNT	INTEREST RATE	INTEREST AMOUNT	DATE PAID	REMARKS	
1	60 da.						6							398 16	7%	4 65	May 6		1
2	60 da.						23							450 00	8%	6 00	May 23	Renewal for $350	2
3	30 da.					4								692 50	8%	4 62	May 4	Sent for coll. 5/2	3
4	90 da.							20						510 00	8%	10 20			4
5	60 da.							22						350 00	8%	4 67		Renewal of note No. 2	5
6																			6
7																			7

Notes Receivable Register (Right Page)

it in blank. If, instead, he writes the words "Pay to the order of" followed by the name of a specified party and his signature, he is giving a special indorsement. The legal effect of both types of indorsement is much the same. However, a blank indorsement makes a note payable to the bearer, while a special indorsement identifies the party to whose order payment is to be made.

Under certain circumstances the maker of a note may arrange for an additional party to join in the promise to pay, either as a *cosigner* or as an indorser of the note. In the first instance, this other party signs his name below that of the maker of the note on its face. In the second case, the other party makes a blank indorsement on the back of the note, called an *accommodation indorsement*. In either event the payee of the note has two persons to look to for payment. This presumably adds security to the note.

If a partial payment is made on a note, it is common practice to record the date of the payment and the amount paid on the back of the note. This is called *indorsing the payment*.

Shown below is a reproduction of the back of a promissory note originally made payable to the order of Clark Munn. The maker of the note (whoever he was) was able to get Thelma West to become an accommodation indorser. Later, the payee, Munn, transferred the note to D. F. Fisher by a special indorsement. On April 15, $200 was paid on the note.

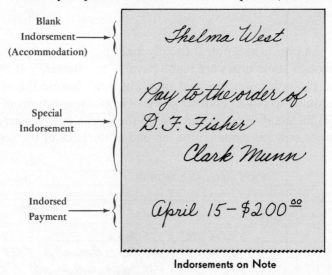

Indorsements on Note

Accounting for notes payable

The following types of transactions involve notes payable:

    (a) Note issued to a supplier in return for an extension of time for payment of obligation

    (b) Note issued as security for cash loan

    (c) Note paid at maturity

    (d) Note renewed at maturity

Note Issued to a Supplier in Return for Extension of Time for Payment.
When a firm wishes to obtain an extension of time for the payment of an account, a note for all or part of the amount due may be acceptable to the supplier. Assume, for example, that the Ridley Hardware Co. owes

Edward & Co. $547.60 and by agreement on May 12 a check on the First National Bank for $47.60 and a 90-day, 7½ percent interest-bearing note for $500 are issued. This transaction should be recorded in the books of the Ridley Hardware Co. by the following general journal entry:

```
May 12. Accounts Payable.................................  547.60
            Cash..........................................           47.60
            Notes Payable.................................          500.00
                 Issued check for $47.60 and note for $500 to Edwards
                 & Co.
```

Note Issued as Security for Cash Loan. Many firms experience periods in which receipts from customers in the usual course of business are not adequate to finance their operations. During such periods, it may be necessary to borrow money from banks. Business firms commonly borrow money from banks on short-term notes to help finance their business operations. Assume, for example, that on May 16, M. B. Ridley borrows $4,000 from the First National Bank on a 60-day, 9 percent interest-bearing note. The transaction should be recorded in general journal form as follows:

```
May 16. Cash..........................................  4,000.00
            Notes Payable.................................           4,000.00
                 Borrowed $4,000 at the bank on a 60-day, 9%
                 note.
```

Commercial banks often deduct interest in advance. If, instead of the transaction described above, Mr. Ridley had issued a $4,000, 60-day, non-interest-bearing note which the bank had discounted at 9 percent, the bank account of the Ridley Hardware Co. would have increased $3,940, and interest expense of $60 would have been recorded as follows:

```
May  6. Cash..........................................  3,940.00
         Interest Expense...............................     60.00
            Notes Payable.................................           4,000.00
                 Discounted at 9% a $4,000, 60-day, non-interest-
                 bearing note.
```

The $60 debit to Interest Expense at this point is really prepaid interest but, since the amount will become interest expense by the end of the accounting period, it is debited immediately to Interest Expense.

It should be noted that, even though the rate of interest was 9 percent in both cases, the money obtained was more expensive in the second case. In the first case, $4,000 was obtained for 60 days at a cost of $60 — exactly 9 percent. ($60 ÷ $4,000 = 1.5% for 60 days; 9% for 360 days.) In the second case, $60 was paid for the use of $3,940 for 60 days — an *effective rate* of nearly 9.14 percent. ($60 ÷ $3,940 = 1.523% for 60 days; 9.138% for 360 days.)

Note Paid at Maturity. When a note payable matures, payment may be made directly to the holder or to a bank where the note was left for collection. The maker will know who the payee is but he may not know who the holder is at maturity because the payee may have transferred the note to another party or he may have left it with a bank for collection. When a note is left with a bank for collection, it is customary for the bank to mail the maker a notice of maturity. For example, the Lawson Store Equipment Co. might forward a one-month, 7 percent note of M. B. Ridley for $650 (dated July 1) to the First National Bank for collection, and the bank might notify Mr. Ridley by sending a notice similar to the one reproduced below.

MAKER – COSIGNER – COLLATERAL	NUMBER	DATE DUE	PRINCIPAL	INTEREST	TOTAL
M. B. Ridley Ridley Hardware Co.	13960	8/1/77	$650.00	$3.79	$653.79

YOUR NOTE DESCRIBED BELOW WILL BE DUE

First National Bank
UNIONTOWN   KANSAS

ENDORSER

TO   M. B. Ridley
Ridley Hardware Co.
1600 Elm Street
Uniontown, KS 66779

NOTE: PLEASE BRING THIS NOTICE WITH YOU.   **PAYABLE AT** First National Bank

Notice of Maturity of Note

If, upon receiving this notice, Mr. Ridley issued a check to the bank for $653.79 in payment of the note and interest, the transaction should be recorded in the books of the Ridley Hardware Co. as indicated by the following general journal entry:

Aug. 1. Notes Payable.....................................	650.00	
Interest Expense....................................	3.79	
Cash..		653.79
Paid note issued July 1 to Lawson Store Equipment Co., plus interest.		

PAGE /   **NOTES PAYABLE REGISTER**

DATE ISSUED	No.	TO WHOM PAYABLE	WHERE PAYABLE		DATE MADE		
			BANK OR FIRM	ADDRESS	Mo.	Day	Year
1977 Mar. 14	1	G. R. Hawkes Co.	First State Bank	Modesto	Mar.	14	'77
Apr. 12	2	County National Bank	County National Bank	Denison	Apr.	12	'77
May 2	3	McAllister Brothers	County National Bank	Denison	May	2	'77

Notes Payable Register (Left Page)

A note made payable to a bank for a loan commonly is paid at that bank upon maturity.

Note Renewed at Maturity. If the maker is unable to pay a note in full at maturity, he may arrange to renew all or a part of the note. For example, on August 10 Mr. Ridley might pay the $9.38 interest and $100 on the principal of the note for $500 issued to Edwards & Co. on May 12 and give them a new 60-day, 7½ percent note for $400. This transaction should be recorded as indicated in the following general journal entry:

Aug. 10.	Notes Payable (old note)............................	500.00	
	Interest Expense....................................	9.38	
	Cash...		109.38
	Notes Payable (new note)...........................		400.00
	Issued a check for $109.38 and a note for $400 to Edwards & Co. in settlement of a note for $500 plus interest.		

Notes payable register

When many notes are issued in the usual course of business, it may be advisable to keep an auxiliary record of such notes that will provide more detailed information than a ledger account. Such an auxiliary record is usually known as a *notes payable register*. One form of such a register is reproduced on the previous page and below. The notes recorded in the illustration were those issued by the L. H. Freeman Co. during the period indicated by the record.

The information recorded in the register may be obtained directly from the note before it is mailed or given to the payee, or from a note stub. Blank notes are usually made up in pads with stubs attached on which spaces are provided for recording such essential information as amount, payee, where payable, date, time, rate of interest, and number. The due date of each note is calculated and entered in the proper When Due column of the register. The interest at maturity is also calculated and entered in the Interest Amount column. When a note is paid, the date is entered in the Date Paid column.

NOTES PAYABLE REGISTER   PAGE 1

	TIME	WHEN DUE J F M A M J J A S O N D	AMOUNT	INTEREST RATE	INTEREST AMOUNT	DATE PAID	REMARKS	
1	60 da.	13	1 826 14	8%	24 35	May 13	Settlement of Jan. 15 inv.	1
2	90 da.	11	500 00	9%	11 250			2
3	30 da.	1	967 35	8%	6 45		Settlement of Mar. 1 inv.	3

Notes Payable Register (Right Page)

Notes payable account

The information recorded in the notes payable account should agree with that recorded in the notes payable register. The following account contains a record of the notes that were entered in the notes payable register of the L. H. Freeman Co.

ACCOUNT *Notes Payable*   ACCOUNT NO. *230*

DATE		ITEM	POST. REF.	DEBIT	CREDIT	BALANCE DEBIT	BALANCE CREDIT
1977							
Mar.	*14*	*No. 1*	*CJ3*		*1826 14*		*1826 14*
Apr.	*12*	*No. 2*	*CJ4*		*5000 00*		*6826 14*
May	*2*	*No. 3*	*CJ5*		*967 35*		
	13	*No. 1*	*CJ5*	*1826 14*			*5967 35*

Proving the notes payable account

Periodically (usually at the end of each month) the notes payable account should be proved by comparing the balance of the account with the total notes outstanding as shown by the notes payable register. A schedule of the notes outstanding on June 30 is given below. Notice that the total of this schedule is the same as the balance of the notes payable account.

SCHEDULE OF NOTES OUTSTANDING

No. 2..........................	$5,000.00
No. 3..........................	967.35
	$5,967.35

Accrued interest receivable

While interest on a note literally accrues day by day, it is impractical to keep a daily record of such accruals. If the life of a note receivable is entirely within the accounting period, no record need be made of interest until the amount is received.

If, however, the business owns some interest-bearing notes receivable at the end of the accounting period, neither the net income for the period nor the assets at the end of the period will be correctly stated unless the interest accrued on notes receivable is taken into consideration. It is, therefore, customary to adjust the accounts by debiting Accrued Interest Receivable and by crediting Interest Earned for the amount of interest that has accrued to the end of the period. The amount of the accrual may be computed by reference to the notes themselves or to the record provided by a notes receivable register. Suppose, for example, that at the end of a fiscal year ending June 30, a business owns four interest-bearing notes. The amount of each note, the date of issue, the rate of interest, the number of days from issue date to June 30, and the interest accrued on June 30 are shown in the schedule at the top of the next page.

SCHEDULE OF ACCRUED INTEREST ON NOTES RECEIVABLE

PRINCIPAL	DATE OF ISSUE	RATE OF INTEREST	DAYS FROM ISSUE DATE TO JUNE 30	ACCRUED INTEREST JUNE 30
$500.00	April 16	7%	75	$ 7.29
300.00	May 4	8%	57	3.80
348.50	May 31	7%	30	2.03
500.00	June 15	7%	15	1.46

Total accrued interest on notes receivable................$14.58

While the amount involved is so small that some accountants would ignore it on the ground of *immateriality*, technical accuracy requires the following entry, in general journal form, as of June 30:

```
June 30. Accrued Interest Receivable.......................    14.58
           Interest Earned................................            14.58
           Interest accrued on notes receivable as of June 30.
```

In preparing the financial statements at the end of the year, the balance of the interest earned account (which will include the $14.58 interest earned but not yet received) will be reported in the income statement, while the balance of the account with Accrued Interest Receivable will be reported in the balance sheet as a current asset.

Accrued interest payable

Neither the expenses of a period nor the liabilities at the end of the period will be correctly stated unless the interest accrued on notes payable is taken into consideration. The mechanics of calculating the amount of interest accrued on notes payable are the same as in the case of notes receivable. If a notes payable register is kept, it should provide the information needed in computing the amount of interest accrued on notes payable. If the total amount of such accrued interest was calculated to be $126.92, and the fiscal period ended June 30, the proper adjusting entry may be made in general journal form as follows:

```
June 30. Interest Expense................................    126.92
           Accrued Interest Payable.......................            126.92
           Interest accrued on notes payable as of June 30.
```

In preparing the financial statements at the end of the year, the balance of the interest expense account (which will include the $126.92 interest incurred but not yet paid) will be reported in the income statement, while the balance of the account with Accrued Interest Payable will be reported in the balance sheet as a current liability.

Report No. 7-1

Complete Report No. 7-1 in the study assignments and submit your working papers to the instructor for approval. Then proceed with the textbook discussion in Chapter 8 until Report No. 8-1 is required.

Chapter 8

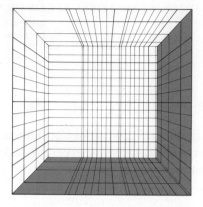

ACCRUAL ACCOUNTING APPLIED TO A RETAIL BUSINESS

A business enterprise that purchases and sells goods on account, maintains a stock of merchandise, and has long-lived assets must account for periodic income or loss on the accrual basis. This is a necessity both for the sake of measuring the success of the business from the standpoint of the owner and in order to comply with federal and state income tax laws. Several of the features of this type of accounting have been introduced in the preceding pages. A more detailed consideration of these procedures and the introduction of the other major practices that constitute accrual accounting will be presented in this and the two following chapters. To make the discussion realistic, it will center around the accounting records of a retail clothing business called Boyd's Clothiers, owned and operated by Lynn C. Boyd. It should be recognized, however, that most of the principles and procedures discussed and illustrated are equally applicable to many other types of businesses.

PRINCIPLES AND PROCEDURES

The discussion will continue to be a blend of accounting principles and bookkeeping practices. It is important to keep in mind that the principles relate to goals and objectives while bookkeeping practices are designed to attain these goals and objectives. Such procedures as double entry and the use of source documents, journals, and ledger accounts are employed to make the record-keeping process complete, orderly, and as error-free as possible. While most accounting principles are broad enough to allow considerable flexibility, it is in the area of bookkeeping procedures that wide latitude is found. Within limits, the records for each business can be styled to meet the particular requirements of the management.

Accrual accounting

The *accrual basis of accounting* consists of recording revenue in the period in which it is earned and expenses in the period in which they are incurred. The receipt or disbursement of cash in the same period may or may not be involved. Revenue is considered to be earned when, in exchange for something of value, money is received or a legal claim to money comes into existence. To a merchant, this normally means the time at which the customer buys the goods and either pays for them or agrees to pay for them. In terms of changes in the accounting elements, revenue arises or accrues when an increase in cash or in a receivable (inflow of assets) causes an increase in owner's equity (except in cases where the increase is due to an investment of assets in the business by the owner). In comparable terms, expense accrues or is incurred when either a reduction in some asset (asset outflow) or an increase in a liability causes the owner's equity to be reduced (except in cases where the owner's withdrawal of assets reduces the owner's equity).

In keeping business records accountants must think in terms of time intervals. They must be sure that revenue and expense are accounted for in the proper accounting period. Within a period, the recognition of many types of revenue and expense at precisely the moment this revenue or expense arises is not so important nor is it usually practicable. For example, the expense of having a salaried employee literally accrues minute by minute during each working day; but if the salary will be paid by the end of the period, no record is made of the expense until it is paid. If, on the other hand, the employee was not paid by the end of the period, the accountant should record the liability and expense at that time. A lag in recording revenue and expense is not serious within the accounting period, but steps must be taken at the end of the period to be sure that all revenue earned and expenses incurred are recorded. These steps consist of making what are called *end-of-period-adjustments* in the accounts. It should be mentioned, however, that adjustments normally are not made for trivial amounts. The *concept of materiality* prevails, which is to ignore matters too small to make any significant difference. Just how small is "too small" is a question that requires judgment on the part of the accountant.

The accrual basis of accounting is widely used because it is suited to the needs of enterprises employing it. It involves the period-by-period matching of revenue with the expenses that caused or aided in producing revenue. The revenue from sales, for example, must be matched against the cost of the goods sold and the various other expenses that were incurred in conducting the business. A simple matching of cash received from customers during a period with the cash paid for goods purchased in that period would be almost meaningless in most cases. The collections might relate to sales of a prior period and the payments to purchases of the current period, or vice versa. The expense related to most long-lived assets does not arise when the property is acquired; the expense occurs as the usefulness of the property is gradually exhausted. The accrual basis recognizes changes in many types of assets and liabilities in computing net income for a specified period — not just changes in the cash account.

The chart of accounts

The importance of classifying accounts in an orderly and systematic manner, identifying each account by assigning it a number to assist in locating it in the ledger, and maintaining a list of the accounts — called a *chart of accounts* — has been discussed and illustrated in preceding chapters. The chart of accounts for the retail business that is used as a basis of the discussion and illustration in this chapter and in the two chapters that follow is shown on page 183.

The pattern of numbers or code shown in the illustration is fairly typical of the arrangement used by many businesses. However, numerous variations are possible. Sometimes letters as well as numbers are made a part of the code. When numbers are used, it is not uncommon for special columns in journals to be headed by just the number, rather than the name, of the account involved. In a system of records that requires numerous accounts, the use of account numbers virtually displaces account names for all but statement purposes. This has been the case for many decades. Furthermore, in recent years account numbers have become essential to the development of a computer-based accounting system. (Note that no account number ends in zero. This is because a zero at the end of a number has no special significance in electronic data processing.)

The nature of many of the accounts included in the chart of accounts for Boyd's Clothiers should be apparent because they have been described in preceding chapters and their use has been illustrated. However, the chart includes certain accounts that are needed in recording several types of transactions and events that have either not yet been considered, or only briefly mentioned. These accounts will be discussed prior to illustrating the accounting records of Boyd's Clothiers.

If this chart of accounts is compared with the accounts in the general ledger illustrated on pages 214–219, it will be noted that the ledger illustration does not include accounts 221, 291, 321, 612, 616, 621, and 622. This is because these accounts are not needed to record routine transactions.

When the matter of adjusting entries and closing entries is discussed and illustrated in the following chapters, these accounts will be shown.

BOYD'S CLOTHIERS

CHART OF ACCOUNTS

*Assets**

Cash
   111 First National Bank
   112 Petty Cash Fund

Receivables
   121 Accounts Receivable
      012 Allowance for Doubtful Accounts

Merchandise Inventory
   131 Merchandise Inventory

Prepaid Expenses
   141 Prepaid Insurance
   151 Supplies

Long-Lived Assets
   181 Store Equipment
      018 Accumulated Depreciation —Store Equipment

Liabilities
   211 Notes Payable
   221 Accrued Interest Payable
   231 Accounts Payable
   241 Sales Tax Payable
   251 FICA Tax Payable
   261 Employees Income Tax Payable
   271 FUTA Tax Payable
   281 State Unemployment Tax Payable
   291 Accrued Bank Credit Card Expense

Owner's Equity
   311 Lynn C. Boyd, Capital
   031 Lynn C. Boyd, Drawing
   321 Expense and Revenue Summary

Revenue from Sales
   411 Sales
      041 Sales Returns and Allowances

Cost of Goods Sold
   511 Purchases
      051 Purchases Returns and Allowances
      052 Purchases Discount

Operating Expenses
   611 Rent Expense
   612 Depreciation Expense
   613 Salaries and Commissions Expense
   614 Payroll Taxes Expense
   615 Heating and Lighting Expense
   616 Supplies Expense
   617 Telephone Expense
   618 Advertising Expense
   619 Bank Credit Card Expense
   621 Uncollectible Accounts Expense
   622 Insurance Expense
   623 Charitable Contributions Expense
   624 Miscellaneous Expense

Other Expenses
   711 Interest Expense

*Words in italics represent headings and not account titles

Accounting for uncollectible accounts receivable

Businesses that sell goods or services on account realize that some of the customers from time to time may not pay all that they owe. The amounts that cannot be collected are called *uncollectible accounts expense*, *bad debts expense*, or *loss from uncollectible accounts*. The last designation is slightly misleading because, while the amounts that cannot be collected are certainly losses, they are losses that may reasonably be expected since they are the direct result of selling on account to encourage a larger volume of sales. The amount of such losses depends to a large degree upon the credit policy of a business. The seller should seek to avoid the two extremes of either having such a "liberal" credit policy that uncollectible accounts become excessive or having such a "tight" credit policy that uncollectible account losses are minimized at the sacrifice of a larger volume of sales and greater net income.

It would be possible to wait until it was certain that the amount due from a customer would never be collected before writing off the amount by a debit to Uncollectible Accounts Expense and by a credit to Accounts Receivable. This procedure is sometimes followed. However, it is considered to be better accounting to estimate the amount of uncollectible account losses that will eventually result from the sales of a period and to treat the estimated amount of expected losses as an expense of that same period. The latter treatment is considered to result in better periodic matching of revenue and expense. The procedure is to use a *contra* account entitled Allowance for Doubtful Accounts (sometimes called Allowance for Bad Debts or Reserve for Bad Debts). This account is contra to the receivable accounts which means its balance will be deducted from the total of the receivable accounts. At the end of the accounting period, an estimate of the expected uncollectible account losses is made, and an adjusting entry is made by debiting Uncollectible Accounts Expense and by crediting Allowance for Doubtful Accounts. To illustrate, suppose that in view of past experience it is expected that there will be a loss of an amount equal to one half of one percent of the sales on account during the year. If such sales amounted to $100,000, the estimated uncollectible account losses would be $500 which should be recorded as follows:

Dec. 31. Uncollectible Accounts Expense.....................	500.00	
Allowance for Doubtful Accounts.................		500.00
Uncollectible accounts expense provision for the year.		

The amount of the debit balance in the uncollectible accounts expense account is reported in the income statement as an operating expense. The amount of the credit balance in the allowance for doubtful accounts is reported in the balance sheet as a deduction from the receivables.

Another technique sometimes used in arriving at the end-of-period adjustment for uncollectible accounts involves a detailed analysis of the receivables. This requires "aging" the receivables. Thus, an analysis is made of the accounts to see what proportions are for recent charges — perhaps those less than a month old — and what proportions are 30–60 days old, 61–90 days old, etc. Then, guided by past experience, estimates are made of the probable amounts of each of the age groups that are likely to be uncollectible. (Generally, the longer a charge has been "on the books," the less likely it is that it will ever be collected.) The estimates can be combined (totaled) to arrive at an amount deemed necessary to have as the end-of-period (credit) balance in the Allowance for Doubtful Accounts. An adjustment is made to give the allowance account the indicated balance. To illustrate, assume that after aging the accounts it is determined that $500 will not be collected. If the allowance account has a credit balance of $50, this means that the adjusting entry must be for the amount of $450. This will bring the allowance account to the desired credit balance. The entry would be as follows:

Dec. 31 Uncollectible Accounts Expense........................... 450
                Allowance for Doubtful Accounts........................   450

Many accountants think that this is the best way to be sure that the net amount shown on the balance sheet (that is, gross receivables less allowance for doubtful accounts) is a realistic estimate of "cash realizable value."

It should be apparent that the credit part of the adjusting entry cannot be made directly to one of the receivable accounts because, at the time this entry is made, there is no way of knowing exactly which of the debtors will not pay. Experience gives virtual assurance that some of the amounts due will be uncollectible but only time will reveal which ones.

When it is determined that a certain account will not be collected, an entry should be made to write off the account and to charge the loss against the allowance. Suppose, for example, that on April 22 of the next year, it is determined that $75 owed by Stuart Palmer cannot be collected. Perhaps he died sometime before and it is found that he left no property, or perhaps he became bankrupt, or left town and cannot be traced. Whatever the circumstance, if it is fairly certain that the amount will not be collected, the following journal entry should be made:

Apr. 22. Allowance for Doubtful Accounts.................... 75.00
                 Accounts Receivable..............................   75.00
                 To write off account of Stuart Palmer found to be
                 uncollectible.

Sometimes the allowance for doubtful accounts will show a debit balance at the end of the accounting period. This happens when the total amount of estimated uncollectible customers' accounts for the year is smaller than the total amount of such accounts actually written off during the year. When this condition is encountered, the adjusting entry for estimated uncollectible accounts must **(1)** cover this debit balance, and **(2)** provide for the expected uncollectible-account losses of the coming year.

In still other cases, it may be found that the allowance account has too large a credit balance, which means that the amount of write-offs has not been as large as was expected. Very often, this is handled by making the amount of the adjustment for the year just ended smaller than it otherwise would be. If substantial amounts are involved (either a very large debit balance or too large an accumulated credit balance), it may be necessary to correct the beginning (first-of-period) balance of the allowance account by either **(1)** a debit to the owner's capital account and a credit to Allowance for Doubtful Accounts in an amount sufficient to eliminate the debit balance in the latter and give it a reasonable credit balance, or **(2)** a debit to the allowance account and a credit to the owner's capital in an amount sufficient to remove the excessive portion of the credit balance in the allowance account. (Such entries are examples of what are called "intra-period correcting entries." Entries of this type are made in an effort to correct past income or loss calculations and the consequent misstatement of some asset, contra asset, or liability account. Such entries are not common.) If the beginning-of-period balance in the Allowance for Doubtful Accounts has been corrected, the end-of-period adjusting entry can be made in the normal manner.

The chart of accounts for Boyd's Clothiers includes Allowance for Doubtful Accounts, Account No. 012, and Uncollectible Accounts Expense, Account No. 621, to provide for recording uncollectible accounts expense and subsequent write-offs of the uncollectible accounts.

Accounting for prepaid expenses

The term *prepaid expense* is largely self-explanatory. It refers to something that has been bought that is properly considered an asset when acquired, but which will eventually be consumed or used up and thus become an expense. Prepaid (unexpired) insurance and supplies of various sorts are leading examples. At the end of the period, the portion of such assets that has expired or has been consumed must be determined and an entry made debiting the proper expense accounts and crediting the proper prepaid expense accounts.

The chart of accounts for Boyd's Clothiers includes two prepaid expense accounts, Prepaid Insurance, Account No. 141, and Supplies, Account No. 151. These accounts are classified as assets in the chart of accounts. The prepaid insurance account should be debited for the cost of the insurance purchased. At the end of the year the account should be credited for the portion of the cost that relates to the year then ending with an offsetting debit to Insurance Expense, Account No. 622. The supplies account should be debited for the cost of supplies purchased. At the end of the year the account should be credited for the cost of supplies consumed or used during the year with an offsetting debit to Supplies Expense, Account No. 616.

Accounting for depreciation

Depreciation accounting is the process of attempting to allocate the cost of most long-lived assets to the periods expected to benefit from the use of these assets. Most long-lived assets eventually become useless to the business either because they wear out or because they become inadequate or obsolete. Sometimes all three of these causes combine to make the assets valueless except, perhaps, for some small salvage value as scrap or junk.

Generally, in computing depreciation, no consideration is given to what these assets might bring if they were to be sold. Assets of this type are acquired to be used and not to be sold. During their useful life their resale value is of no consequence unless the business is about to cease. For a going business, the idea is to allocate the net cost of such assets over the years they are expected to serve. By "net cost" is meant original cost less estimated scrap or salvage value. Inasmuch as the possibility of scrap or salvage value is commonly ignored, it is usually the original cost of the assets that is allocated.

It should be apparent that depreciation expense can be no more than an estimate. Usually there is no way of knowing just how long an asset will serve. However, with past experience as a guide, the estimates can be reasonably reliable.

There are several ways of calculating the periodic depreciation write-off. Traditionally, the so-called *straight-line method* has been widely used. With this method, the original cost (or cost less any expected scrap value) of an asset is divided by the number of years the asset is expected to serve to find the amount that is to be considered as depreciation expense each year. It is common practice to express depreciation as a percentage of the original cost of the asset. For example, in the case of an asset with a 10-year life, 10 percent of the original cost should be written off each year; for a 20-year asset, 5 percent should be written off.

There are some depreciation methods that permit larger write-offs in the earlier years of the life of the asset. In 1954 the Internal Revenue Code was revised to permit taxpayers to use certain of these methods in calculating net income subject to tax, though these methods primarily are useful only in the case of new assets. This change in the law stimulated the use of these "reducing-charge" methods. ("Reducing-charge" means a successively smaller write-off each year.) However, the straight-line method has been very popular in the past, and it has a number of virtues including simplicity. Straight-line depreciation is widely used. The straight-line method of accounting for depreciation is used by Boyd's Clothiers.

Depreciation expense is recorded by an end-of-period adjusting entry that involves debiting one or more depreciation expense accounts and crediting one or more accumulated depreciation (sometimes called allowance for depreciation) accounts. The latter accounts are contra accounts — contra to the accounts for the assets that are being depreciated. In theory there would be no objection to making the credits directly to the asset accounts themselves (in the same way that the asset accounts for prepaid expenses are credited to record their decreases). However, in order that the original cost of the assets will be clearly revealed, any portions of this cost written off are credited to the contra accounts. The amounts of the credit balances of the contra accounts are reported in the balance sheet as deductions from the costs of the assets to which they relate.

The credit balances in the accumulated depreciation accounts get larger year by year. When the amounts become equal to the cost of the related assets, no more depreciation may be taken.

The difference between the allowance for doubtful accounts and the accumulated depreciation account should be recognized. Both are credited by adjusting entries at the end of the period. In both cases, the offsetting debits go to expense accounts. In both cases, the balances in the contra accounts are shown in the balance sheet as subtractions from the amounts of the assets to which they relate. However, Allowance for Doubtful Accounts is debited whenever anticipated uncollectibles materialize. The balance of this allowance account does not get continually larger. (If it does, this indicates that the estimate of uncollectible account losses has been excessive.) In contrast, the credit balances of the accumulated depreciation accounts will get larger year by year, often for many years. The credit balances remain in these accounts for as long as the assets to which they relate are kept in service.

Since Boyd's Clothiers has only one class of long-lived assets that is subject to depreciation — store equipment — there is only one contra account, Accumulated Depreciation—Store Equipment, Account No. 018. Depreciation expense is debited to an account so named, Account No. 612.

Purchases discount   Purchase invoices representing purchases on account may be subject to discount if paid within a specified time. Retailers may be allowed a discount by wholesalers on invoices that are paid within a specified time, such as five days, ten days, or fifteen days, from the date of the invoice. This is known as a *cash discount* and it should not be confused with trade discounts allowed by wholesalers.

Trade discounts are the discounts allowed retailers from the list or catalog prices of wholesalers. Such trade discounts are usually shown as deductions on the invoice and only the net amount is recorded as the purchase price. If the invoice is subject to an additional discount for cash, it will be indicated on the invoice under the heading of "Terms." For example, the terms may be specified as "2/10, n/30," which means that if paid within ten days from the date of the invoice a discount of 2 percent may be deducted; otherwise the net amount of the invoice (after any trade discounts) is payable within thirty days. Stated terms of "3/10 EOM" means that if the invoice is paid no later than 10 days after the end of the current month, 3 percent discount may be taken.

To facilitate the payment of invoices in time to be entitled to any discount offered, Ms. Boyd follows the policy of filing each invoice in an unpaid invoice file according to the date it should be paid. It is, therefore, only necessary to refer to the file each day to determine which invoices are due on that date and which may be subject to discount. Any amount of cash discount deducted when paying an invoice should be recorded as a credit to Purchases Discount, Account No. 052. Thus, if an invoice for $140, subject to a discount of 6 percent if paid within ten days, is paid within the specified time, the payment should be recorded by debiting Accounts Payable for $140, by crediting the bank account for $131.60, and by crediting Purchases Discount for $8.40. The purchases discount account has a credit balance and (along with Purchases Returns and Allowances) is reported as a deduction from the gross amount of purchases in the cost of goods sold section of the income statement. Some businesses report the credit balance in the purchases discount account as "other revenue." Although this latter practice is not uncommon, the trend definitely favors the practice of regarding discount earned for prompt payment of purchase invoices as a deduction from the gross amount of purchases rather than as other revenue.

Accounts with suppliers and customers

As previously explained, a record of the amounts due to suppliers for purchases on account and the amounts due from customers for sales on account may be kept without maintaining a separate ledger account for each supplier and for each customer. A file of unpaid vendors' invoices and another of sales slips for sales on account may suffice. Many merchants, however, prefer to keep a separate ledger account for each supplier and for each customer.

Subsidiary Ledgers. When the character of the enterprise and the volume of business are such that it is necessary to keep relatively few accounts, it may be satisfactory to keep all of the accounts together in a single general ledger, which may be bound, loose-leaf, or a set of cards. However, when the volume of business and the number of transactions warrant employment of more than one bookkeeper to keep the records, it may be advisable to subdivide the ledger. In some businesses it is necessary to keep separate accounts with thousands of customers and suppliers. In such cases it usually is considered advisable to segregate the accounts with customers and the accounts with suppliers from the other accounts and to keep them in separate ledgers known as *subsidiary ledgers.*

Three-Column Account Form. A special account form known as the three-column account form is widely used in keeping the individual accounts with customers and suppliers. While the standard account form shown in the illustration on page 12, or the four-column form, illustrated on page 145, may be used satisfactorily for customers' and suppliers' accounts, most accountants favor the use of the *three-column account form* shown below for such accounts. It will be noted that three parallel amount columns are provided for recording debits, credits, and balances. The nature of the account determines whether its usual balance is a debit or a credit. Accounts with customers almost always have debit balances; accounts with suppliers nearly always have credit balances. Following each entry the new balance may be determined and recorded in the Balance column, or if preferred, the balance may be determined and recorded at the end of each month.

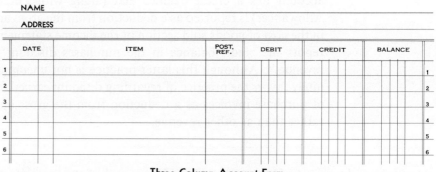

Three-Column Account Form

Control accounts
When subsidiary ledgers are kept for suppliers and for customers, it is customary to keep *control accounts* for the subsidiary ledgers in the general ledger. Thus, if accounts with suppliers are kept in a subsidiary accounts payable ledger, a control account for accounts payable should be kept in the general ledger; if accounts with customers are kept in a subsidiary accounts receivable ledger, a control account for accounts receivable should be kept in the general ledger. The use of control accounts in the general ledger makes it possible to take a trial balance of the general ledger accounts without reference to the subsidiary ledgers.

Accounts Payable Control. The accounts payable control account provides a summary of the information recorded in the individual accounts with suppliers kept in a subsidiary accounts payable ledger. Transactions affecting suppliers' accounts are posted separately to the individual accounts in the subsidiary ledger. These transactions may also be posted separately, or may be summarized periodically and the totals posted, to the control account in the general ledger. The balance of the accounts payable control account may be proved by preparing a schedule of the individual account balances in the accounts payable ledger.

Accounts with suppliers normally have credit balances. If a supplier's account has a debit balance, the balance may be circled or be written in red ink. In preparing the schedule of accounts payable, the total of the accounts with debit balances should be deducted from the total of the accounts with credit balances, and the difference should agree with the balance of the accounts payable control account.

Accounts Receivable Control. The accounts receivable control account provides a summary of the information recorded in the individual accounts with customers kept in a subsidiary accounts receivable ledger. Transactions affecting customers' accounts are posted separately to the individual accounts in the subsidiary ledger. These transactions may also be posted separately, or may be summarized periodically and the totals posted to the control account in the general ledger. The balance of the accounts receivable control account may be proved by preparing a schedule of the individual account balances in the accounts receivable ledger.

Accounts with customers normally have debit balances. If a customer's account has a credit balance, the balance may be circled or be written in red ink. In preparing the schedule of accounts receivable, the total of the accounts with credit balances should be deducted from the total of the accounts with debit balances and the difference should agree with the balance of the accounts receivable control account.

Posting from the books of original entry

Posting to the individual accounts with suppliers and customers in the respective subsidiary ledgers may be done either from the books of original entry or directly from vouchers or other documents that represent the transactions. When the posting is done from the books of original entry, each item should, of course, be posted separately to the proper account and as the posting is completed the proper cross-reference should be made in the Posting Reference column of the book of original entry and in the Posting Reference column of the ledger account. Under this plan the voucher or other document that represents the transaction may be filed after the transaction is recorded in the appropriate book of original entry. As each transaction is recorded in a book of original entry, care must be taken to enter all of the information that will be needed when posting.

Posting from vouchers or other documents

When the posting is done directly from the vouchers or other documents that represent the transactions, the transactions usually will be recorded first in the proper books of original entry, after which the vouchers or other documents will be referred to the bookkeeper in charge of the suppliers' and customers' accounts for direct posting.

Posting to the individual accounts with suppliers

It is necessary to post all items that represent increases or decreases in the amount owed to each supplier. A list of vouchers or other documents that usually represent transactions completed with suppliers is shown below. The usual posting reference is also indicated.

VOUCHER OR DOCUMENT	TRANSACTION REPRESENTED	POSTING REFERENCE
(a) Purchase invoice No. 1	Purchase	P 1
(b) Charge-back invoice No. 1	Return or allowance	CB 1
(c) Check stub No. 1	Payment on account	Ck 1

The purchase invoices and charge-back invoices are usually numbered consecutively as they are received and issued. These numbers should not be confused with the numbers used by the vendor (supplier). The check stubs should be numbered consecutively to agree with the numbers of the checks issued. As the posting is completed, the proper cross-reference should be made in the Posting Reference column of the account and on the voucher or other document. If a loose-leaf ledger is used and accounts with suppliers are kept in alphabetic order, the posting may be indicated by means of a distinctive check mark on the voucher or other document.

Posting to the individual accounts with customers

It is necessary to post all items that represent increases or decreases in the amount owed by each customer. Following is a list of vouchers or other documents that usually represent transactions completed with customers. The usual posting reference is also indicated.

VOUCHER OR DOCUMENT	TRANSACTION REPRESENTED	POSTING REFERENCE
(a) Sale ticket No. 1	Sale	S 1
(b) Credit memo No. 1	Return or allowance	CM 1
(c) Remittance received	Collection on account	C

The sales tickets usually are prepared in duplicate or triplicate and are numbered consecutively. Each salesperson may use a different series of numbers. One copy is retained for the use of the bookkeeper and another copy is given to the customer.

Credit memorandums issued to customers in connection with sales returns or allowances are usually prepared in duplicate and are numbered consecutively. One copy goes to the customer and the other copy is retained for the use of the bookkeeper.

Remittances received from customers may consist of cash or cash items, such as checks, bank drafts, and money orders. When the remittance is in the form of cash, it is customary to issue a receipt. The receipt may be issued in duplicate, in which case the duplicate copy will provide the information needed for the purpose of posting to the customer's account. Sometimes receipt stubs are used to record the information for posting purposes. When the remittance is in the form of a check, it is not necessary to issue a receipt as the canceled check will serve as a receipt for the customer.

Posting a credit to the customer's account may be made directly from the check or from a list of checks received. Sometimes all remittances received daily are listed in such a manner as to provide the information needed for posting purposes. When this plan is followed, the bookkeeper need not handle the remittances at all. It is a quite common practice to use a form of monthly statement of account in which the upper portion (containing the customer's name and address) is to be detached and sent in along with the remittance. The amount of the remittance is noted on this slip of paper which then contains all the information needed to post the correct credit to the proper customer's account. If the customer does not send in (or bring in) the top part of the statement, a receipt or memo is prepared to serve the same purpose. This procedure is especially suitable when it is possible to separate the functions of **(1)** handling the cash and cash items, and **(2)** recording the credits to the customers' accounts.

As the posting is completed, the proper cross-reference should be made in the Posting Reference column of the account and on the voucher or other document. If a loose-leaf ledger is used and accounts with customers are kept in alphabetic order, the posting may be indicated by means of a distinctive check mark or by initialing the voucher or other document.

Accountants generally prefer to post from the basic documents rather than from the books of original entry to the individual accounts with suppliers and customers because such procedure provides better control and promotes accuracy. When a purchase invoice is recorded in a purchases journal by one person and is posted directly from the invoice to the proper supplier's account by another person, it is unlikely that both persons will make the same mistake. Even if the posting is done by the person who also keeps the purchases journal, there is less likelihood of making a mistake than when the posting is done from the purchases journal. If a mistake were made in recording the amount of the invoice in the purchases journal, the same mistake would almost certainly be made in posting from the purchases journal to the supplier's account. The same reasoning may be applied to the recording of sales transactions and all other transactions that affect accounts with suppliers and customers.

Statement of account   When merchandise is sold on account, it is customary to render a monthly statement of account to each charge customer. Usually the statements are mailed as soon as they can be completed following the close of each month or at a time during the month determined by the billing cycle. (The use of "billing cycles" is limited, generally, to businesses with hundreds or thousands of customers.) In order that statements may be mailed promptly, some firms follow the policy of including transactions completed up to the 25th of the preceding month or five days before the close of the customer's billing cycle. Such statements are an aid to collection. When a remittance is not received from the customer within the usual credit period, a copy of the statement of account may be referred to the credit department for such action as the credit manager may wish to take. A model filled-in copy of a statement of account is reproduced below. This is a statement of the account of W. D. Ross for the month ended October 31. It shows **(1)** the balance at the beginning of the month amounting to $64.60; **(2)** a charge of $173.25 (for a sale of $165.00 plus tax of $8.25) made on October 24, **(3)** a credit of $150 for cash received on October 27; and **(4)** the balance at the close of the month amounting to $87.85. Note that the customer is asked to tear off the upper portion of the statement and to send it along with his remittance.

STATEMENT

BOYD'S
CLOTHIERS

600 Olive Street
St. Louis, Missouri 63101

W. D. ROSS
9719 ECHO
ST. LOUIS, MO   63114

PLEASE DETACH THIS PORTION AND RETURN WITH YOUR REMITTANCE ▼

DATE	DESCRIPTION	CHARGES	CREDITS	BALANCE
Oct. 1			BALANCE FORWARD	64.60
24	Mdse.	173.25		237.85
27	Cash		150.00	87.85

Statement of Account

Report No. 8-1	Complete Report No. 8-1 in the study assignments and submit your working papers to the instructor for approval. After completing the report, continue with the following textbook discussion until the next report is required.

APPLICATION OF ACCOUNTING PRINCIPLES

The accrual basis of accounting as applied to a merchandising enterprise is illustrated on the following pages by a reproduction of the records of Boyd's Clothiers, owned and operated by Lynn C. Boyd. The records include the following:

BOOKS OF ORIGINAL ENTRY

Combined cash journal
Purchases journal
Sales journal

BOOKS OF FINAL ENTRY

General ledger
Accounts receivable ledger
Accounts payable ledger

AUXILIARY RECORDS

Petty cash disbursements record
Checkbook
Employees' earnings records

Combined cash journal

The form of combined cash journal used is similar to the one illustrated on pages 160 and 161. However, in Boyd's journal the first two amount columns are used in recording banking transactions including deposits, checks, and bank charges. These columns serve the same purpose as though they were headed Cash Receipts and Disbursements. Ms. Boyd follows the practice of depositing all cash receipts in a checking account at the First National Bank and of making all disbursements by check (except for the payment of small items, which may be paid from a petty cash fund, and a few charges made directly by the bank). For these reasons, a bank account rather than a cash account is kept in the general ledger. The posting to the bank account is from the combined cash journal, the account being debited for the total receipts (deposits) and being credited for the total disbursements (checks and bank charges). The journal also differs from the one on pages 106 and 107 in that Boyd's has a Purchases Discount Credit column immediately to the right of the Bank Credit column.

All items entered in the General Debit and Credit columns of the combined cash journal are posted individually to the proper accounts in the general ledger. No individual posting to the general ledger is required from any of the other amount columns. Instead, the totals of these columns are posted at the end of the month.

Purchases journal

The form of purchases journal used is the same as the one illustrated on page 144. It was described in detail in Chapter 6. All transactions involving the purchase of merchandise *on account* are recorded in this journal. Because the posting of the individual credits to the accounts with suppliers is done directly from the purchase invoices, the only posting required from the purchases journal is the total purchases for each month. This involves a debit to Purchases, Account No. 511, and a credit to Accounts Payable, Account No. 231.

Sales journal

The form of sales journal used is the same as the one illustrated on page 152. It was described in detail in Chapter 6. All transactions involving the sale of merchandise *on account* are recorded in this journal. Because the posting of individual charges to the accounts with customers is done directly from the sales tickets, the only posting required from the sales journal is the total sales for each month. This involves a debit to Accounts Receivable, Account No. 121, and credits to Sales, Account No. 411, and to Sales Tax Payable, Account No. 241.

General ledger

A general ledger with the accounts arranged in numerical order is used. A chart of the accounts appears on page 183. The four-column account form is used in the general ledger.

Accounts receivable ledger

An accounts receivable ledger with the accounts for customers arranged in alphabetic order is used. The three-column account form is used in this ledger. Posting to the individual accounts with customers is done directly from the sales tickets or other documents. As each item is posted, the balance is extended immediately so that reference to the account of any customer at any time will reveal without any delay the amount due.

This is important since it is often necessary to determine the status of a particular customer's account before extending additional credit.

Accounts payable ledger

An accounts payable ledger with the accounts for suppliers arranged in alphabetic order is used. The three-column account form also is used in this ledger. Posting to the individual accounts with suppliers is done directly from the invoices or other documents. As each item is posted, the balance is extended immediately so that reference to the account of any supplier at any time will reveal the amount owed to that supplier.

Auxiliary records

As previously stated, certain auxiliary records are used, including a petty cash disbursements record and a checkbook. The form of petty cash disbursements record is similar to that illustrated on pages 50 and 51. A record of deposits made and checks issued is kept on the check stubs as well as in the combined cash journal. At the end of each month, when the summary posting from the combined cash journal has been completed, the balance of the bank checking account in the ledger should be the same as the balance recorded on the check stubs. The earnings records maintained for each of Ms. Boyd's four employees are similar to the one illustrated on pages 80 and 81. (To conserve space, these records are not reproduced in this chapter.)

Accounting procedure

The books of account containing a record of the transactions completed during the month of December are reproduced on pages 208 to 225. These books include the combined cash journal, the purchases journal, the sales journal, the petty cash disbursements record, the general ledger, the accounts receivable ledger, and the accounts payable ledger. Before recording any transactions for December, the balance of the bank checking account was entered in the combined cash journal and the balance in the petty cash fund was entered in the petty cash disbursements record. The balance at the beginning of the month of December is shown in each of the accounts in the general, accounts receivable, and accounts payable ledgers. These balances along with those at the end of the month are summarized in the trial balances and schedules reproduced on pages 225 and 226.

Following is a narrative of the transactions completed during December. Transactions of a type that have not been previously introduced are analyzed to show their effect upon the accounts.

BOYD'S CLOTHIERS

NARRATIVE OF TRANSACTIONS

Monday, December 2

Issued checks as follows:

No. 867, Dolan Realty Co., $700, in payment of December rent.

No. 868, The Penn-Central Railroad Co., $53.18, in payment of freight on merchandise purchased.

No. 869, Aris Glove Co., $330, in payment of invoice of November 5, no discount.

It will be noted that all three checks were recorded in the combined cash journal. Check No. 867 was recorded by debiting Rent Expense, Account No. 611, and by crediting the bank account. Check No. 868 was recorded by debiting Purchases, Account No. 511, and by crediting the bank account. Since the freight charge increases the cost of the merchandise, the purchases account should be debited. Note that the account titles were written in the Description column. The account numbers were inserted in the Posting Reference column when the individual posting was completed at the end of the week.

Check No. 869 was recorded by debiting Accounts Payable and crediting the bank account, the name of the supplier being written in the Description column. A check mark was placed in the Posting Reference column to indicate that checks issued to suppliers are not posted individually from the combined cash journal. Such checks are posted directly to the proper suppliers' accounts in the accounts payable ledger from the information on the check stubs.

Tuesday, December 3

Received the following invoices for merchandise purchased on account:

Daniel Hays Co., Johnstown, NY 12095, $228, per Invoice No. 204 of November 30. Terms, net 30 days.

Hanes Corporation, Winston-Salem, NC 27102, $744, per Invoice No. 205 of November 30. Terms, 8/10 EOM.

Julius Resnick, Inc., 46 E. 32d St., New York, NY 10016, $1,488, per Invoice No. 206 of November 30. Terms, 3/10 EOM.

It will be noted that after receiving the merchandise and checking the invoices, the transactions were recorded in the purchases journal. Check marks were placed in the Posting Reference column to indicate that individual posting is not done from the purchases journal. The invoices were then posted directly to the credit of the three suppliers' accounts in the accounts payable ledger, after which the invoices were filed in an unpaid invoice file according to their due dates.

Wednesday, December 4

Received check from D. P. Walsh, $317.23.

Note that the credit was immediately posted to the customer's account. The remittance was then recorded in the combined cash journal by debiting the bank account and by crediting Accounts Receivable. The name of the customer was written in the Description column. Since the credit had already been posted to the customer's account, a check mark was placed in the Posting Reference column.

Received a notice from the First National Bank that $235.42 had been deducted from the account of Boyd's Clothiers, representing a discount of

3 percent of the net amount of BankAmericard and Master Charge vouchers that had been deposited by Boyd's relating to such sales (less credits issued to customers for returns) during the preceding month.

> Note that this was recorded in the combined cash journal as a debit to Bank Credit Card Expense, Account No. 619, and a credit in the Bank "Checks Cr." column. (Even though the reduction in the Bank balance was not accomplished by issuing a check, the effect was the same. A subtraction of the amount was made on the next check stub.)

Thursday, December 5

Sold merchandise on account as follows:

No. 271A, D. P. Walsh, 113 Grether, St. Louis, MO 63135, $432.39, tax, $21.62.

No. 257B, J. J. Anders, 11939 Rocky, St. Louis, MO 63141, $85.12, tax, $4.26.

No. 235C, J. L. Burnett, 15 Forester, St. Louis, MO 63011, $537.95, tax $26.90.

> Unless otherwise specified, all charge sales are payable on the 10th of the following month. No cash discount is allowed. Note that these transactions were recorded in the sales journal. A check mark was placed in the Posting Reference column to indicate that individual posting is not done from the sales journal. The sales tickets were then posted directly to the proper customers' accounts in the accounts receivable ledger, after which each ticket was filed under the name of the customer for future reference. The numbers of the sales tickets indicate that there are four salespersons identified by the letters A, B, C, and D. Each of these persons uses a separate pad of sales tickets numbered consecutively.

Issued Checks as follows:

No. 870, Brown Shoe Co., $460.60, in payment of invoice of November 27, $470 less discount of $9.40.

No. 871, Damon, Inc., $432.40, in payment of invoice of November 26, $460 less discount of $27.60.

No. 872, El Jay Co., $2,079.20, in payment of invoice of November 29, $2,260 less discount of $180.80.

No. 873, Marx Neuman Co., $784, in payment of invoice of November 27, $800 less discount of $16.

No. 874, Schoeneman, Inc., $1,128, in payment of invoice of November 29, $1,200 less discount of $72.

No. 875, Smart Pants, Inc., $1,258.56, in payment of invoice of November 27, $1,368 less discount of $109.44.

> Each of the six checks was recorded in the combined cash journal by crediting the bank account, crediting Purchases Discount in the column provided, and debiting Accounts Payable for the gross amount. The name of the supplier was written in the description column and a check mark was placed in the Posting Reference column to indicate that the posting to the individual supplier's account in the accounts payable ledger was not made from this journal. The check stubs provided the information for posting. In posting the suppliers' accounts, one line was used for the amount of the check and another for the amount of the discount.

Friday, December 6

Issued checks as follows:

> No. 876, Post Publishing Co., $61.04, in payment for circulars to be used for advertising purposes.
>
> No. 877, State Treasurer, $912.14, in payment of sales taxes for November.

> Both checks were recorded in the combined cash journal by debiting the proper accounts and by crediting the bank account. Check No. 876 was charged to Advertising Expense and Check No. 877 was charged to Sales Tax Payable. The numbers of the checks were written in the Check No. column and the titles of the accounts to be charged were written in the Description column.

Bought merchandise from Damon, Inc., 16 E. 34th St., New York, NY 10016, $1,150, per Invoice No. 207 of December 4. Terms, 6/10, n/30.

Sold merchandise on account as follows:

> No. 259B, J. F. Yager, 5 Brookston Ct., Kirkwood, MO 63122, $106.32, tax $5.32.

Saturday, December 7

Cash (including bank credit card) sales for the week:

SALESPERSON	MERCHANDISE	TAX	TOTAL
A	$ 840.15	$ 42.01	$ 882.16
B	762.18	38.11	800.29
C	1,041.73	52.09	1,093.82
D	628.40	31.42	659.82
	$3,272.46	$163.63	$3,436.09

> As each cash sale was completed a sales ticket and a BankAmericard or Master Charge voucher, if necessary, were prepared. This ticket provided the information needed in recording the sale on the cash register when ringing up the amount of cash or vouchers received. As each amount was thus recorded it was added to the previous total of cash sales made by each salesperson on a mechanical accumulator in the register. Usually the total cash sales are recorded daily, but to save time and to avoid unnecessary duplication of entries the total cash sales are here recorded at the end of each week and on the last day of the month. This transaction was recorded in the combined cash journal by debiting the bank account for $3,436.09 and by crediting Sales for $3,272.46 and Sales Tax Payable for $163.63.

Made petty cash disbursements as follows:

> Postage stamps, $10. Petty Cash Voucher No. 73.
>
> Messenger fee, $3. Petty Cash Voucher No. 74.

> All disbursements from the petty cash fund are recorded in the petty cash disbursements record. This record is ruled so as to facilitate the classification of such expenditures. It will be noted that the cost of the postage stamps was recorded as a charge to Supplies, Account No. 151, and the messenger fees to Miscellaneous Expense, Account No. 624.

END-OF-THE-WEEK WORK

(1) Proved the footings of the combined cash journal. **(2)** Deposited $3,753.32 in the First National Bank and proved the bank balance ($7,621.61). **(3)** Posted each entry individually from the General Debit and Credit columns of the combined cash journal to the proper general ledger accounts. **(4)** Proved the footings of the petty cash disbursements record and proved the balance of the petty cash fund ($87). **(5)** Proved the footings of the sales journal.

Monday, December 9

Issued checks as follows:

No. 878 to Daniel Hays Co., $684, in payment of invoice of November 15, no discount.

No. 879, Hanes Corporation, $684.48, in payment of invoice of November 30, $744 less discount of $59.52.

No. 880, Julius Resnick, Inc., $1,443.36, in payment of invoice of November 30, $1,488 less discount of $44.64.

A customer who had used her Master Charge card to purchase a dress (sales price, $84.95; sales tax, $4.25) two days before, returned it having decided it was the wrong color. Ms. Boyd agreed to take it back and prepared a Master Charge credit voucher for the full amount, $89.20.

> Since the original transaction had been handled as a cash sale, the return was recorded in the combined cash journal as a credit of $89.20 in the Bank "Checks Cr." column with a debit of $84.95 to Sales Returns and Allowances, Account No. 041, and a debit of $4.25 to Sales Tax Payable, Account No. 241. (At the time of the next bank deposit, the amount of the credit voucher will be treated as a deduction from the amount of the vouchers being deposited.)

Tuesday, December 10

Issued Check No. 881 for $500.68 to the First National Bank, a U.S. depositary, in payment of the following taxes:

Employees' income tax withheld during November.............		$284.40
FICA tax imposed —		
On employees (withheld during November).................	$108.14	
On the employer......................................	108.14	216.28
Total..		$500.68

> This transaction resulted in decreases in FICA tax payable and in employees income tax payable with a corresponding decrease in the bank account; hence, it was recorded in the combined cash journal by debiting FICA Tax Payable for $216.28 and Employees Income Tax Payable for $284.40, and by crediting the bank account for $500.68.

Sold merchandise on account as follows on page 202.

No. 243D, R. D. Williams, 617 Rebecca, St. Charles, MO 63301, $246.05, tax $12.30.

Wednesday, December 11

Received the following remittances from customers:

J. E. Buelt, $300, on account.
L. V. Freeman, $200, on account.
K. E. Vivian, $82.11, in full settlement of account.

Thursday, December 12

Issued Check No. 882 to Damon, Inc., $1,081, in payment of invoice of December 4, $1,150 less discount of $69.

Made the following disbursements from the petty cash fund:

Boy Scouts of America, $5. Petty Cash Voucher No. 75.
Lynn C. Boyd, $10, for personal use. Petty Cash Voucher No. 76.

Friday, December 13

Received the following invoices for merchandise purchased on account:

Aris Glove Co., 10 E. 38th St., New York, NY 10016, $412.50, per Invoice No. 208 of December 10. Terms, net 30 days.

El Jay Co., 411 Anderson, Fairview, NJ 07022, $1,695, per Invoice No. 209 of December 10. Terms, 8/10, n/30.

Huk-a-Poo, Inc., 411 Broadway, New York, NY 10012, $543.75, per Invoice No. 210 of December 11. Terms, 8/10, n/30.

Saturday, December 14

Cash and bank credit card sales for the week:

SALESPERSON	MERCHANDISE	TAX	TOTAL
A	$ 830.12	$ 41.51	$ 871.63
B	1,215.05	60.75	1,275.80
C	728.80	36.44	765.24
D	411.60	20.58	432.18
	$3,185.57	$159.28	$3,344.85

Issued Check No. 883 payable to Payroll for $705.24.

Ms. Boyd follows the policy of paying her employees on the 15th and last day of each month. Since December 15 fell on Sunday, the employees were paid on the 14th. The following statement was prepared from the payroll record:

PAYROLL STATEMENT FOR PERIOD ENDED DECEMBER 15

Total wages and commissions earned during period............		$892.70
Employees' taxes to be withheld:		
Employees' income tax.................................	$133.90	
FICA tax 6% of $892.70..............................	53.56	187.46
Net amount payable to employees.........................		$705.24
Employer's payroll taxes:		
FICA tax, 6% of $892.70..............................		$ 53.56
Unemployment compensation taxes —		
State unemployment tax, 2.7% of $104.80...............		2.83
FUTA tax, 0.5% of $104.80...........................		.52
Total...		$ 56.91

None of the earnings of the four employees had reached the $15,000 point. Accordingly, all of the wages and commissions earned during the period are subject to the FICA tax. All but one employee (a part-time employee) had reached the $4,200 State Unemployment and FUTA tax limits in an earlier month. As a result, only $104.80 of wages and commissions earned during the period is subject to these unemployment taxes.

Two entries were required to record the payroll in the combined cash journal — one to record the total earnings of the employees, the amounts withheld for FICA tax and income tax, and the net amount paid; the other to record the social security tax imposed on the employer.

END-OF-THE-WEEK WORK

(1) Proved the footings of the combined cash journal. **(2)** Deposited $3,837.76 ($3,926.96 − $89.20 credit of December 9) in the First National Bank and proved the bank balance ($6,360.61). **(3)** Posted each entry individually from the General Debit and Credit columns of the combined cash journal to the proper general ledger accounts. **(4)** Proved the footings of the petty cash disbursements record and proved the balance of the petty cash fund ($72). **(5)** Proved the footings of the sales journal.

Tuesday, December 17

Received the following remittances from customers:

J. F. Yager, $213.52, on account.
S. W. Novak, $369.90, in full settlement of account.
C. E. Wuller, $367.57 in full settlement of account.

(Since a page of the combined cash journal was filled at this point, the totals of the amount columns were recorded on the double ruled line at the bottom of the page, after which they were carried forward and entered at the top of the next page.)

Wednesday, December 18

Sold merchandise on credit as follows:

No. 239C, K. E. Vivian, 1830 Patterson Rd., Florissant, MO 63031, $329.90, tax $16.50.

No. 246D, E. E. Palmer, 1129 Mackinac, St. Louis, MO 63141, $68.15, tax $3.41.

No. 277A, W. R. Price, 1629 Rathford Ct., St. Louis, MO 63141, $154.11, tax $7.71.

Thursday, December 19

Issued checks as follows:

No. 884, El Jay Co., $1,559.40, in payment of invoice of December 10, $1,695 less discount of $135.60.

No. 885, Huk-a-Poo, Inc., $500.25, in payment of invoice of December 11, $543.75 less discount of $43.50.

Made petty cash disbursements as follows:

Advertising, $6.29. Petty Cash Voucher No. 77.

Supplies, $8.35. Petty Cash Voucher No. 78.

Miscellaneous expense, $1.75. Petty Cash Voucher No. 79.

Friday, December 20

Issued Charge-Back Invoice No. 291 for $66 to Aris Glove Co., for merchandise returned; to be applied on Invoice No. 208 received December 13.

This transaction was recorded in the combined cash journal by debiting Accounts Payable and by crediting Purchases Returns and Allowances. It was also posted directly to the account of the Aris Glove Co. in the accounts payable ledger from the charge-back invoice.

Saturday, December 21

Issued Check No. 886 for $1,000 to Ms. Boyd for personal use.

Cash and bank credit card sales for the week:

SALESPERSON	MERCHANDISE	TAX	TOTAL
A	$ 982.50	$ 49.13	$1,031.63
B	801.30	40.07	841.37
C	714.75	35.74	750.49
D	840.05	42.00	882.05
	$3,338.60	$166.94	$3,505.54

END-OF-THE-WEEK WORK

(1) Proved the footings of the combined cash journal. **(2)** Deposited $4,456.53 in the First National Bank and proved the bank balance ($7,757.49). **(3)** Posted each entry individually from the General Debit and Credit columns of the combined cash journal to the proper general ledger accounts. **(4)** Proved the footings of the petty cash disbursements record and proved the balance of the petty cash fund ($55.61). **(5)** Proved the footings of the sales journal.

Monday, December 23

Issued Check No. 887 for $16.80 to United Parcel Service in payment of statement for delivery service for month ended December 15.

> Very few of the customers of Boyd's Clothiers wish to have their purchases delivered. In some special circumstances, Ms. Boyd or one of the employees handles deliveries. In some cases, United Parcel Service is used. Since the monthly amount is small, Miscellaneous Expense is debited when the charge is paid.

Tuesday, December 24

Sold merchandise on credit as follows:

No. 262B, D. P. Walsh, 113 Grether, St. Louis, MO 63135, $18.55, tax $.93.

No. 249D, C. W. Reed, 761 Cella, St. Louis, MO 63124, $191.42, tax $9.57.

No. 256C, L. V. Freeman, 7362 S. Yorkshire, St. Louis, MO 63126, $17.95, tax $.90.

Thursday, December 26

Received the following remittances from customers:

W. R. Price, $100, on account.
C. W. Reed, $300, on account.

Made petty cash disbursements as follows:

Advertising, $4.80. Petty Cash Voucher No. 80.
Supplies, $9.13. Petty Cash Voucher No. 81.
Miscellaneous expense, $2.90. Petty Cash Voucher No. 82.

Friday, December 27

Issued Credit Memorandum No. 12 for $22.58 to W. R. Price for merchandise returned. (Sales price of merchandise, $21.50, tax $1.08.)

Issued Check No. 888 for $421.30 to the Post Publishing Co. in payment of advertising bill.

Received a notice from the First National Bank that $369.90 had been deducted from the account of Boyd's Clothiers, since a check from S. W. Novak deposited a few days before had not been paid by Mr. Novak's bank (not sufficient funds). Mr. Novak's check was enclosed with the notice.

> The amount of the check was debited immediately to Mr. Novak's account in the accounts receivable ledger with the notation "NSF." An entry was made in the

combined cash journal debiting Accounts Receivable with a credit in the Bank "Checks Cr." column. A deduction was made on the following check stub.

Saturday, December 28

Cash and bank credit card sales for the week:

SALESPERSON	MERCHANDISE	TAX	TOTAL
A	$ 795.40	$ 39.77	$ 835.17
B	867.50	43.38	910.88
C	403.10	20.16	423.26
D	642.35	32.12	674.47
	$2,708.35	$135.43	$2,843.78

Issued checks as follows:

No. 889, The Central States Bell Telephone Co., $32.15, for telephone service.

No. 890, The United Gas & Electric Co., $73.28, for gas and electricity.

No. 891, Daniel Hays Co., $228 in payment of invoice of November 30, no discount.

END-OF-THE-WEEK WORK

(1) Proved the footings of the combined cash journal. **(2)** Deposited $3,243.78 in the First National Bank and proved the bank balance, ($9,859.84). **(3)** Posted each entry individually from the General Debit and Credit columns of the combined cash journal to the proper general ledger accounts. **(4)** Proved the footings of the petty cash disbursements record and proved the balance of the petty cash fund ($38.78). **(5)** Proved the footings of the sales journal.

Monday, December 30

Received invoice from Jacob Siegel Co., 4725 N. Broad St., Philadelphia, PA 19141, $1,300, for merchandise purchased per Invoice No. 211 of December 27. Terms, 6/10, n/30.

Tuesday, December 31

Received the following invoices:

Brown Shoe Co., 8300 Maryland Ave., St. Louis, MO 63105, $705 per Invoice No. 212 of December 27. Terms, 2/10, n/30.

El Jay Co., 411 Anderson, Fairview, NJ 07022, $678 per Invoice No. 213 of December 26. Terms, 8/10, n/30.

Hanes Corporation, Winston-Salem, NC 27102, $148.80 per Invoice No. 214 of December 27. Terms, 8/10 EOM.

Marx Neuman Co., 9 W. 57th St., New York, NY 10019, $600 per Invoice No. 215 of December 26. Terms, 2/10, n/30.

Webster Safe & Lock Co., 916 Washington Ave., St. Louis, MO 63101, $562, safe purchased per invoice of December 30. Terms 2/30, n/60.

The first four invoices were recorded in the purchases journal in the usual manner. The invoice received from the Webster Safe & Lock Co. was recorded in the combined cash journal by debiting Store Equipment and by crediting Accounts Payable. In this enterprise the purchases journal is used only for recording invoices covering merchandise purchased on account.

Cash and bank credit card sales:

SALESPERSON	MERCHANDISE	TAX	TOTAL
A	$ 511.70	$25.59	$ 537.29
B	340.65	17.03	357.68
C	320.30	16.02	336.32
D	296.90	14.85	311.75
	$1,469.55	$73.49	$1,543.04

Issued Check No. 892 payable to Payroll for $698.55.

PAYROLL STATEMENT FOR PERIOD ENDED DECEMBER 31

Total wages and commissions earned during period............		$884.20
Employees' taxes to be withheld:		
Employees' income tax..................................	$132.60	
FICA tax, 6% of $884.20..............................	53.05	185.65
Net amount payable to employees.........................		$698.55
Employer's payroll taxes:		
FICA tax, 6% of $884.20..............................		$ 53.05
Unemployment compensation taxes —		
State unemployment tax, 2.7% of $103.60................		2.80
FUTA tax, 0.5% of $103.60............................		.52
Total...		$ 56.37

Issued Check No. 893 for $61.22 to replenish the petty cash fund.

STATEMENT OF PETTY CASH DISBURSEMENTS FOR DECEMBER

Lynn C. Boyd, drawing	$10.00
Supplies	27.48
Advertising expense	11.09
Charitable contributions expense	5.00
Miscellaneous expense	7.65
Total disbursements	$61.22

Before the above statement was prepared the petty cash disbursements record was proved by footing the amount columns, the totals were entered in ink, and the record was ruled with single and double lines. The balance was then brought down below the double rules. The amount received to replenish the fund was added to the balance and the total, $100, was entered in the Description column.

The amount of the check issued was entered in the combined cash journal by debiting the proper accounts and by crediting the bank account. It should be remembered that no posting is done from the petty cash disbursements record; the proper accounts

PURCHASES JOURNAL   PAGE 32

	DATE	INVOICE NO.	FROM WHOM PURCHASED	POST. REF.	AMOUNT	
1	19-- Dec. 3	204	Daniel Hays Co.	✓	228 00	1
2	3	205	Hanes Corporation	✓	744 00	2
3	3	206	Julius Resnick, Inc.	✓	1488 00	3
4	6	207	Damon, Inc.	✓	1150 00	4
5	13	208	Aris Glove Co.	✓	412 50	5
6	13	209	El Jay Co.	✓	1695 00	6
7	13	210	Huk-a-Poo, Inc.	✓	543 75	7
8	30	211	Jacob Siegel Co.	✓	1300 00	8
9	31	212	Brown Shoe Co.	✓	705 00	9
10	31	213	El Jay Co.	✓	678 00	10
11	31	214	Hanes Corporation	✓	148 80	11
12	31	215	Mary Neuman Co.	✓	600 00	12
13			Purchases Dr.-Accounts Payable Cr.	511 231	9693 05	13
14						14
15						15
16						16
17						17
18						18
19						19
20						20
21						21
22						22
23						23

Boyd's Clothiers — Purchases Journal

will be charged for the petty cash disbursements when the posting is completed from the combined cash journal.

ROUTINE END-OF-THE-MONTH WORK

(1) Proved the footings and entered the totals in the combined cash journal and the sales journal; entered the total in the purchases journal. **(2)** Deposited $1,543.04 in the First National Bank and proved the bank balance ($10,643.11). **(3)** Completed the individual posting from the General Debit and Credit columns of the combined cash journal. **(4)** Completed the summary posting of the columnar totals of the combined cash journal, the purchases journal, and the sales journal to the proper accounts in the general ledger. **(5)** Ruled the combined cash journal, the purchases journal, and the sales journal. **(6)** Prepared a trial balance and schedules of accounts receivable and accounts payable.

SALES JOURNAL   PAGE 44

	DATE	SALE NO.	TO WHOM SOLD	POST. REF.	ACCOUNTS RECEIVABLE DR.	SALES CR.	SALES TAX PAYABLE CR.	
1	19-- Dec. 5	271A	D. P. Walsh	✓	454 01	432 39	2 62	1
2	5	257B	J. J. Anders	✓	89 38	85 12	4 26	2
3	5	235C	J. L. Burnett	✓	564 85	537 95	26 90	3
4	6	259B	J. F. Yager	✓	111 64 / 1 2 1 9 88	106 32 / 1 1 6 1 78	5 32 / 5 8 10	4
5	10	243D	C. D. Williams	✓	258 35 / 1 4 7 8 23	246 05 / 1 4 0 7 83	12 30 / 7 0 40	5
6	18	239C	K. E. Vivian	✓	346 40	329 90	16 50	6
7	18	246D	E. E. Palmer	✓	71 56	68 15	3 41	7
8	18	277A	W. R. Price	✓	161 82 / 2 0 5 8 01	154 11 / 1 9 5 2 99	7 71 / 9 8 02	8
9	24	262B	D. P. Walsh	✓	19 48	18 55	93	9
10	24	249D	C. W. Reed	✓	200 99	191 42	9 57	10
11	24	256C	L. V. Freeman	✓	18 85 / 2 2 9 7 33	17 95 / 2 1 8 7 91	90 / 1 0 9 42	11
12					2297 33	2187 91	109 42	12
13					(121)	(411)	(244)	13

Boyd's Clothiers — Sales Journal

47 PAGE   COMBINED CASH JOURNAL

	FIRST NATIONAL BANK		PURCHASES DISCOUNT 052 CR.	CK. NO.	DAY	DESCRIPTION	POST. REF.	
	DEPOSITS 111 DR.	CHECKS 111 CR.						
1						AMOUNTS FORWARDED *Balance* 12,302.83		1
2		700 00		867	2	Rent Expense	611	2
3		53 18		868	2	Purchases	511	3
4		330 00		869	2	Aris Glove Co.	✓	4
5	317 23				4	D. P. Walsh	✓	5
6		235 42			4	Bank Credit Card Expense	619	6
7		460 60	9 40	870	5	Brown Shoe Co.	✓	7
8		432 40	27 60	871	5	Damon, Inc.	✓	8
9		2079 20	180 80	872	5	El Jay Co.	✓	9
10		784 00	16 00	873	5	Mary Neuman Co.	✓	10
11		1128 00	72 00	874	5	Schoeneman, Inc.	✓	11
12		1258 56	109 44	875	5	Smart Pants, Inc.	✓	12
13		61 04		876	6	Advertising Expense	618	13
14		912 14		877	6	Sales Tax Payable	241	14
15	3436 09				7	Cash + bank credit card sales forwk.	✓	15
16	3753 32	8434 54	415 24			7623.61		16
		684 00		878	9	Daniel Hays Co.	✓	
17		684 48	59 52	879	9	Hanes Corporation	✓	17
18		1443 36	44 64	880	9	Julius Resnick	✓	18
19		89 20			9	Sales Returns & Allowances	041	19
20						Sales Tax Payable	241	20
21		500 68		881	10	FICA Tax Payable	251	21
22						Employees Income Tax Pay.	261	22
23	300 00				11	J. E. Buelt	✓	23
24	200 00				11	L. V. Freeman	✓	24
25	82 11				11	K. E. Vivian	✓	25
26		1081 00	69 00	882	12	Damon, Inc.	✓	26
27	3344 85				14	Cash + bank credit card sales forwk.	✓	27
28		705 24		883	14	Salaries + Commissions Exp.	613	28
29						FICA Tax Payable	251	29
30						Employees Income Tax Pay.	261	30
31					14	Payroll Taxes Payable	614	31
32						FICA Tax Payable	251	32
33						FUTA Tax Payable	271	33
34	7680 28	13622 50	588 40			State Unemployment Tax Pay. 6360.61	281	34
35	213 52				17	J. F. Yager	✓	35
36	369 90				17	S. W. Novak	✓	36
37	367 57				17	C. E. Wuller	✓	37
38	8631 27	13622 50	588 40		17	Carried forward		38

Boyd's Clothiers — Combined Cash Journal (Left Page)
(*continued on next page*)

FOR MONTH OF *December* 19 —　　PAGE 47

#	GENERAL DEBIT	GENERAL CREDIT	ACCOUNTS PAYABLE 231 Dr.	ACCOUNTS RECEIVABLE 121 Cr.	SALES 411 Cr.	SALES TAX PAYABLE 241 Cr.	#
1							1
2	70000						2
3	5318						3
4			33000				4
5				31723			5
6	23542						6
7			47000				7
8			46000				8
9			226000				9
10			80000				10
11			120000				11
12			136800				12
13	6104						13
14	91214						14
15	196175		68500	31723	327246 / 327246	16363 / 16363	15
16			68400				16
17			74400				17
18			148800				18
19	8495						19
20	425						20
21	21628						21
22	28440						22
23				30000			23
24				20000			24
25				8211			25
26			115000				26
27					318557	15928	27
28	89270						28
29		5356					29
30		13390					30
31	5691						31
32		5356					32
33		52					33
34		283					34
35	350127	24437	1095400	89934 / 21352	645803	32291	35
36				36990			36
37				36757			37
38	350127	24437	1095400	185033	645803	32291	38

Boyd's Clothiers — Combined Cash Journal (Right Page)
(*continued on next page*)

48 PAGE   COMBINED CASH JOURNAL

| FIRST NATIONAL BANK | | PURCHASES DISCOUNT 052 CR. | CK. NO. | DAY | DESCRIPTION | POST. REF. |
DEPOSITS 111 DR.	CHECKS 111 CR.					
8631 27	13622 50	588 40			AMOUNTS FORWARDED	
	1559 40	135 60	884	19	El Jay Co.	✓
	500 25	43 50	885	19	Hik-a-Poo, Inc.	✓
				20	Purchs. R&A-Aris Glove Co.	051
	1000 00		886	21	Lynn C. Boyd, Drawing	031
3505 54				21	Cash + bank credit card sales for wk.	✓
12136 81	16682 15	767 50				
	16 80		887	23	Miscellaneous Expense 1,157.44	624
100 00				26	W.R. Price	✓
300 00				26	C.W. Reed	✓
				27	Sales R&A-W.R. Price	041
					Sales Tax Payable	241
	421 30		888	27	Advertising Expense	618
	369 90			27	Accounts Rec.-S.W. Novak	121
2843 78				28	Cash + bank credit card sales for wk.	✓
	32 15		889	28	Telephone Expense	617
	73 28		890	28	Heating & Lighting Exp.	615
	228 00		891	28	Daniel Hays Co.	✓
15380 59	17323 58	767 50		31	Store Equipment 9,859.84	181
					Accts. Pay.-Webster Safe+Lock Co	231
1543 04				31	Cash + bank, credit card sales for wk.	✓
	698 55		892	31	Salaries + Commissions Exp.	613
					FICA Tax Payable	251
					Employees Income Tax Pay.	261
				31	Payroll Tax Expense	614
					FICA Tax Payable	251
					FUTA Tax Payable	271
					State Unemployment Tax Pay.	281
	61 22		893	31	Lynn C. Boyd, Drawing	031
					Supplies	151
					Advertising Expense	618
					Charitable Contributions Exp.	623
					Miscellaneous Expense 10,643.11	624
16923 63	18583 35	767 50				
(111)	(111)	(052)				

Boyd's Clothiers — Combined Cash Journal (Left Page)
(concluded)

FOR MONTH OF *December* 19 —   PAGE 48

	GENERAL DEBIT	GENERAL CREDIT	ACCOUNTS PAYABLE 231 Dr.	ACCOUNTS RECEIVABLE 121 Cr.	SALES 411 Cr.	SALES TAX PAYABLE 241 Cr.	
1	3501 27	244 37	10954 00	1850 33	6458 03	322 91	1
2			1695 00				2
3			543 75				3
4		66 00	66 00				4
5	1000 00						5
6					3338 60	166 94	6
7	4501 27 / 16 80	310 37	13268 75	1850 33	9796 63	489 85	7
8				100 00			8
9				300 00			9
10	21 50			22 58			10
11	1 08						11
12	421 30						12
13	369 90						13
14					2708 35	135 43	14
15	32 15						15
16	73 28						16
17	5437 28	310 37	228 00 / 13486 75	2272 91	12504 98	625 28	17
18	562 00						18
19		562 00					19
20					1469 55	73 49	20
21	884 20						21
22		53 05					22
23		132 60					23
24	56 37						24
25		53 05					25
26		52					26
27		2 80					27
28	10 00						28
29	27 48						29
30	11 09						30
31	5 00						31
32	7 65						32
33	7001 07	1114 39	13486 75	2272 91	13974 53	698 77	33
34	(✓)	(✓)	(231)	(121)	(411)	(241)	34
35							35
36							36
37							37

Boyd's Clothiers — Combined Cash Journal (Right Page)
(concluded)

PAGE 28　　　　　　　　　PETTY CASH DISBURSEMENTS

	DAY	DESCRIPTION	VOU. NO.	TOTAL AMOUNT	031	151	
1		AMOUNTS FORWARDED					1
2	7	Postage stamps　　Balance 100.00	73	10 00		10 00	2
3	7	Messenger fee	74	3 00			3
4	12	Boy Scouts of America　87.00	75	5 00		10 00	4
5	12	Lynn C. Boyd, personal use　72.00	76	10 00	10 00	10 00	5
6	19	Advertising	77	6 29			6
7	19	Supplies	78	8 35		8 35	7
8	19	Miscellaneous expense　55.61	79	1 75			8
9	26	Advertising	80	4 80	10 00	18 35	9
10	26	Supplies	81	9 13		9 13	10
11	26	Miscellaneous expense　38.78	82	2 90			11
12				61 22	10 00	27 48	12
13	31	Balance		38.78			13
14	31	Received in fund		61.22			14
15		Total		100.00			15

Boyd's Clothiers — Petty Cash Disbursements Record (Left Page)

ACCOUNT First National Bank　　　　　　　ACCOUNT NO. 111

DATE	ITEM	POST. REF.	DEBIT	CREDIT	BALANCE DEBIT	BALANCE CREDIT
19-- Dec. 1	Balance	✓			1230283	
31		CJ48	1692363			
31		CJ48		1858335	1064311	

ACCOUNT Petty Cash Fund　　　　　　　ACCOUNT NO. 112

DATE	ITEM	POST. REF.	DEBIT	CREDIT	BALANCE DEBIT	BALANCE CREDIT
19-- Dec. 1	Balance	✓			10000	

ACCOUNT Accounts Receivable　　　　　　　ACCOUNT NO. 121

DATE	ITEM	POST. REF.	DEBIT	CREDIT	BALANCE DEBIT	BALANCE CREDIT
19-- Dec. 1	Balance	✓			296599	
27		CJ48	36990			
31		S44	229733			
31		CJ48		227291	336031	

ACCOUNT Allowance for Doubtful Accounts　　　　　　　ACCOUNT NO. 012

DATE	ITEM	POST. REF.	DEBIT	CREDIT	BALANCE DEBIT	BALANCE CREDIT
19-- Dec. 1	Balance	✓				5922

Boyd's Clothiers — General Ledger

FOR MONTH OF *December* 19--   PAGE 28

DISTRIBUTION OF CHARGES

	618	623	624				ACCOUNT	AMOUNT	
1									1
2									2
3			3 00 / 3 00						3
4		5 00							4
5		5 00	3 00						5
6	6 29								6
7									7
8	6 29	5 00	1 75 / 4 75						8
9	4 80								9
10									10
11	11 09	5 00	2 90 / 7 65						11
12	11 09	5 00	7 65						12
13									13
14									14
15									15

Boyd's Clothiers — Petty Cash Disbursements Record (Right Page)

ACCOUNT *Merchandise Inventory*   ACCOUNT NO. 131

DATE	ITEM	POST. REF.	DEBIT	CREDIT	BALANCE DEBIT	BALANCE CREDIT
19-- Dec. 1	Balance	✓			27632 40	

ACCOUNT *Prepaid Insurance*   ACCOUNT NO. 141

DATE	ITEM	POST. REF.	DEBIT	CREDIT	BALANCE DEBIT	BALANCE CREDIT
19-- Dec. 1	Balance	✓			562 60	

ACCOUNT *Supplies*   ACCOUNT NO. 151

DATE	ITEM	POST. REF.	DEBIT	CREDIT	BALANCE DEBIT	BALANCE CREDIT
19-- Dec. 1	Balance	✓			230 28	
31		CJ48	27 48		257 76	

ACCOUNT *Store Equipment*   ACCOUNT NO. 181

DATE	ITEM	POST. REF.	DEBIT	CREDIT	BALANCE DEBIT	BALANCE CREDIT
19-- Dec. 1	Balance	✓			5031 60	
31		CJ48	562 00		5593 60	

Boyd's Clothiers — General Ledger (*continued*)

ACCOUNT *Accumulated Depreciation – Store Equipment* ACCOUNT NO. *018*

DATE	ITEM	POST. REF.	DEBIT	CREDIT	BALANCE DEBIT	BALANCE CREDIT
19-- Dec. 1	Balance	✓				86210

ACCOUNT *Notes Payable* ACCOUNT NO. *211*

DATE	ITEM	POST. REF.	DEBIT	CREDIT	BALANCE DEBIT	BALANCE CREDIT
19-- Dec. 1	Balance	✓				300000

ACCOUNT *Accounts Payable* ACCOUNT NO. *231*

DATE	ITEM	POST. REF.	DEBIT	CREDIT	BALANCE DEBIT	BALANCE CREDIT
19-- Dec. 1	Balance	✓				757200
31		CJ48		56200		
31		P32		969305		
31		CJ48	1348675			434030

ACCOUNT *Sales Tax Payable* ACCOUNT NO. *241*

DATE	ITEM	POST. REF.	DEBIT	CREDIT	BALANCE DEBIT	BALANCE CREDIT
19-- Dec. 1	Balance	✓				91214
6		CJ47	91214		—0—	—0—
9		CJ47	425			
27		CJ48	108			
31		S44		10942		
31		CJ47		69877		80286

ACCOUNT *FICA Tax Payable* ACCOUNT NO. *251*

DATE	ITEM	POST. REF.	DEBIT	CREDIT	BALANCE DEBIT	BALANCE CREDIT
19-- Dec. 1	Balance	✓				21628
10		CJ47	21628		—0—	—0—
14		CJ47		5356		
14		CJ47		5356		
31		CJ48		5305		
31		CJ48		5305		21322

ACCOUNT *Employees Income Tax Payable* ACCOUNT NO. *261*

DATE	ITEM	POST. REF.	DEBIT	CREDIT	BALANCE DEBIT	BALANCE CREDIT
19-- Dec. 1	Balance	✓				28440
10		CJ47	28440		—0—	—0—
14		CJ47		13390		
31		CJ48		13260		26650

Boyd's Clothiers — General Ledger (*continued*)

ACCOUNT *FUTA Tax Payable*   ACCOUNT NO. *271*

DATE		ITEM	POST. REF.	DEBIT	CREDIT	BALANCE	
						DEBIT	CREDIT
19-- Dec.	1	Balance	✓				82 96
	14		CJ47		52		
	31		CJ48		52		84 00

ACCOUNT *State Unemployment Tax Payable*   ACCOUNT NO. *281*

DATE		ITEM	POST. REF.	DEBIT	CREDIT	BALANCE	
						DEBIT	CREDIT
19-- Dec.	1	Balance	✓				107 77
	14		CJ47		283		
	31		CJ48		280		113 40

ACCOUNT *Lynn C. Boyd, Capital*   ACCOUNT NO. *311*

DATE		ITEM	POST. REF.	DEBIT	CREDIT	BALANCE	
						DEBIT	CREDIT
19-- Dec.	1	Balance	✓				25 635 19

ACCOUNT *Lynn C. Boyd, Drawing*   ACCOUNT NO. *031*

DATE		ITEM	POST. REF.	DEBIT	CREDIT	BALANCE	
						DEBIT	CREDIT
19-- Dec.	1	Balance	✓			22 405 80	
	21		CJ48	1 000 00			
	31		CJ48	10 00		23 415 80	

ACCOUNT *Sales*   ACCOUNT NO. *411*

DATE		ITEM	POST. REF.	DEBIT	CREDIT	BALANCE	
						DEBIT	CREDIT
19-- Dec.	1	Balance	✓				186 581 21
	31		S44		2 187 91		
	31		CJ48		13 974 53		202 743 65

ACCOUNT *Sales Returns and Allowances*   ACCOUNT NO. *041*

DATE		ITEM	POST. REF.	DEBIT	CREDIT	BALANCE	
						DEBIT	CREDIT
19-- Dec.	1	Balance	✓			2 854 85	
	9		CJ47	84 95			
	27		CJ48	21 50		2 961 30	

Boyd's Clothiers — General Ledger (*continued*)

ACCOUNT *Purchases*   ACCOUNT NO. 511

DATE	ITEM	POST. REF.	DEBIT	CREDIT	BALANCE DEBIT	BALANCE CREDIT
19-- Dec. 1	Balance	✓			1185127 2	
2		CJ47	53 18			
31		P32	9693 05		1282589 5	

ACCOUNT *Purchases Returns and Allowances*   ACCOUNT NO. 051

DATE	ITEM	POST. REF.	DEBIT	CREDIT	BALANCE DEBIT	BALANCE CREDIT
19-- Dec. 1	Balance	✓				16551 0
20		CJ48		66 00		17211 0

ACCOUNT *Purchases Discount*   ACCOUNT NO. 052

DATE	ITEM	POST. REF.	DEBIT	CREDIT	BALANCE DEBIT	BALANCE CREDIT
19-- Dec. 1	Balance	✓				69220 4
31		CJ48		767 50		76895 4

ACCOUNT *Rent Expense*   ACCOUNT NO. 611

DATE	ITEM	POST. REF.	DEBIT	CREDIT	BALANCE DEBIT	BALANCE CREDIT
19-- Dec. 1	Balance	✓			77000 0	
2		CJ47	7000 00		84000 0	

ACCOUNT *Salaries and Commissions Expense*   ACCOUNT NO. 613

DATE	ITEM	POST. REF.	DEBIT	CREDIT	BALANCE DEBIT	BALANCE CREDIT
19-- Dec. 1	Balance	✓			1953950	
14		CJ47	8927 0			
31		CJ48	8842 0		213164 0	

ACCOUNT *Payroll Taxes Expense*   ACCOUNT NO. 614

DATE	ITEM	POST. REF.	DEBIT	CREDIT	BALANCE DEBIT	BALANCE CREDIT
19-- Dec. 1	Balance	✓			17033 0	
14		CJ47	569 1			
31		CJ48	563 7		18165 8	

ACCOUNT *Heating and Lighting Expense*   ACCOUNT NO. 615

DATE	ITEM	POST. REF.	DEBIT	CREDIT	BALANCE DEBIT	BALANCE CREDIT
19-- Dec. 1	Balance	✓			6863 6	
28		CJ48	732 8		7596 4	

Boyd's Clothiers — General Ledger (*continued*)

ACCOUNT *Telephone Expense*   ACCOUNT NO. *617*

DATE		ITEM	POST. REF.	DEBIT	CREDIT	BALANCE DEBIT	BALANCE CREDIT
19-- Dec.	1	Balance	✓			340 15	
	28		CJ48	32 15		372 30	

ACCOUNT *Advertising Expense*   ACCOUNT NO. *618*

DATE		ITEM	POST. REF.	DEBIT	CREDIT	BALANCE DEBIT	BALANCE CREDIT
19-- Dec.	1	Balance	✓			8219 82	
	6		CJ47	61 04			
	27		CJ48	421 30			
	31		CJ48	11 09		8713 25	

ACCOUNT *Bank Credit Card Expense*   ACCOUNT NO. *619*

DATE		ITEM	POST. REF.	DEBIT	CREDIT	BALANCE DEBIT	BALANCE CREDIT
19-- Dec.	1	Balance	✓			2179 92	
	4		CJ47	235 42		2415 34	

ACCOUNT *Charitable Contributions Expense*   ACCOUNT NO. *623*

DATE		ITEM	POST. REF.	DEBIT	CREDIT	BALANCE DEBIT	BALANCE CREDIT
19-- Dec.	1	Balance	✓			345 00	
	31		CJ48	5 00		350 00	

ACCOUNT *Miscellaneous Expense*   ACCOUNT NO. *624*

DATE		ITEM	POST. REF.	DEBIT	CREDIT	BALANCE DEBIT	BALANCE CREDIT
19-- Dec.	1	Balance	✓			461 20	
	23		CJ48	16 80			
	31		CJ48	7 65		485 65	

ACCOUNT *Interest Expense*   ACCOUNT NO. *711*

DATE		ITEM	POST. REF.	DEBIT	CREDIT	BALANCE DEBIT	BALANCE CREDIT
19-- Dec.	1	Balance	✓			116 09	

Boyd's Clothiers — General Ledger (*concluded*)

NAME *J. J. Anders*
ADDRESS *11939 Rocky, St. Louis, MO 63141*

DATE	ITEM	POST. REF.	DEBIT	CREDIT	BALANCE
19-- Dec. 5		S2578	8938		8938

NAME *J. E. Buelt*
ADDRESS *9140 Fox Estates, St. Louis, MO 63126*

DATE	ITEM	POST. REF.	DEBIT	CREDIT	BALANCE
19-- Dec. 1	Dr. Balance	✓			61486
11		C		30000	31486

NAME *J. L. Burnett*
ADDRESS *15 Forester, St. Louis, MO 63011*

DATE	ITEM	POST. REF.	DEBIT	CREDIT	BALANCE
19-- Dec. 5		S235C	56485		56485

NAME *L. V. Freeman*
ADDRESS *7362 S. Yorkshire, St. Louis, MO 63126*

DATE	ITEM	POST. REF.	DEBIT	CREDIT	BALANCE
19-- Dec. 1	Dr. Balance	✓			43240
11		C		20000	23240
24		S256C	1885		25125

NAME *S. W. Novak*
ADDRESS *216 Hawkesbury, St. Louis, MO 63135*

DATE	ITEM	POST. REF.	DEBIT	CREDIT	BALANCE
19-- Dec. 1	Dr. Balance	✓			36990
17		C		36990	—0—
27	N S F	✓	36990		36990

NAME *E. E. Palmer*
ADDRESS *1129 Mackinac, St. Louis, MO 63141*

DATE	ITEM	POST. REF.	DEBIT	CREDIT	BALANCE
19-- Dec. 1	Dr. Balance	✓			11215
18		S246D	7156		18371

Boyd's Clothiers — Accounts Receivable Ledger

NAME *W. R. Price*

ADDRESS *1629 Rathford Court, St. Louis, MO 63141*

DATE		ITEM	POST. REF.	DEBIT	CREDIT	BALANCE
19-- Dec.	1	Dr. Balance	✓			14219
	18		S277Q	16182		30401
	26		C		10000	20401
	27		CM.12		2258	18143

NAME *C. W. Reed*

ADDRESS *761 Cella, St. Louis, MO 63124*

DATE		ITEM	POST. REF.	DEBIT	CREDIT	BALANCE
19-- Dec.	1	Dr. Balance	✓			31406
	24		S249D	20099		51505
	26		C		30000	21505

NAME *K. E. Vivian*

ADDRESS *1830 Patterson Rd., Florissant, MO 63031*

DATE		ITEM	POST. REF.	DEBIT	CREDIT	BALANCE
19-- Dec.	1	Dr. Balance	✓			8211
	11		C		8211	-0-
	18		S239C	34640		34640

NAME *D. P. Walsh*

ADDRESS *113 Grether, St. Louis, MO 63135*

DATE		ITEM	POST. REF.	DEBIT	CREDIT	BALANCE
19-- Dec.	1	Dr. Balance	✓			31723
	4		C		31723	-0-
	5		S271Q	45401		45401
	24		S262B	1948		47349

NAME *C. D. Williams*

ADDRESS *617 Rebecca, St. Charles, MO 63301*

DATE		ITEM	POST. REF.	DEBIT	CREDIT	BALANCE
19-- Dec.	10		S243D	25835		25835

Boyd's Clothiers — Accounts Receivable Ledger (*continued*)

NAME *C. E. Wuller*
ADDRESS *10711 St. Mathew Ln., St. Ann, MO 63074*

DATE	ITEM	POST. REF.	DEBIT	CREDIT	BALANCE
19-- Dec. 1	Dr. Balance	✓			36757
17		C		36757	—0—

NAME *J. F. Yager*
ADDRESS *5 Brookston Ct., Kirkwood, MO 63122*

DATE	ITEM	POST. REF.	DEBIT	CREDIT	BALANCE
19-- Dec. 1	Dr. Balance	✓			21352
6		S2598	11164		32516
17		C		21352	11164

Boyd's Clothiers — Accounts Receivable Ledger (*concluded*)

NAME *Aris Glove Co.*
ADDRESS *10 East 38th. St., New York, NY 10016*

DATE	ITEM	POST. REF.	DEBIT	CREDIT	BALANCE
19-- Dec. 1	Cr. Balance	✓			33000
2		Ck869	33000		—0—
13	12/10, n/30	P208		41250	41250
20		CB291	6600		34650

NAME *Brown Shoe Co.*
ADDRESS *8300 Maryland Ave., St. Louis, MO 63105*

DATE	ITEM	POST. REF.	DEBIT	CREDIT	BALANCE
19-- Dec. 1	Cr. Balance	✓			47000
5		Ck870	46060		
5	Discount		940		—0—
31		P212		70500	70500

NAME *Damon, Inc.*
ADDRESS *16 E. 34th. St., New York, NY 10016*

DATE	ITEM	POST. REF.	DEBIT	CREDIT	BALANCE
19-- Dec. 1	Cr. Balance	✓			46000
5		Ck871	43240		
5	Discount		2760		—0—
6	12/4–6/10, n/30	P207		115000	115000
12		Ck882	108100		
12	Discount		6900		—0—

Boyd's Clothiers — Accounts Payable Ledger

NAME *Daniel Hays Co.*
ADDRESS *Johnstown, N.Y. 12095*

DATE		ITEM	POST. REF.	DEBIT	CREDIT	BALANCE
19-- Dec.	1	Cr. Balance	✓			68400
	3	11/30 – n/30	P204		22800	91200
	9		Ck878	68400		22800
	28		Ck891	22800		—0—

(Gen Ledger) NAME *El Jay Co.*
ADDRESS *411 Anderson, Fairview, N.J. 07022*

DATE		ITEM	POST. REF.	DEBIT	CREDIT	BALANCE
19-- Dec.	1	Cr. Balance	✓			226000
	5		Ck872	207920		
	5	Discount		18080		—0—
	13	12/10 – 8/10, n/30	P209		169500	169500
	19		Ck884	155940		
	19	Discount		13560		—0—
	31	12/26 – 8/10, n/30	P213		67800	67800

NAME *Hanes Corporation*
ADDRESS *Winston-Salem, N.C. 27102*

DATE		ITEM	POST. REF.	DEBIT	CREDIT	BALANCE
19-- Dec.	3	11/30 – 8/10 EOM	P205		74400	74400
	9		Ck879	68448		
	9	Discount		5952		—0—
	31	12/27 – 8/10 EOM	P214		148880	148880

NAME *Huk-a-Poo, Inc.*
ADDRESS *411 Broadway, New York, N.Y. 10012*

DATE		ITEM	POST. REF.	DEBIT	CREDIT	BALANCE
19-- Dec.	13	12/11 – 8/10, n/30	P210		54375	54375
	19		Ck885	50025		
	19	Discount		4350		—0—

Boyd's Clothiers — Accounts Payable Ledger (*continued*)

NAME *Mary Neuman Co.*
ADDRESS *9 W. 57th St., New York, N.Y. 10019*

DATE	ITEM	POST. REF.	DEBIT	CREDIT	BALANCE
19-- Dec. 1	Cr. Balance	✓			80000
5		Ck 873	78400		
5	Discount		1600		—0—
31		P 215		60000	60000

NAME *Julius Resnick, Inc.*
ADDRESS *46 E. 32d St., New York, N.Y. 10016*

DATE	ITEM	POST. REF.	DEBIT	CREDIT	BALANCE
19-- Dec. 3	11/30 - 3/10 EOM	P 206		148800	148800
9		Ck 880	144336		
9	Discount		4464		—0—

NAME *Schoeneman, Inc.*
ADDRESS *Box 17, Owings Mills, M.D. 21117*

DATE	ITEM	POST. REF.	DEBIT	CREDIT	BALANCE
19-- Dec. 1	Cr. Balance	✓			120000
5		Ck 874	112800		
5	Discount		7200		—0—

NAME *Jacob Siegel Co.*
ADDRESS *4725 N. Broad St., Philadelphia, PA 19141*

DATE	ITEM	POST. REF.	DEBIT	CREDIT	BALANCE
19-- Dec. 30	12/27 - 6/10, n/30	P 211		130000	130000

NAME *Smart Pants, Inc.*
ADDRESS *1407 Broadway, New York, N.Y. 10012*

DATE	ITEM	POST. REF.	DEBIT	CREDIT	BALANCE
19-- Dec. 1	Cr. Balance	✓			136800
5		Ck 875	125856		
5	Discount		10944		—0—

Boyd's Clothiers — Accounts Payable Ledger (*continued*)

NAME *Webster, Safe & Lock Co*

ADDRESS *916 Washington Ave., St. Louis, MO 63101*

DATE	ITEM	POST. REF.	DEBIT	CREDIT	BALANCE
19-- Dec. 31	12/30 – 2/30, n/60	CJ48		56200	56200

Boyd's Clothiers — Accounts Payable Ledger (*concluded*)

Boyd's Clothiers
Trial Balance

Account	Acct. No.	November 30, 19— Dr. Balance	November 30, 19— Cr. Balance	December 31, 19— Dr. Balance	December 31, 19— Cr. Balance
First National Bank	111	1230283		1064311	
Petty Cash Fund	112	10000		10000	
Accounts Receivable	121	296599		336031	
Allow. for Doubt. Accts.	012		5922		5922
Merchandise Inventory	131	2763240		2763240	
Prepaid Insurance	141	56260		56260	
Supplies	151	23028		25776	
Store Equipment	181	503160		559360	
Accum. Depr.-Store Equip.	018		86210		86210
Notes Payable	211		300000		300000
Accounts Payable	231		757200		434030
Sales Tax Payable	241		91214		80286
FICA Tax Payable	251		21628		21322
Employees Inc. Tax Pay.	261		28440		26650
FUTA Tax Payable	271		8296		8400
State Unemp. Tax Pay.	281		10777		11340
Lynn C. Boyd, Capital	311		2563519		2563519
Lynn C. Boyd, Drawing	031	2240580		2341580	
Sales	411		18658121		20274365
Sales Ret. and Allow.	041	285485		296130	
Purchases	511	11851272		12825895	
Pur. Ret. and Allow.	051		165510		172110
Purchases Discount	052		692204		768954
Rent Expense	611	770000		840000	
Sal. and Comm. Exp.	613	1953950		2131640	
Payroll Taxes Expense	614	170330		181658	
Heating and Light Exp.	615	68636		75964	
Telephone Expense	617	34015		37230	
Advertising Expense	618	821982		871325	
Bank Credit Card Exp.	619	217992		241534	
Charitable Cont. Exp.	623	34500		35000	
Miscellaneous Exp.	624	46120		48565	
Interest Expense	711	11609		11609	
		23389041	23389041	24753108	24753108
		23389041	23389041	24753108	24753108

Boyd's Clothiers — Trial Balance

Boyd's Clothiers
Schedule of Accounts Receivable

	Nov. 30, 19-	Dec. 31, 19-
J. J. Anders		89.38
J. E. Buelt	614.86	314.86
J. L. Burnett		564.85
L. V. Freeman	432.40	251.25
S. W. Novak	369.90	369.90
E. E. Palmer	112.15	183.71
W. B. Price	142.19	181.43
C. W. Reed	314.06	215.05
K. E. Vivian	82.11	346.40
D. P. Walsh	317.23	473.49
R. D. Williams		258.35
C. E. Wuller	367.57	
J. F. Yager	213.52	111.64
	2965.99	3360.31

Boyd's Clothiers — Schedule of Accounts Receivable

Boyd's Clothiers
Schedule of Accounts Payable

	Nov. 30, 19-	Dec. 31, 19-
Aris Glove Co.	330.00	346.50
Brown Shoe Co.	470.00	705.00
Damon, Inc.	460.00	
El Jay Co	2260.00	678.00
Hanes Corporation		148.80
Daniel Hays Co	684.00	
Mary Neuman Co.	800.00	600.00
Schoeneman, Inc.	1200.00	
Jacob Siegel Co.		1300.00
Smart Pants, Inc.	1368.00	
Webster Safe & Lock Co.		562.00
	7572.00	4340.30

Boyd's Clothiers — Schedule of Accounts Payable

Report No. 8-2

Complete Report No. 8-2 in the study assignments and submit your working papers to the instructor for approval. After completing this report, continue with the textbook discussion in Chapter 9 until the next report is required.

Chapter 9

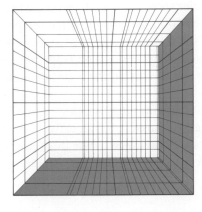

THE PERIODIC SUMMARY

One of the major reasons for keeping accounting records is to accumulate information that will make it possible to prepare periodic summaries of both **(1)** the revenue and expenses of the business during a specified period and **(2)** the assets, liabilities, and owner's equity of the business at a specified date. A trial balance of the general ledger accounts will provide most of the information that is required for these summaries (the income statement and the balance sheet). However, the trial balance does not supply the data in a form that is easily interpreted, nor does it reflect changes in the accounting elements that have not been represented by ordinary business transactions. Therefore, at the end of a fiscal period it is necessary, first, to determine the kind and amounts of changes that the accounts do not reflect and to adjust the accounts accordingly and, second, to recast the information into the form of an income statement and a balance sheet. These two steps are often referred to as "the periodic summary."

END-OF-PERIOD WORK SHEET

It has already been mentioned that an end-of-period work sheet is a device that assists the accountant in three ways. It facilitates **(1)** the preparing of the financial statements, **(2)** the making of needed adjustments in the accounts, and **(3)** the closing of the temporary owner's equity accounts.

In most cases the accountant is under some pressure to produce the income statement and the balance sheet as soon as possible after the period has ended. The end-of-period work sheet is of greatest assistance in helping the accountant meet this need for promptness. The help that the work sheet gives in making adjustments and in closing the accounts is secondary in importance.

Work sheets are not financial statements; they are devices used to assist the accountant in performing certain tasks. Ordinarily it is only the accountant who uses (or even sees) a work sheet. For this reason a work sheet (sometimes called a *working trial balance*) is usually prepared in pencil.

A work sheet for a retail store

While an end-of-period work sheet can be in any one of several forms, a common and widely used arrangement involves ten amount columns. The amount columns are used in pairs. The first pair of amount columns is for the trial balance. The data to be recorded consist of the name, number, and debit or credit balance of each account. Debit balances should be entered in the left-hand column and credit balances in the right-hand column. The second pair of amount columns is used to record needed end-of-period adjustments. The third pair of amount columns is used to show the account balances as adjusted. This pair of amount columns is headed "Adjusted Trial Balance" because its purpose is to show that the debit and credit account balances as adjusted are equal in amount. The fourth pair of amount columns is for the adjusted balances of the expense and revenue accounts. This pair of columns is headed "Income Statement" since the amounts shown will be reported in that statement. The fifth, and last, pair of amount columns is headed "Balance Sheet" and shows the adjusted account balances that will be reported in that statement.

To illustrate the preparation and use of the end-of-period work sheet, the example of the accounts of Boyd's Clothiers will be continued. The journals and ledgers for this business for the month of December were reproduced in the preceding chapter. In this chapter the income statement for the year and the balance sheet at the end of the year will be reproduced, showing the use of a work sheet as a device for summarizing the data to be presented in those statements.

The work sheet for Boyd's Clothiers

The end-of-year work sheet for this business is reproduced on pages 230 and 231. Following is a description and discussion of the steps that were followed in the preparation of this work sheet. Each step should be studied carefully with frequent reference to the work sheet itself.

Trial Balance Columns. The trial balance of the general ledger accounts as of December 31 was entered in the first pair of amount columns. This trial balance is the same as the one shown on page 225 except that all of the account titles were included in the work sheet list even though certain of the accounts had no balances at this point.

The Trial Balance Debit and Credit columns were totaled. The totals should be equal. If not, the cause of any discrepancy must be found and corrected before the preparation of the work sheet can proceed.

Adjustments Columns. The second pair of amount columns on the work sheet was used to record certain entries that were necessary to reflect various changes that had occurred during the year in some of the accounting elements. In this case, adjustments were needed: **(1)** to remove the amount of the beginning-of-year merchandise inventory and to record the amount of the end-of-year inventory; **(2)** to record the amount of interest expense incurred but not paid; **(3)** to record the amount of bank credit card expense for December that will not be deducted from the bank account until early in the following month; **(4)** to record the portions of prepaid insurance expired and of supplies used during the year; **(5)** to record the estimated depreciation expense for the year; and **(6)** to record the estimated amount of expected losses from uncollectible accounts.

Eight complete entries were made in the Adjustments columns to reflect these changes. When an account was debited, the amount was entered on the same horizontal line as the name of the account and in the Adjustments Debit column. Amounts credited were entered, of course, in the Credit column. Each such entry made on the work sheet was identified by a small letter in parentheses to facilitate cross-reference. Following is an explanation of each of the entries:

Entry (a): In order to remove the amount of the beginning inventory of merchandise from the asset account and at the same time to include it in the determination of net income for the current year, Expense and Revenue Summary, Account No. 321, was debited, and Merchandise Inventory, Account No. 131, was credited for $27,632.40. This amount was the calculated cost of the inventory at the end of the preceding year (the beginning of the year under consideration). The amount had been in the merchandise inventory account as a debit since the accounts were adjusted as of December 31 a year ago.

Entry (b): This entry recorded the calculated cost of the merchandise on hand December 31 — often referred to as the year-end inventory. The calculation was based on a physical count of the merchandise in stock at the close of the year. The cost of the merchandise in stock was recorded by debiting Merchandise Inventory, Account No. 131, and by crediting Expense and Revenue Summary, Account No. 321, for $25,074.05.

Boyd's Clothiers
Work Sheet
For the Year Ended December 31, 19—

No.	Account	Acct. No.	Trial Balance Debit	Trial Balance Credit	Adjustments Debit	Adjustments Credit	Adj. Trial Balance Debit	Adj. Trial Balance Credit	Income Statement Debit	Income Statement Credit	Balance Sheet Debit	Balance Sheet Credit
1	First National Bank	111	1064311				1064311				1064311	
2	Petty Cash Fund	112	10000				10000				10000	
3	Accounts Receivable	121	336031				336031				336031	
4	Allowance for Doubtful Accts.	012		5922		(a) 25098		31020				31020
5	Merchandise Inventory	131	2763240		(b) 2507405	(b) 2763240	2507405				2507405	
6	Prepaid Insurance	141	56260			(c) 28130	28130				28130	
7	Supplies	151	26776			(f) 19776	6000				6000	
8	Store Equipment	181	559360				559360				559360	
9	Accum. Deprec.—Store Equip.	018		86210		(g) 50316		136526				136526
10	Notes Payable	211		300000				300000				300000
11	Accrued Interest Payable	221				(e) 3733		3733				3733
12	Accounts Payable	231		434030				434030				434030
13	Sales Tax Payable	241		80286				80286				80286
14	F.I.C.O. Tax Payable	251		21322				21322				21322
15	Employees Income Tax Pay.	261		26650				26650				26650
16	F.U.T.O. Tax Payable	271		8400				8400				8400
17	State Unemployment Tax Pay.	281		1340				1340				1340
18	Accrued Bank Credit Card Exp.	291				(d) 20962		20962				20962
19	Lynn C. Boyd, Capital	311		2563519				2563519				2563519
20	Lynn C. Boyd, Drawing	031	2341580				2341580				2341580	
21	Exp. and Rev. Summary	321			(b1) 2763240	(b2) 2507405	2763240	2507405	2763240	2507405		
22	Sales	411		20214365				20214365		20214365		
23	Sales Returns and Allow.	041	296130				296130		296130			
24	Purchases	511	12825895				12825895		12825895			
25	Purchases Returns and Allow.	051		172110				172110		172110		
26	Purchases Discount	052		768954				768954		768954		
27	Rent Expense	611	840000				840000		840000			
28	Depreciation Expense	612			(g) 50316		50316		50316			
29	Sal. and Commissions Exp.	613	2131640				2131640		2131640			

Account Title	Acct. No.	Trial Balance Debit	Trial Balance Credit	Adjustments Debit	Adjustments Credit	Adjusted Trial Balance Debit	Adjusted Trial Balance Credit	Income Statement Debit	Income Statement Credit	Balance Sheet Debit	Balance Sheet Credit
Payroll Taxes Expense	614	181653				181653		181653			
Heating and Lighting Exp.	615	75964				75964		75964			
Supplies Expense	616			(A) 19776		19776		19776			
Telephone Expense	617	37230				37230		37230			
Advertising Expense	618	871325				871325		871325			
Bank Credit Card Expense	619	241534		(A) 20962		262496		262496			
Uncollectible Accounts Exp.	621			(A) 25098		25098		25098			
Insurance Expense	622			(A) 28130		28130		28130			
Charitable Contributions Exp.	623	35000				35000		35000			
Miscellaneous Expense	624	48565				48565		48565			
Interest Expense	711	11609		(B) 3733		15342		15342			
	12	24753108		5418660	5418660	27360622	27360622	20507805	23722834	6852817	3637788
Net Income	13							3215029			3215029
	14							23722834	23722834	6852817	6852817

Boyd's Clothiers — Ten Column Work Sheet

Entry (*c*): This entry recorded the accrued interest expense that had been incurred but not paid by debiting Interest Expense, Account No. 711, and by crediting Accrued Interest Payable, Account No. 221, for $37.33. The December 31 trial balance shows that Notes Payable had a credit balance of $3,000. This related to an 8 percent, 6-month note dated November 5. From November 5 to December 31 was 56 days. Interest at the rate of 8 percent per year on $3,000 for 56 days is $37.33.

Entry (*d*): This entry recorded the expense of the deduction that will be made by the bank during January for BankAmericard and Master Charge vouchers deposited during December. These amounted to $6,987.27. The bank will deduct 3 percent of this amount from the checking account. Since the amount, $209.62 (3 percent of $6,987.27), is really an expense for the year just ended, this adjustment gets it into the calculation of the net income for the past year. The adjustment was recorded by a debit to Bank Credit Card Expense, Account No. 619, and a credit to Accrued Bank Credit Card Expense, Account No. 291.

Entry (*e*): This entry recorded the insurance expense for the year by debiting Insurance Expense, Account No. 622, and by crediting Prepaid Insurance, Account No. 141, for $281.30. The December 31 trial balance shows that Prepaid Insurance had a debit balance of $562.60. This amount was the cost of a two-year policy dated January 2 of the year under consideration. By December 31 one year had elapsed and, thus, one half of the premium paid had become an expense.

Entry (*f*): This entry recorded the calculated cost of the supplies used during the year by debiting Supplies Expense, Account No. 616, and by crediting Supplies, Account No. 151, for $197.76. The December 31 trial balance shows that Supplies had a debit balance of $257.76. This amount was the sum of the cost of any supplies on hand at the start of the year, plus the cost of supplies purchased during the year. A physical count of the supplies on hand December 31 was made and the cost determined to be $60. Thus, supplies that cost $197.76 ($257.76 − $60) had been used during the year.

Entry (*g*): This entry recorded the calculated depreciation expense for the year by debiting Depreciation Expense, Account No. 612, and by crediting Accumulated Depreciation — Store Equipment, Account No. 018, for $503.16. The December 31 trial balance shows that Store Equipment had a debit balance of $5,593.60. This balance represented the $5,031.60 cost of various items of property that had been owned the entire year plus the $562 cost of the safe that was purchased on December 31. Ms. Boyd follows the policy of not calculating any depreciation on assets that have been owned for less than a month. Thus, depreciation expense for the year on store equipment relates to property that had been owned for the entire year. Its cost was $5,031.60. This equipment is being depreciated at the rate of 10 percent a year. Ten percent of $5,031.60 is $503.16.

Entry (h): This entry recorded the estimated uncollectible accounts expense for the year by debiting Uncollectible Accounts Expense, Account No. 621, and by crediting Allowance for Doubtful Accounts, Account No. 012, for $250.98. Guided by past experience, Ms. Boyd estimated that uncollectible accounts losses will be approximately one percent of the total sales on account for the year. Investigation of the records revealed that such sales amounted to $25,098.13. One percent of this amount is $250.98.

After making the required entries in the Adjustments columns of the work sheet, the columns were totaled to prove the equality of the debit and credit entries.

Adjusted Trial Balance Columns. The third pair of amount columns of the work sheet was used for the *adjusted trial balance*. To determine the balance of each account after making the required adjustments, it was necessary to take into consideration the amounts recorded in the first two pairs of amount columns. When an account balance was not affected by entries in the Adjustments columns, the amount in the Trial Balance columns was extended directly to the Adjusted Trial Balance columns.

When an account balance was affected by an entry in the Adjustments columns, the balance recorded in the Trial Balance columns was increased or decreased, as the case might be, by the amount of the adjusting entry. For example, Accumulated Depreciation — Store Equipment was listed in the Trial Balance Credit column as $862.10. Since there was an entry of $503.16 in the Adjustments Credit column, the amount extended to the Adjusted Trial Balance Credit column was found by addition to be $1,365.26 ($862.10 + $503.16). Prepaid Insurance was listed in the Trial Balance Debit column as $562.60. Since there was an entry of $281.30 in the Adjustments Credit column, the amount to be extended to the Adjusted Trial Balance Debit column was found by subtraction to be $281.30 ($562.60 − $281.30).

There is one exception to the procedure just described that relates to the debit and the credit on the line for Expense and Revenue Summary, Account No. 321, in the Adjustments columns. While the $2,558.35 excess of the $27,632.40 debit (the amount of the beginning-of-year merchandise inventory) over the $25,074.05 credit (the amount of the end-of-year merchandise inventory) could be extended to the Adjusted Trial Balance Debit column, it is better to extend both the debit and the credit amounts into the Adjusted Trial Balance columns. The reason is that both amounts are used in the preparation of the income statement and, accordingly, it is helpful to have both amounts appear in the Income Statement columns. Therefore, both amounts are shown in the Adjusted Trial Balance columns.

The Adjusted Trial Balance columns were totaled to prove the equality of the debits and credits.

Income Statement Columns. The fourth pair of amount columns of the work sheet was used to show the amounts that will be reported in the income statement. The manner of extending the debit and credit amounts on the line for Expense and Revenue Summary was mentioned previously. The amounts for sales, purchases returns and allowances, and purchases discount were extended to the Income Statement Credit column. The amounts for sales returns and allowances, purchases, and all of the expenses were extended to the Income Statement Debit column.

The Income Statement columns were totaled. The difference between the totals of these columns is the amount of the increase or the decrease in owner's equity due to net income or net loss during the accounting period. If the total of the credits exceeds the total of the debits, the difference represents the increase in owner's equity due to net income; if the total of the debits exceeds the total of the credits, the difference represents the decrease in owner's equity due to net loss.

Reference to the Income Statement columns of Boyd's Clothiers work sheet will show that the total of the credits amounted to $237,228.34 and the total of the debits amounted to $205,078.05. The difference, amounting to $32,150.29, was the amount of the net income for the year.

Balance Sheet Columns. The fifth pair of amount columns of the work sheet was used to show the amounts that will be reported in the balance sheet. The Balance Sheet columns were totaled. The difference between the totals of these columns also is the amount of the net income or the net loss for the accounting period. If the total of the debits exceeds the total of the credits, the difference represents a net income for the accounting period; if the total of the credits exceeds the total of the debits, the difference represents a net loss for the period. This difference should be the same as the difference between the totals of the Income Statement columns.

Reference to the Balance Sheet columns of the work sheet will show that the total of the debits amounted to $68,528.17 and the total of the credits amounted to $36,377.88. The difference of $32,150.29 represented the amount of the net income for the year.

Completing the Work Sheet. The difference between the totals of the Income Statement columns and the totals of the Balance Sheet columns should be recorded on the next horizontal line below the totals. If the difference represents net income, it should be so designated and recorded in the Income Statement Debit and in the Balance Sheet Credit columns. If, instead, a net loss has been the result, the amount should be so designated and entered in the Income Statement Credit and in the Balance Sheet

Debit columns. Finally, the totals of the Income Statement and Balance Sheet columns, after the net income (or net loss) has been recorded, are entered, and a double line is ruled immediately below the totals.

Proving the Work Sheet. The work sheet provides proof of the arithmetical accuracy of the data that it summarizes. The totals of the Trial Balance columns, the Adjustments columns, and the Adjusted Trial Balance columns must be equal. The amount of the difference between the totals of the Income Statement columns must be exactly the same as the amount of the difference between the totals of the Balance Sheet columns.

The reason why the same amount must be inserted to cause both the Income Statement columns and the Balance Sheet columns to be in balance was mentioned in Chapter 5. Stated slightly differently, the explanation is found in the basic difference between the balance sheet accounts and the income statement accounts, and in an understanding of the real nature of net income (or net loss). The reality of net income is that the assets have increased, or that the liabilities have decreased, or that some combination of both events has taken place during a period of time. Day by day most of these changes have been recorded in the asset and liability accounts in order that they may be kept up to date. However, the effect of the changes on the owner's equity element is not recorded in the permanent owner's equity account. Instead, the changes are recorded in the temporary owner's equity accounts — the revenue and expense accounts.

Thus, at the end of the period after the accounts have been adjusted, each of the asset and liability accounts reflects the amount of that element *at the end of the period.* If, however, there have been no capital investments during the period and any withdrawals have been charged to a drawing account, the balance of the owner's capital account is the amount of the equity *at the beginning of the period.* (All of the changes in owner's equity are shown in the revenue and expense accounts and in the drawing account.)

As applied to the work sheet, this must mean that the Balance Sheet column totals are out of balance by the amount of the change in owner's equity that is due to net income or net loss for the period involved. If there was net income, the assets, in total, are either that much larger, or the liabilities are that much smaller, or some combination of such changes has resulted. In other words, the asset and liability accounts reflect the net income of the period, but the owner's capital account at this point does not. It is only after the temporary accounts are closed at the end of the period and the amount of the net income for the period has been transferred to the owner's capital account that the latter account reflects the net income of the period.

The owner's capital account lacks two things to bring its balance up to date (as are the balances of the asset and liability accounts): **(1)** the decrease due to any withdrawals during the period which is reflected in the debit balance of the drawing account and **(2)** the increase due to any net income for the period. On the work sheet the debit balance of the drawing account is extended to the Balance Sheet Debit column. Thus, all that is needed to cause the Balance Sheet columns to be equal is the amount of the net income for the year — the same amount that is the difference between the totals of the Income Statement columns.

Report No. 9-1

Complete Report No. 9-1 in the study assignments and submit your working papers to the instructor for approval. After completing the report, continue with the following textbook discussion until the next report is required.

THE FINANCIAL STATEMENTS

The financial statements usually consist of **(1)** an income statement and **(2)** a balance sheet. The purpose of an income statement is to summarize the results of operations during an accounting period. The income statement provides information as to the sources of revenue, types of expenses, and the amount of the net income or the net loss for the period. The purpose of a balance sheet is to provide information as to the status of a business at a specified date. The balance sheet shows the kinds and amounts of assets and liabilities and the owner's equity in the business at a specified point in time — usually at the close of business on the last day of the accounting period.

The income statement

A formal statement of the results of the operation of a business during an accounting period is called an *income statement*. Other titles commonly used for this statement include *profit and loss statement*, *income and expense statement*, *revenue and expense statement*, *operating statement*, and *report of earnings*. Whatever the title, the purpose of the statement or report is to show the types and amounts of revenue and expenses that the business had during the period involved, and the resulting net income or net loss for this accounting period.

Importance of the Income Statement. The income statement is now generally considered to be the most important financial statement of a business. A business cannot exist indefinitely unless it has profit or net income. The income statement is essentially a "report card" of the enterprise. The statement provides a basis for judging the overall effectiveness of the management. Decisions as to whether to continue a business, to expand it, or to contract it are often based upon the results as reported in the income statement. Actual and potential creditors are interested in income statements because one of the best reasons for extending credit or for making a loan is that the business is profitable.

Various government agencies are interested in income statements of businesses for a variety of reasons. Regulatory bodies are concerned with the earnings of the enterprises they regulate, because a part of the regulation usually relates to the prices, rates, or fares that may be charged. If the enterprise is either exceptionally profitable or unprofitable, some change in the allowed prices or rates may be needed. Income tax authorities — federal, state, and local — have an interest in business income statements. Net income determination for tax purposes differs somewhat from the calculation of net income for other purposes, but, for a variety of reasons, the tax authorities are interested in both sets of calculations.

Form of the Income Statement. The form of the income statement depends, in part, upon the type of business. For merchandising businesses, the so-called "ladder type" is commonly used. This name is applied because the final net income is calculated on a step-by-step basis. The amount of gross sales is shown first with sales returns and allowances deducted. The difference is *net sales.* Cost of goods sold is next subtracted to arrive at *gross margin* (sometimes called *gross profit*). The portion of the statement down to this point is sometimes called the "trading section." Operating expenses are next listed, and the total of their amounts is subtracted to arrive at the amount of the *operating income.* Finally, the amounts of any "other" revenue are added and any "other" expenses are subtracted to arrive at the final amount of net income (or net loss).

It is essential that the statement be properly headed. The name of the business (or of the individual if it is a professional practice or if the business is operated in the owner's name) should be shown first. The name of the statement is then shown followed by the period of time that the statement covers. It is common practice to state this as, for example, "For the Year Ended December 31, 1977" (or whatever the period and ending date happen to be).

The income statement presented to the owner (or owners) of a business, and to potential creditors or other interested parties is usually in type-written form. Very often, however, the accountant prepares the original statement in pencil or ink on ruled paper. This is used by the typist in preparing typewritten copies. The income statement for Boyd's Clothiers

BOYD'S CLOTHIERS

Income Statement

For the Year Ended December 31, 19—

Operating revenue:			
Sales.....................................			$202,743.65
Less sales returns and allowances....			2,961.30
Net sales..............................			$199,782.35
Cost of goods sold:			
Merchandise inventory, January 1.......		$ 27,632.40	
Purchases.............................	$128,258.95		
Less: Purch. ret. and allow. $1,721.10			
Purchases discounts.. 7,689.54	9,410.64		
Net purchases.........................		118,848.31	
Merchandise available for sale.........		$146,480.71	
Less merchandise inv., December 31...		25,074.05	
Cost of goods sold...................			121,406.66
Gross margin on sales...................			$ 78,375.69
Operating expenses:			
Rent expense...........................		$ 8,400.00	
Depreciation expense...................		503.16	
Salaries and commissions expense.......		21,316.40	
Payroll taxes expense..................		1,816.58	
Heating and lighting expense...........		759.64	
Supplies expense.......................		197.76	
Telephone expense......................		372.30	
Advertising expense....................		8,713.25	
Bank credit card expense...............		2,624.96	
Uncollectible accounts expense.........		250.98	
Insurance expense......................		281.30	
Charitable contributions expense.......		350.00	
Miscellaneous expense..................		485.65	
Total operating expenses.............			46,071.98
Operating income........................			$ 32,303.71
Other expenses:			
Interest expense.......................			153.42
Net income..............................			$ 32,150.29

Boyd's Clothiers — Income Statement

for the year ended December 31, 19--, is shown above. The information needed in preparing the statement was obtained from the work sheet shown on pages 230 and 231.

Income Statement Analysis. There are various procedures employed to assist in the interpretation of income statements. One device is to present income statements for two or more comparable periods in comparative form. If the figures for two periods are shown in adjacent columns, a third column showing the amount of increase or decrease in each element may be shown. This will call attention to changes of major significance.

Another analytical device is to express all, or at least the major, items on the statement as a percent of net sales and then to compare these percentages for two or more periods. For example, if the net sales of $199,782.35 for Boyd's Clothiers for the year just ended are treated as 100 percent, the cost of goods sold which amounted to $121,406.66 was equal to 60.77 percent of net sales; the gross margin on sales which amounted to $78,375.69 was equal to 39.23 percent of net sales; operating expenses which amounted to $46,071.98 were equal to 23.06 percent of net sales; operating income (gross margin less operating expenses) which amounted to $32,303.71 was equal to 16.17 percent of net sales; and net income which amounted to $32,150.29 was equal to 16.09 percent of net sales. A comparison of these percentages with the same data for one or more prior years would reveal trends that would surely be of interest, and perhaps of real concern, to the management of the business.

The balance sheet

A formal statement of the assets, liabilities, and owner's equity in a business at a specified date is known as a *balance sheet*. The title of the statement had its origin in the equality of the elements, that is, in the balance between the sum of the assets and the sum of the liabilities and owner's equity. Sometimes the balance sheet is called a *statement of assets and liabilities*, a *statement of condition*, or a *statement of financial position*. Various other titles are used occasionally.

Importance of the Balance Sheet. The balance sheet of a business is of considerable interest to various parties for several reasons. The owner or owners of a business are interested in the kinds and amounts of assets and liabilities, and the amount of the owner's equity or capital element.

Creditors of the business are interested in the financial position of the enterprise, particularly as it pertains to the claims they have and the prospects for prompt payment. Potential creditors or possible lenders are concerned about the financial position of the business. Their decision as to whether to extend credit or to make loans to the business may depend, in large part, upon the condition of the enterprise as revealed by a balance sheet.

Persons considering buying an ownership interest in a business are greatly interested in the character and amount of the assets and liabilities, though this interest is probably secondary to their concern about the future earnings possibilities.

Finally, various regulatory bodies are interested in the financial position of the businesses that are under their jurisdiction. Examples of regulated businesses include banks, insurance companies, public utilities, railroads, and airlines.

Form of the Balance Sheet. Traditionally, balance sheets have been presented either in *account form* or in *report form*. When the account form is followed, the assets are listed on the left side of the page (or on the left of two facing pages) and the liabilities and owner's equity are listed on the right. This form is similar to the debit-side and credit-side arrangement of the standard ledger account. The balance sheet of Boyd's Clothiers as of December 31, 19––, in account form is reproduced on pages 242 and 243. The data for the preparation of the statement were secured from the work sheet.

When the report form of the balance sheet is followed, the assets, liabilities, and owner's equity elements are exhibited in that order on the page. The balance sheet of John H. Roberts, Management Consultant, was shown in report form on page 117. This arrangement is generally superior when the statement is typed on regular letter-size paper (8½" x 11").

Whichever form is used, it is essential that the statement have the proper heading. This means that three things must be shown: **(1)** The name of the business must be given (or the name of the individual if the business or professional practice is carried on in the name of an individual), followed by **(2)** the name of the statement — usually just "Balance Sheet," and finally **(3)** the date — month, day, and year. Sometimes the expression "As of Close of Business December 31, 1977" (or whatever date is involved) is included. It must be remembered that a balance sheet relates to a particular moment of time.

Classification of Data in the Balance Sheet. The purpose of the balance sheet and of all other financial statements and reports is to convey as much information as possible. This aim is furthered by some classification of the data being reported. As applied to balance sheets, it has become almost universal practice to classify both assets and liabilities as between those that are considered "current" and those that are considered "noncurrent" or "long-lived."

Current Assets. *Current Assets* include cash and all other assets that may be reasonably expected to be realized in cash or sold or consumed during the normal operating cycle of the business. In a merchandising business the current assets usually will include cash, receivables (such as accounts receivable), merchandise inventory, and temporary investments. Prepaid expenses, such as unexpired insurance and unused supplies, are also generally treated as current assets. This is not because such items will be realized in cash, but because they will probably be consumed in a relatively short time.

The asset cash may be represented by one or more accounts, such as bank checking accounts, bank savings accounts, or a petty cash fund.

Reference to Boyd's Clothiers balance sheet will show that cash is listed at $10,743.11. Reference to the work sheet will show that this is made up of two items: the balance in the checking account at the First National Bank, $10,643.11, and the amount of the petty cash fund, $100.

Temporary investments refer to those assets that have been acquired with money that would otherwise have been temporarily idle and unproductive. Such investments usually take the form of corporate stocks, bonds, or notes, or any of several types of government bonds. Quite often the policy is to invest in securities that can be liquidated in a short time with little chance of loss. So-called *marketable securities* are often favored. Assets of the same type may be owned by a business for many years, and, under such circumstances, they would not be classified as temporary investments. It is the matter of intention that indicates whether the investments are to be classified as temporary and included in the current assets or considered as long-term investments and either included in the long-lived asset classification or in a separate classification entitled *Permanent Investments.*

Reference to the balance sheet of Boyd's Clothiers on pages 242 and 243 reveals that the current assets of this business consisted of cash, accounts receivable, merchandise inventory, prepaid insurance, and supplies.

Long-Lived Assets. Property that is used in the operation of a merchandising business may include such assets as land, buildings, office equipment, store equipment, and delivery equipment. Such assets are called *long-lived assets*. Of these assets only land is really permanent; however, all of these assets have a useful life that is comparatively long.

Reference to the balance sheet of Boyd's Clothiers will show that the long-lived assets of the business consist of store equipment. The amount of the accumulated depreciation is shown as a deduction from the cost of the equipment. The difference represents the *undepreciated cost* of the equipment — the amount that will be written off as depreciation expense in future periods.

Current Liabilities. *Current liabilities* include those obligations that will be due in a short time and paid with monies provided by the current assets. As of December 31, the current liabilities of Boyd's Clothiers consisted of notes payable, accrued interest payable, accounts payable, sales tax payable, FICA tax payable, employees income tax payable, FUTA tax payable, state unemployment tax payable and accrued bank credit card expense.

Long-Term Liabilities. *Long-term liabilities* (sometimes called *fixed liabilities*) include those obligations that will not be due for a relatively long time. The most common of the long-term liabilities is mortgages payable.

A mortgage payable is a debt or an obligation that is secured by a *mortgage*, which provides for the conveyance of certain property upon failure to pay the debt at maturity. When the debt is paid, the mortgage becomes void. It will be seen, therefore, that a mortgage payable differs little from an account payable or a note payable except that the creditor holds the mortgage as security for the payment of the debt. Usually debts secured by mortgages run for a longer period of time than ordinary notes payable or accounts payable. A mortgage payable should be classified as a long-term liability if the maturity date extends beyond the normal operating cycle of the business (usually a year). Boyd's Clothiers has no long-term liabilities.

Owner's Equity. As previously explained, accounts relating to the owner's equity element may be either permanent or temporary owner's equity accounts. The permanent owner's equity accounts used in recording the operations of a particular enterprise depend upon the type of legal organization, that is, whether the enterprise is organized as a sole proprietorship, as a partnership, or as a corporation.

BOYD'S
Balance
December

Assets

Current assets:

Cash		$10,743.11
Accounts receivable	$ 3,360.31	
Less allowance for doubtful accounts	310.20	3,050.11
Merchandise inventory		25,074.05
Prepaid insurance		281.30
Supplies		60.00
Total current assets		$39,208.57

Long-lived assets:

Store equipment		$ 5,593.60
Less accumulated depreciation		1,365.26
Total long-lived assets		4,228.34
Total assets		$43,436.91

Boyd's Clothiers — Balance Sheet (Left Side)

In the case of a sole proprietorship, one or more accounts representing the owner's interest or equity in the assets may be kept. Reference to the chart of accounts, shown on page 183, will reveal that the following accounts are classified as owner's equity accounts:

Account No. 311, Lynn C. Boyd, Capital
Account No. 031, Lynn C. Boyd, Drawing
Account No. 321, Expense and Revenue Summary

Account No. 311 reflects the amount of Ms. Boyd's equity. It may be increased by additional investments or by the practice of not withdrawing cash or other assets in an amount as large as the net income of the enterprise; it may be decreased by withdrawals in excess of the amount of the net income or by sustaining a net loss during one or more accounting periods. Usually there will be no changes in the balance of this account during the accounting period, in which case the balance represents the owner's investment in the business as of the beginning of the accounting period and until such time as the books are closed at the end of the accounting period.

Account No. 031 is Ms. Boyd's drawing account. This account is charged for any withdrawals of cash or other property for personal use. It is a temporary account in which is kept a record of the owner's personal

```
CLOTHIERS
Sheet
31, 19--
                                Liabilities
Current liabilities:

  Notes payable.........................      $ 3,000.00
  Accrued interest payable..............           37.33
  Accounts payable......................        4,340.30
  Sales tax payable.....................          802.86
  FICA tax payable......................          213.22
  Employees income tax payable..........          266.50
  FUTA tax payable......................           84.00
  State unemployment tax payable........          113.40
  Accrued bank credit card expense......          209.62
                                                ---------
    Total current liabilities...........                     $ 9,067.23

                              Owner's Equity

Lynn C. Boyd, capital:

  Capital, January 1....................              $25,635.19
  Net income............................  $32,150.29
    Less withdrawals....................   23,415.80    8,734.49
                                           ---------   ---------
  Capital, December 31..................                          34,369.68
                                                                  ---------
Total liabilities and owner's equity.....                        $43,436.91
                                                                  =========
```

Boyd's Clothiers — Balance Sheet (Right Side)

drawings during the accounting period. Ordinarily such drawings are made in anticipation of earnings rather than as withdrawals of capital. The balance of the account, as shown by the trial balance at the close of an accounting period, represents the total amount of the owner's drawings during the period.

Reference to the work sheet shown on pages 230 and 231 will reveal that the balance of Ms. Boyd's drawing account is listed in the Balance Sheet Debit column. This is because there is no provision on a work sheet for making deductions from owner's equity except by listing them in the Debit column. Since the balance of the owner's capital account is listed in the Balance Sheet Credit column, the listing of the balance of the owner's drawing account in the Debit column is equivalent to deducting the amount from the balance of the owner's capital account.

Account No. 321 is used only at the close of the accounting period for the purpose of summarizing the temporary owner's equity accounts. Sometimes this account is referred to as a *clearing account*. No entries should appear in the account before the books are closed at the end of the accounting period.

The owner's equity section of the balance sheet of Boyd's Clothiers is arranged to show the major changes that took place during the year in the owner's equity element of the business. Ms. Boyd's interest in the business amounted to $25,635.19 at the beginning of the period. Her interest was increased $32,150.29 as the result of profitable operations, and decreased $23,415.80 as the result of withdrawals during the year. Thus, the owner's equity element of the business on December 31 amounted to $34,369.68.

Balance Sheet Analysis. The information provided by a balance sheet can be analyzed in several ways to assist in judging the financial position and soundness of the business. A few of the major analytical procedures will be briefly considered.

A balance sheet as of one date may be compared with a balance sheet as of another date to determine the amount of the increase or the decrease in any of the accounts or groups of accounts. Sometimes balance sheets as of two or more dates are prepared in comparative form by listing the amounts as of different dates in parallel columns. Thus, if balance sheets as of the close of two succeeding calendar years are compared, it is possible to determine the amount of the increase or the decrease during the intervening period in any of the accounts or groups of accounts involved. If such a comparison reveals an increase in accounts receivable, it may indicate that collections during the later period were not as favorable as they were during the preceding period. If the comparison reveals an increase in accounts payable, it may indicate an inability to pay current bills because of insufficient cash. If the comparison reveals an increase in the current assets without a corresponding increase in the liabilities, it may indicate an improved financial position or status.

Too much emphasis should not be placed upon an increase or a decrease in cash. Some individuals are inclined to judge the results of operations largely by the cash balance. This practice may be misleading. The net results of operations can be properly determined only by comparison of all the assets and the liabilities. The ability of a business to meet its current obligations may be determined largely by an analysis of its current assets, particularly those assets that are sometimes referred to as the quick assets. *Quick assets* include cash and all other current assets that are readily realizable in cash, such as temporary investments in the form of marketable securities.

The relation of an account, a group of accounts, or an accounting element to another account, group of accounts, or accounting element may be referred to as the *ratio*. For example, if the total current assets amount to twice as much as the total current liabilities, the ratio is said to be 2 to 1. Ratios may be expressed in percentages or on a unit basis. Fractions of units may be expressed by means of common fractions or decimals as, for example, 7¾ to 1 or 7.75 to 1.

In an enterprise in which capital invested is a material revenue-producing factor, such as is the case in a merchandising enterprise, the ratio of the current assets to the current liabilities may be important. Reference to the balance sheet shown on pages 242 and 243 reveals that the total current assets amount to $39,208.57 and the total current liabilities amount to $9,067.23, a ratio of over 4 to 1. The total assets amount to $43,436.91 and the total liabilities amount to $9,067.23, a ratio of nearly 5 to 1. These ratios are sufficiently high to indicate a very favorable financial position.

Banks often consider the ratio of current assets to current liabilities when considering the advisability of making a loan. It is not expected that the long-lived assets will be sold to realize sufficient funds with which to pay a short-term loan. If the balance sheet seems to indicate that a sufficient amount of cash will not be realized from the collection of accounts receivable or from the sales of service or merchandise to repay a loan at maturity, the bank may consider the loan inadvisable. The excess of the amount of the current assets over the amount of the current liabilities is called *net current assets* or *working capital*.

It is difficult to estimate what the proper ratio of current assets to current liabilities should be, because of the variations in enterprises and industries. A 2 to 1 ratio of current assets to current liabilities may be more than sufficient in some enterprises but entirely insufficient in others. In the milk distributing business, for example, a 1 to 1 ratio of current assets to current liabilities is considered satisfactory. The reasons are that very little capital is tied up in inventory, the amount of accounts receivable is comparatively small, and the terms on which the milk is purchased from farmers are such that settlements are slow and comparatively large amounts are due to farmers at all times. Another reason is that a large amount of capital is invested in long-lived assets, such as equipment for treating the milk and for delivering it to customers.

Generally speaking, the ratio of the current assets to the current liabilities should be maintained in a range from 2 to 1 to 5 to 1. While a standard ratio cannot be established for all enterprises, a knowledge of the working capital requirements of a particular enterprise will be helpful in determining what the ratio of current assets to current liabilities should be.

A comparison of the relationships between certain amounts in the income statement and certain amounts in the balance sheet may be informative. The leading example of this type is the ratio of net income to owner's equity in the business. The owner's equity of Boyd's Clothiers was $25,635.19 on January 1. The net income for the year of $32,150.29 was over 125 percent of this amount. A comparison of this ratio with the ratio of net income to capital invested in prior years should be of interest to the owner. It may also be of interest to compare the ratio of the net income of Boyd's Clothiers to the amount of capital invested by Ms. Boyd with the same ratio for other stores of comparable nature and size. It is important to note, however, that the net income of Boyd's Clothiers was computed without regard to any salary or other compensation for the services of Ms. Boyd. In comparing the results of operations of Boyd's Clothiers with those of other retail clothing businesses, some appropriate adjustment of the data might be needed to make the comparison valid.

Inventory turnover

A merchant is usually interested in knowing the rate of *inventory turnover* for each accounting period. This has reference to the number of times the merchandise available for sale is turned during the accounting period. The rate of turnover is found by dividing the cost of goods sold for the period by the average inventory. Where an inventory is taken only at the end of each accounting period, the average inventory for the period may be found by adding the beginning and ending inventories together and dividing by two. The turnover of Boyd's Clothiers for the year ended December 31 may be computed as follows:

Beginning inventory	$ 27,632.40
Ending inventory	25,074.05
Cost of goods sold for the period	121,406.66

$27,632.40 + $25,074.05 ÷ 2 = $26,353.23, average inventory
$121,406.66 ÷ $26,353.23 = 4.6, rate of turnover

This calculation indicates that, on the average, the merchandise turns over about once every 2½ months. A careful analysis of the theory involved in computing the rate of turnover will indicate that the greater the sales the smaller the margin need be on each dollar of sales in order to produce a satisfactory dollar amount of gross margin.

Report No. 9-2

Complete Report No. 9-2 in the study assignments and submit your working papers to the instructor for approval. After completing the report, you may continue with the textbook discussion in Chapter 10 until the next report is required.

Chapter 10

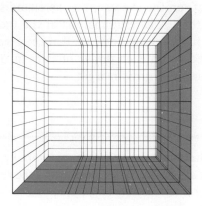

ADJUSTING AND CLOSING ACCOUNTS AT END OF ACCOUNTING PERIOD

As explained in the preceding chapter, the adjustment of certain accounts at the end of the accounting period is required because of changes that have occurred during the period that are not reflected in the accounts. Since the purpose of the temporary owner's equity accounts is to assemble information relating to a specified period of time, at the end of the period the balances of these accounts must be removed to cause the accounts to be ready to perform their function in the following period. In other words, accounts of this type must be "closed."

ADJUSTING ENTRIES

In preparing the work sheet for Boyd's Clothiers (reproduced on pages 230 and 231), adjustments were made to accomplish the following purposes:

    (a) To transfer the amount of the merchandise inventory at the beginning of the accounting period to the expense and revenue summary.

    (b) To record the calculated cost of the merchandise inventory at the end of the accounting period.

    (c) To record the amount of interest accrued on notes payable.

    (d) To record the amount of accrued bank credit card expense.

    (e) To record the amount of insurance premium expired during the year.

(f) To record the cost of supplies used during the year.

(g) To record the estimated amount of depreciation of long-lived assets (store equipment) for the year.

(h) To record the amount of losses from uncollectible accounts expected to result from the sales on account made during the year.

The effect of these adjustments was reflected in the financial statements reproduced on pages 238, 242, and 243. To bring the ledger into agreement with the financial statements, the adjustments should be recorded in the proper accounts. It is customary, therefore, at the end of each accounting period to journalize the adjustments and to post them to the accounts.

Journalizing the adjusting entries

Adjusting entries may be recorded in either a general journal or a combined cash journal. If the entries are made in a combined cash journal, the only amount columns used are the General Debit and Credit columns. A portion of a page of a combined cash journal showing the adjusting entries of Boyd's Clothiers is reproduced below. It should be noted that when the adjusting entries are recorded in the combined cash journal, they are entered in exactly the same manner as they would be entered in

COMBINED CASH JOURNAL FOR MONTH OF *December* 19 —   PAGE *49*

	DAY	DESCRIPTION	POST. REF.	GENERAL DEBIT	GENERAL CREDIT	
1		AMOUNTS FORWARDED				1
2	31	*Adjusting Entries*				2
3		Expense and Revenue Summary	321	2763240		3
4		Merchandise Inventory	131		2763240	4
5		Merchandise Inventory	131	2507405		5
6		Expense and Revenue Summary	321		2507405	6
7		Interest Expense	711	3733		7
8		Accrued Interest Payable	221		3733	8
9		Bank Credit Card Expense	619	20962		9
10		Accrued Bank Credit Card Expense	291		20962	10
11		Insurance Expense	622	28130		11
12		Prepaid Insurance	141		28130	12
13		Supplies Expense	616	19776		13
14		Supplies	151		19776	14
15		Depreciation Expense	612	50316		15
16		Accum. Deprec.—Store Equip.	018		50316	16
17		Uncollectible Accounts Expense	621	25098		17
18		Allowance for Doubtful Accounts	012		25098	18
19				5418660	5418660	19

Boyd's Clothiers — Adjusting Entries

a general journal. Since the heading "Adjusting Entries" explains the nature of the entries, a separate explanation of each adjusting entry is unnecessary. The information needed in journalizing the adjustments was obtained from the Adjustments columns of the work sheet reproduced on pages 230 and 231. The account numbers were not entered in the Posting Reference column at the time of journalizing; they were entered as the posting was completed.

Posting the adjusting entries

The adjusting entries should be posted individually to the proper general ledger accounts. The accounts of Boyd's Clothiers that were affected by the adjusting entries are reproduced below and on pages 251 and 252. The entries in the accounts for December transactions that were posted prior to posting the adjusting entries are the same as appeared in the accounts reproduced on pages 214–219. The number of the combined cash journal page on which the adjusting entries were recorded was entered in the Posting Reference column of the general ledger accounts affected, and the account numbers were entered in the Posting Reference column of the combined cash journal as the posting was completed. This provided a cross-reference in both books.

ACCOUNT *Allowance for Doubtful Accounts*   ACCOUNT NO. 012

DATE	ITEM	POST. REF.	DEBIT	CREDIT	BALANCE DEBIT	BALANCE CREDIT
19-- Dec. 1	Balance	✓				5922
31		CJ49		25098		31020

ACCOUNT *Merchandise Inventory*   ACCOUNT NO. 131

DATE	ITEM	POST. REF.	DEBIT	CREDIT	BALANCE DEBIT	BALANCE CREDIT
19-- Dec. 1	Balance	✓			2763240	
31		CJ49		2763240		
31		CJ49	2507405		2507405	

ACCOUNT *Prepaid Insurance*   ACCOUNT NO. 141

DATE	ITEM	POST. REF.	DEBIT	CREDIT	BALANCE DEBIT	BALANCE CREDIT
19-- Dec. 1	Balance	✓			56260	
31		CJ49		28130	28130	

Boyd's Clothiers — General Ledger Accounts After Posting Adjusting Entries

ACCOUNT *Supplies*   ACCOUNT NO. *151*

DATE		ITEM	POST. REF.	DEBIT	CREDIT	BALANCE	
						DEBIT	CREDIT
19-- Dec.	1	Balance	✓			23028	
	31		CJ48	2748		25776	
	31		CJ49		19776	6000	

ACCOUNT *Accumulated Depreciation – Store Equipment*   ACCOUNT NO. *018*

DATE		ITEM	POST. REF.	DEBIT	CREDIT	BALANCE	
						DEBIT	CREDIT
19-- Dec.	1	Balance	✓				86210
	31		CJ49		50316		136526

ACCOUNT *Accrued Interest Payable*   ACCOUNT NO. *221*

DATE		ITEM	POST. REF.	DEBIT	CREDIT	BALANCE	
						DEBIT	CREDIT
19-- Dec.	31		CJ49		3733		3733

ACCOUNT *Accrued Bank Credit Card Expense*   ACCOUNT NO. *291*

DATE		ITEM	POST. REF.	DEBIT	CREDIT	BALANCE	
						DEBIT	CREDIT
19-- Dec.	31		CJ49		20962		20962

ACCOUNT *Expense and Revenue Summary*   ACCOUNT NO. *321*

DATE		ITEM	POST. REF.	DEBIT	CREDIT	BALANCE	
						DEBIT	CREDIT
19-- Dec.	31		CJ49	2763240			
			CJ49		2507405		

ACCOUNT *Depreciation Expense*   ACCOUNT NO. *612*

DATE		ITEM	POST. REF.	DEBIT	CREDIT	BALANCE	
						DEBIT	CREDIT
19-- Dec.	31		CJ49	50316		50316	

Boyd's Clothiers — General Ledger Accounts After Posting Adjusting Entries (*continued*)

ACCOUNT *Supplies Expense*   ACCOUNT NO. 616

DATE	ITEM	POST. REF.	DEBIT	CREDIT	BALANCE DEBIT	BALANCE CREDIT
19-- Dec. 31		CJ49	19776		19776	

ACCOUNT *Bank Credit Card Expense*   ACCOUNT NO. 619

DATE	ITEM	POST. REF.	DEBIT	CREDIT	BALANCE DEBIT	BALANCE CREDIT
19-- Dec. 1	Balance	✓			217992	
4		CJ47	23542		241534	
31		CJ49	20962		262496	

ACCOUNT *Uncollectible Accounts Expense*   ACCOUNT NO. 621

DATE	ITEM	POST. REF.	DEBIT	CREDIT	BALANCE DEBIT	BALANCE CREDIT
19-- Dec. 31		CJ49	25098		25098	

ACCOUNT *Insurance Expense*   ACCOUNT NO. 622

DATE	ITEM	POST. REF.	DEBIT	CREDIT	BALANCE DEBIT	BALANCE CREDIT
19-- Dec. 31		CJ49	28130		28130	

ACCOUNT *Interest Expense*   ACCOUNT NO. 711

DATE	ITEM	POST. REF.	DEBIT	CREDIT	BALANCE DEBIT	BALANCE CREDIT
19-- Dec. 1	Balance	✓			11609	
31		CJ49	3733		15342	

Boyd's Clothiers — General Ledger Accounts After Posting Adjusting Entries (*concluded*)

Report No. 10-1	Complete Report No. 10-1 in the study assignments and submit your working papers to the instructor for approval. Continue with the following textbook discussion until Report No. 10-2 is required.

CLOSING PROCEDURE

After the adjusting entries have been posted, all of the temporary owner's equity accounts should be closed. This means that the accountant must remove ("close out") **(1)** the balance of every account that enters into the calculation of the net income (or net loss) for the accounting period and **(2)** the balance of the owner's drawing account. The purpose of the closing procedure is to transfer the balances of the temporary owner's equity accounts to the permanent owner's equity account. This could be accomplished simply by debiting or crediting each account involved with an offsetting credit or debit to the permanent owner's equity account. However, it is considered better practice to transfer the balances of all accounts that enter into the net income or net loss determination to a summarizing account called Expense and Revenue Summary (sometimes called *Income Summary*, *Profit and Loss Summary*, or just *Profit and Loss*). Then, the resulting balance of the expense and revenue summary account (which will be the amount of the net income or net loss for the period) is transferred to the permanent owner's equity account.

The final step in the closing procedure is to transfer the balance of the owner's drawing account to the permanent owner's equity account. After this is done, only the asset accounts, the liability accounts, and the permanent owner's equity account have balances. If there has been no error, the sum of the balances of the asset accounts (less balances of any contra accounts) will be equal to the sum of the balances of the liability accounts plus the balance of the permanent owner's equity account. The accounts will agree exactly with what is shown in the balance sheet as of the close of the period. Reference to the balance sheet of Boyd's Clothiers reproduced on pages 242 and 243 will show that the assets, liabilities, and owner's equity as of December 31 may be expressed in equation form as follows:

$$\text{ASSETS} = \text{LIABILITIES} + \text{OWNER'S EQUITY}$$
$$\$43,436.91 \qquad \$9,067.23 \qquad \$34,369.68$$

Journalizing the closing entries

Closing entries, like adjusting entries, may be recorded in either a general journal or a combined cash journal. If the entries are made in a combined cash journal, only the General Debit and Credit columns are used. A portion of a page of a combined cash journal showing the closing entries for Boyd's Clothiers is reproduced below. Since the heading

COMBINED CASH JOURNAL FOR MONTH OF *December* 19 —   PAGE *50*

	DAY	DESCRIPTION	POST. REF.	GENERAL DEBIT	GENERAL CREDIT	
1		AMOUNTS FORWARDED				1
2	31	*Closing Entries*				2
3		Sales	411	202743 65		3
4		Purchases Returns + Allowances	051	1721 10		4
5		Purchases Discount	052	7689 54		5
6		Expense and Revenue Summary	321		212154 29	6
7		Expense and Revenue Summary	321	177445 65		7
8		Sales Returns + Allowances	041		2961 30	8
9		Purchases	511		128258 95	9
10		Rent Expense	611		8400 00	10
11		Depreciation Expense	612		503 16	11
12		Salaries and Commissions Exp.	613		21316 40	12
13		Payroll Taxes Expense	614		1816 58	13
14		Heating and Lighting Expense	615		759 64	14
15		Stationery and Supplies Expense	616		197 76	15
16		Telephone and Telegraph Expense	617		372 30	16
17		Advertising Expense	618		8713 25	17
18		Bank Credit Card Expense	619		2624 96	18
19		Uncollectible Accounts Expense	621		250 98	19
20		Insurance Expense	622		281 30	20
21		Charitable Contributions Expense	623		350 00	21
22		Miscellaneous Expense	624		485 65	22
23		Interest Expense	711		153 42	23
24		Expense and Revenue Summary	321	32150 29		24
25		Lynn C. Boyd, Capital	311		32150 29	25
26		Lynn C. Boyd, Capital	311	23415 80		26
27		Lynn C. Boyd, Drawing	031		23415 80	27
				445166 03	445166 03	

Boyd's Clothiers — Closing Entries

"Closing Entries" explains the nature of the entries, a separate explanation of each closing entry is not necessary. The information required in preparing the closing entries was obtained from the work sheet illustrated on pages 230 and 231.

The first closing entry was made to close the sales, purchases returns and allowances, and purchases discount accounts. Since these accounts have credit balances, each account must be debited for the amount of its balance in order to close it. The debits to these three accounts are offset by a credit of $212,154.29 to Expense and Revenue Summary.

The second closing entry was made to close the sales returns and allowances, purchases, and all of the expense accounts. Since these accounts have debit balances, each account must be credited for the amount of its balance in order to close it. The credits to these accounts are offset by a debit of $177,445.65 to Expense and Revenue Summary.

Since the posting of the first two adjusting entries and the first two closing entries causes the expense and revenue summary account to have a credit balance of $32,150.29 (the net income for the year), the account has served its purpose and must be closed. The third closing entry accomplishes this by debiting the expense and revenue summary account with an offsetting credit to Lynn C. Boyd, Capital, for $32,150.29.

The fourth closing entry was made to close the Lynn C. Boyd drawing account. Since this account has a debit balance, it must be credited to close it. The offsetting entry is a debit of $23,415.80 to Lynn C. Boyd, Capital.

The account numbers shown in the Posting Reference column were not entered at the time of journalizing the closing entries — they were entered as the posting was completed.

Posting the closing entries

Closing entries are posted in the usual manner and proper cross-references are provided by using the Posting Reference columns of the combined cash journal and the ledger accounts. After all the closing entries have been posted, the accounts affected appear as shown on pages 256–261. Note that as each account was closed, the "no balance" symbol "—0—" was placed in each column.

It may be observed that the first two adjusting entries described and illustrated earlier in the chapter actually qualify both as "adjusting" and as "closing" entries. They serve to adjust the merchandise inventory account by removing the amount of the beginning inventory and by recording the amount of the ending inventory. They facilitate the closing process in that they cause two amounts that enter into the calculation of net income or net loss to be entered in the Expense and Revenue Summary. It matters little which descriptive term is applied; the important thing is to be sure that needed adjustments are made and that the temporary owner's equity accounts are closed as of the end of the accounting period.

ACCOUNT *Lynn C. Boyd, Capital*   ACCOUNT NO. 311

DATE		ITEM	POST. REF.	DEBIT	CREDIT	BALANCE DEBIT	BALANCE CREDIT
19-- Dec.	1	Balance	✓				2563519
	31		CJ50		3215029		
	31		CJ50	2341580			3436968

ACCOUNT *Lynn C. Boyd, Drawing*   ACCOUNT NO. 031

DATE		ITEM	POST. REF.	DEBIT	CREDIT	BALANCE DEBIT	BALANCE CREDIT
19-- Dec.	1	Balance	✓			2240580	
	21		CJ48	100000			
	31		CJ48	1000		2341580	
	31		CJ50		2341580	—0—	—0—

ACCOUNT *Expense and Revenue Summary*   ACCOUNT NO. 321

DATE		ITEM	POST. REF.	DEBIT	CREDIT	BALANCE DEBIT	BALANCE CREDIT
19-- Dec.	31		CJ49	2763240			
	31		CJ49		2507405		
	31		CJ50		2121 5429		
	31		CJ50	17744565			
	31		CJ50	3215029		—0—	—0—

Boyd's Clothiers — Partial General Ledger

ACCOUNT *Sales*   ACCOUNT NO. *411*

DATE		ITEM	POST. REF.	DEBIT	CREDIT	BALANCE	
						DEBIT	CREDIT
19-- Dec.	1	Balance	✓				18658121
	31		J44		218791		
	31		CJ48		1397453		20274365
	31		CJ50	20274365		—0—	—0—

ACCOUNT *Sales Returns and Allowances*   ACCOUNT NO. *041*

DATE		ITEM	POST. REF.	DEBIT	CREDIT	BALANCE	
						DEBIT	CREDIT
19-- Dec.	1	Balance	✓			285485	
	9		CJ47	8495			
	27		CJ48	2150		296130	
	31		CJ50		296130	—0—	—0—

ACCOUNT *Purchases*   ACCOUNT NO. *511*

DATE		ITEM	POST. REF.	DEBIT	CREDIT	BALANCE	
						DEBIT	CREDIT
19-- Dec.	1	Balance	✓			11851272	
	2		CJ47	5318			
	31		P32	969305		12825895	
	31		CJ50		12825895	—0—	—0—

ACCOUNT *Purchases Returns and Allowances*   ACCOUNT NO. *051*

DATE		ITEM	POST. REF.	DEBIT	CREDIT	BALANCE	
						DEBIT	CREDIT
19-- Dec.	1	Balance	✓				165510
	20		CJ48		6600		172110
	31		CJ50	172110		—0—	—0—

Boyd's Clothiers — Partial General Ledger (*continued*)

ACCOUNT *Purchases Discount*   ACCOUNT NO. *052*

DATE		ITEM	POST. REF.	DEBIT	CREDIT	BALANCE	
						DEBIT	CREDIT
19-- Dec.	1	Balance	✓				692204
	31		CJ48		76750		768954
	31		CJ50	768954		—0—	—0—

ACCOUNT *Rent Expense*   ACCOUNT NO. *611*

DATE		ITEM	POST. REF.	DEBIT	CREDIT	BALANCE	
						DEBIT	CREDIT
19-- Dec.	1	Balance	✓			770000	
	2		CJ47	70000		840000	
	31		CJ50		840000	—0—	—0—

ACCOUNT *Depreciation Expense*   ACCOUNT NO. *612*

DATE		ITEM	POST. REF.	DEBIT	CREDIT	BALANCE	
						DEBIT	CREDIT
19-- Dec.	31		CJ49	50316		50316	
	31		CJ50		50316	—0—	—0—

ACCOUNT *Salaries and Commissions Expense*   ACCOUNT NO. *613*

DATE		ITEM	POST. REF.	DEBIT	CREDIT	BALANCE	
						DEBIT	CREDIT
19-- Dec.	1	Balance	✓			1953950	
	14		CJ47	89270			
	31		CJ48	88420		2131640	
	31		CJ50		2131640	—0—	—0—

Boyd's Clothiers — Partial General Ledger (*continued*)

ACCOUNT *Payroll Taxes Expense*   ACCOUNT NO. 614

DATE		ITEM	POST. REF.	DEBIT	CREDIT	BALANCE	
						DEBIT	CREDIT
19-- Dec.	1	Balance	✓			170330	
	14		CJ47	5691			
	31		CJ48	5637		181658	
	31		CJ50		181658	—0—	—0—

ACCOUNT *Heating and Lighting Expense*   ACCOUNT NO. 615

DATE		ITEM	POST. REF.	DEBIT	CREDIT	BALANCE	
						DEBIT	CREDIT
19-- Dec.	1	Balance	✓			68636	
	28		CJ48	7328		75964	
	31		CJ50		75964	—0—	—0—

ACCOUNT *Supplies Expense*   ACCOUNT NO. 616

DATE		ITEM	POST. REF.	DEBIT	CREDIT	BALANCE	
						DEBIT	CREDIT
19-- Dec.	31		CJ49	19776		19776	
	31		CJ50		19776	—0—	—0—

ACCOUNT *Telephone Expense*   ACCOUNT NO. 617

DATE		ITEM	POST. REF.	DEBIT	CREDIT	BALANCE	
						DEBIT	CREDIT
19-- Dec.	1	Balance	✓			34015	
	28		CJ48	3215		37230	
	31		CJ50		37230	—0—	—0—

Boyd's Clothiers — Partial General Ledger (*continued*)

ACCOUNT *Advertising Expense*   ACCOUNT NO. 618

DATE	ITEM	POST. REF.	DEBIT	CREDIT	BALANCE DEBIT	BALANCE CREDIT
19-- Dec. 1	Balance	✓			821982	
6		CJ47	6104			
27		CJ48	42130			
31		CJ48	1109		871325	
31		CJ50		871325	—0—	—0—

ACCOUNT *Bank Credit Card Expense*   ACCOUNT NO. 619

DATE	ITEM	POST. REF.	DEBIT	CREDIT	BALANCE DEBIT	BALANCE CREDIT
19-- Dec. 1	Balance	✓			217992	
4		CJ47	23542		241534	
31		CJ49	20962		262496	
31		CJ50		262496	—0—	—0—

ACCOUNT *Uncollectible Accounts Expense*   ACCOUNT NO. 621

DATE	ITEM	POST. REF.	DEBIT	CREDIT	BALANCE DEBIT	BALANCE CREDIT
19-- Dec. 31		CJ49	25098		25098	
31		CJ50		25098	—0—	—0—

ACCOUNT *Insurance Expense*   ACCOUNT NO. 622

DATE	ITEM	POST. REF.	DEBIT	CREDIT	BALANCE DEBIT	BALANCE CREDIT
19-- Dec. 31		CJ49	28130		28130	
31		CJ50		28130	—0—	—0—

Boyd's Clothiers — Partial General Ledger (*continued*)

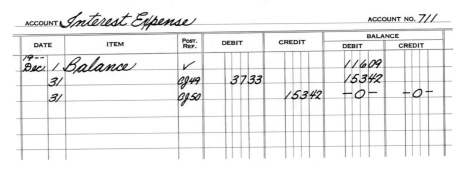

ACCOUNT *Charitable Contributions Expense*   ACCOUNT NO. 623

DATE	ITEM	POST. REF.	DEBIT	CREDIT	BALANCE DEBIT	BALANCE CREDIT
19-- Dec. 1	Balance	✓			34500	
31		CJ48	500		35000	
31		CJ50		35000	—0—	—0—

ACCOUNT *Miscellaneous Expense*   ACCOUNT NO. 624

DATE	ITEM	POST. REF.	DEBIT	CREDIT	BALANCE DEBIT	BALANCE CREDIT
19-- Dec. 1	Balance	✓			46120	
23		CJ48	1680			
31		CJ48	765		48565	
31		CJ50		48565	—0—	—0—

ACCOUNT *Interest Expense*   ACCOUNT NO. 711

DATE	ITEM	POST. REF.	DEBIT	CREDIT	BALANCE DEBIT	BALANCE CREDIT
19-- Dec. 1	Balance	✓			11609	
31		CJ49	3733		15342	
31		CJ50		15342	—0—	—0—

Boyd's Clothiers — Partial General Ledger (concluded)

Trial balance after closing

    A trial balance of the general ledger accounts that remain open after the temporary owner's equity accounts have been closed is usually referred to as a *post-closing trial balance*. The purpose of the post-closing trial balance is to prove that the general ledger is in balance at the beginning of a new accounting period. It is advisable to know that such is the case before any transactions for the new accounting period are recorded.

    The post-closing trial balance should contain the same accounts and amounts as appear in the Balance Sheet columns of the work sheet, except that **(1)** the owner's drawing account is omitted because it has been closed, and **(2)** the owner's capital account has been adjusted for the amount of the net income (or net loss) and the amount of his drawings.

A post-closing trial balance of the general ledger of Boyd's Clothiers is shown below. Some accountants advocate that the post-closing trial balance should be dated as of the close of the old accounting period, while others advocate that it should be dated as of the beginning of the new accounting period. In this illustration the trial balance is dated December 31, the end of the period.

Account	Acct. No.	Dr. Balance	Cr. Balance
Boyd's Clothiers			
Post-Closing Trial Balance			
December 31, 19--			
First National Bank	111	10643 11	
Petty Cash Fund	112	100 00	
Accounts Receivable	121	3360 31	
Allowance for Doubtful Accounts	012		310 20
Merchandise Inventory	131	25074 05	
Prepaid Insurance	141	281 30	
Supplies	151	60 00	
Store Equipment	181	5593 60	
Accumulated Depr.—Store Equipment	018		1365 26
Notes Payable	211		3000 00
Accrued Interest Payable	221		37 33
Accounts Payable	231		4340 30
Sales Tax Payable	241		802 86
F I C A Tax Payable	251		213 22
Employees Income Tax Payable	261		266 50
F U T A Tax Payable	271		84 00
State Unemployment Tax Payable	281		113 40
Accrued Bank Credit Card Expense	291		209 62
Lynn C. Boyd, Capital	311		34369 68
		45112 37	45112 37

Boyd's Clothiers — Post-Closing Trial Balance

Reversing entries for accrual adjustments   Many accountants reverse the adjusting entries for accruals. The purpose of such reversing entries (sometimes called "readjusting entries") is to make possible the recording of the transactions of the succeeding accounting period in a routine manner and to assure that the proper amount of revenue will be credited to the period in which earned and that the proper amount of expenses will be charged to the period in which incurred.

A case in point is the matter of interest expense. When cash is disbursed in payment of interest, the routine manner of recording the transaction is to debit Interest Expense and to credit Cash (or Bank). If any portion of such interest was accrued in the preceding accounting period and the adjusting entry had not been reversed at the beginning of the current accounting period, the amount debited to Interest Expense would not represent the proper amount of expense incurred in the current period. If, however, the adjusting entry at the end of the preceding period had been reversed, the interest expense account would be credited for the amount accrued and, after recording the interest paid in the current period as a debit to Interest Expense, the balance of the account would represent the correct amount of the interest expense for the current period.

Journalizing the reversing entries

Reversing entries, like adjusting and closing entries, may be recorded in either a general journal or a combined cash journal. If the entries are made in a combined cash journal, the only amount columns used are the General Debit and Credit columns. A portion of a page of a combined cash journal showing the reversing entries of Boyd's Clothiers is reproduced below. Usually the reversing entries are made immediately after closing the books at the end of an accounting period. However, it is customary to date the entries as of the first day of the succeeding accounting period. Thus, the reversing entries for Boyd's Clothiers are dated January 1. Since the heading "Reversing Entries" explains the nature of the entries, a separate explanation of each reversing entry is unnecessary. Following is a discussion of each of the reversing entries.

COMBINED CASH JOURNAL FOR MONTH OF *January* 19 — PAGE *51*

	DAY	DESCRIPTION	POST. REF.	GENERAL DEBIT	GENERAL CREDIT	
1		AMOUNTS FORWARDED				1
2	1	*Reversing Entries*				2
3		*Accrued Interest Payable*	221	37 33		3
4		*Interest Expense*	711		37 33	4
5		*Accrued Bank Credit Card Expense*	291	209 62		5
6		*Bank Credit Card Expense*	619		209 62	6
7				2 46 95	2 46 95	7
8						8
9						9
10						10
11						11
12						12
13						13
14						14

Boyd's Clothiers — Reversing Entries

Accrued Interest Payable. Reference to the adjusting entries for Boyd's Clothiers reproduced on page 249 will reveal that Interest Expense, Account No. 711, was debited and Accrued Interest Payable, Account No. 221, was credited for $37.33 to record the interest accrued on an 8 percent interest-bearing note for $3,000 issued November 5. To reverse the adjusting entry it was necessary to debit Accrued Interest Payable, Account No. 221, and to credit Interest Expense, Account No. 711, for $37.33. The accounts affected by this entry are reproduced below.

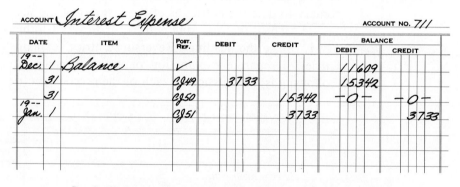

Boyd's Clothiers — Accrued Interest Payable and Interest Expense
After Posting of Reversing Entry

It will be noted that after posting the reversing entry, the account Accrued Interest Payable has a zero balance and the account Interest Expense has a credit balance of $37.33. If the note for $3,000 plus interest is paid when due on May 5, the payment will be $3,120 (principal of note $3,000, plus interest at 8 percent for 6 months, $120). To record the payment it is necessary only to debit Notes Payable, Account No. 211, for $3,000 and Interest Expense, Account No. 711, for $120 and to credit First National Bank, Account No. 111, for $3,120. After posting this entry, the interest expense account will have a debit balance of $82.67 ($120 minus $37.33). This balance represents the amount of interest expense incurred in the year in which the note matures. If the adjusting entry had not been reversed, it would be necessary to make an analysis before recording the payment on May 5 in order to determine the amount of interest expense incurred in the preceding year and the amount of interest expense incurred in the current year. This would reveal that it would be necessary to debit Accrued Interest Payable for $37.33 and Interest Expense for $82.67 so that each year might be charged with the correct interest expense. When the adjustment is reversed, the need for this analysis is eliminated.

The reversal procedure is particularly useful if the year-end adjustment for interest expense incurred but not paid related to interest accrued on several interest-bearing obligations. When the adjustment is reversed, all future payments of interest can be debited to the interest expense account without any concern as to when each amount paid was incurred. The portion of any payments that is an expense of the new period will automatically emerge as the balance of the interest expense account.

Accrued Bank Credit Card Expense. In the adjusting entries for Boyd's Clothiers, Bank Credit Card Expense, Account No. 619, was debited and Accrued Bank Credit Card Expense, Account No. 291, was credited for $209.62 to record the amount of the expense for December which the bank will not deduct from Boyd's checking account until early in January. The reversing entry (as of January 1) was a debit to the accrual account (No. 291) and a credit to the expense account (No. 619) for the same amount. Because the debit balance of the expense account (including the December expense not yet paid) had been closed, the result of the reversing entry was to remove the credit balance in the liability account and give the expense account a credit balance of $209.62. Below and on page 266 are the accounts after the reversing entry has been posted.

ACCOUNT *Accrued Bank Credit Card Expense*   ACCOUNT NO. *291*

DATE	ITEM	POST. REF.	DEBIT	CREDIT	BALANCE DEBIT	BALANCE CREDIT
19-- Dec. 31		CJ49		209 62		209 62
19-- Jan. 1		CJ51	209 62		—0—	—0—

Boyd's Clothiers — Accrued Bank Credit Card Expense
After Posting of Reversing Entry

ACCOUNT *Bank Credit Card Expense*   ACCOUNT NO. 619

DATE		ITEM	POST. REF.	DEBIT	CREDIT	BALANCE DEBIT	BALANCE CREDIT
19-- Dec.	1	Balance	✓			217992	
	4		CJ47	23542		241534	
	31		CJ49	20962		262496	
	31		CJ50		262496	—0—	—0—
19-- Jan.	1		CJ51		20962		20962

Boyd's Clothiers — Bank Credit Card Expense
After Posting of Reversing Entry

The regular entry to record the bank's deduction for this expense is a debit to Bank Credit Card Expense and a credit to the bank account. If such an entry is made in early January for the calculated amount, $209.62, the expense account will be in balance. This is what is wanted — the amount is an expense of the year just ended, not the new year. If the reversing entry had not been made, the accountant would have had to remember that the January debit was to be different from the other eleven months. This is not a serious problem, but it is better whenever possible not to disturb the regular routine of recording transactions. Reversing entries for accrued expenses and revenue help accomplish this objective.

The accounting cycle

The steps involved in handling the effect of all transactions and events completed during an accounting period, beginning with entries in the books of original entry and ending with the reversing entries, collectively comprise the *accounting cycle*. In Chapter 5 (pages 125 and 126) nine steps were listed. A tenth step — journalizing and posting the reversing entries — needs to be added if the accrual basis of accounting is being followed.

Income and self-employment taxes

The discussion of accounting for the revenue and expenses of a business enterprise has included frequent references to income tax considerations. It is important to note that an unincorporated business owned by one person is not taxed. The owner — not the business — is subject to income taxes. However, the amounts of business revenue and business expenses must be reported on the owner's personal tax return regardless of the amount of money or other property that has actually been withdrawn from the business during the year. As mentioned earlier, in the case of a sole proprietorship, there is no legal distinction between the business and its owner.

In order to bring a large class of self-employed individuals into the federal social security program, the law requires all self-employed persons (except those specifically exempted) to pay a self-employment tax. The rate of tax is 2 percent more than the prevailing FICA rate, but the base of the "self-employment income tax" is the same as the base for the FICA tax. (If it is assumed that the combined FICA tax rate is 6 percent, the self-employment income tax rate would be 8 percent on the assumed base of $15,000.) The actual rate and base of the tax may be changed by Act of Congress at any time. In general, *self-employment income* means the net income of a trade or business conducted by an individual or a partner's distributive share of the net income of a partnership whether or not any cash is distributed. Earnings of less than $400 from self-employment are ignored.

A taxable year for the purpose of the tax on self-employment income is the same as the taxpayer's taxable year for federal income tax purposes. The self-employment tax is reported along with the regular federal income tax. For calendar-year taxpayers, the tax return and full or final payment is due on April 15 following the close of the year. Like the personal income tax, the self-employment tax is treated as a personal expense of the owner. If the taxes are paid with business funds, the amount should be charged to the owner's drawing account.

Report No. 10-2   Complete Report No. 10-2 in the study assignments and submit your working papers to the instructor for approval. You will then be given instructions as to the work to be done next.

Chapters 6-10

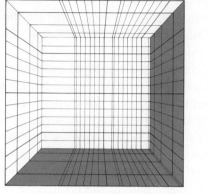

PRACTICAL ACCOUNTING PROBLEMS

Problem 6-A   Ms. Elinor Spiller decides to open a dress shop under the name of Elinor's Shop. The books of original entry include a purchases journal, a sales journal, and a combined cash journal. This problem involves the use of the purchases journal and the combined cash journal only. The following selected transactions were completed during the month of October:

Oct. 1. Invested $8,000 in the business.

1. Received Invoice No. 262 dated Sept. 29 from Mini Midi Maxi, Inc., for merchandise purchased, $95.50. Terms, 30 days net.

3. Received Invoice No. 263 dated Sept. 29 from Terre Brothers for merchandise purchased, $232.41. Terms, 10 days net.

5. Purchased a cash register for cash, $124.75. (Debit Furniture and Fixtures.)

6. Received Invoice No. 264 dated October 4 from Boes, Inc., for merchandise purchased, $126.80. Terms, 30 days net.

10. Purchased merchandise for cash, $61.65.

11. Received Invoice No. 265 dated October 8 from Mini Midi Maxi, Inc., for merchandise purchased, $161.30. Terms, 30 days net.

12. Paid Terre Brothers $232.41 in full for Invoice No. 263, dated Sept. 29.

13. Returned defective merchandise to Mini Midi Maxi, Inc., $32.50.

17. Received invoice dated October 15 from the American Showcase Co. for showcases purchased, $1,843.12. Terms, 15 days net.

24. Received Invoice No. 266 dated October 18 from Terre Brothers for merchandise purchased, $286.74. Terms, 10 days net.

Oct. 25. Purchased merchandise for cash, $136.18.
   31. Received Invoice No. 267 dated October 26 from Kay Francis for merchandise purchased, $52.40. Terms, 30 days net.

REQUIRED: **(1)** Record each transaction in the proper journal using the following accounts:

111 Cash	311 Elinor Spiller, Capital
151 Furniture and Fixtures	511 Purchases
231 Accounts Payable	051 Purchases Returns and Allowances

For the purchases journal, use a sheet of paper ruled like that shown in the illustration on page 144. For the combined cash journal, use a sheet of paper like that shown in the illustration on pages 160 and 161. (The Check No. column will not be used in this problem.) Number the pages of the journals. **(2)** Prove the combined cash journal by footing the amount columns; then total and rule this journal. Total the purchases journal and rule. **(3)** Open the necessary accounts using the four-column form of ledger paper. Post the combined cash journal and purchases journal entries for October, foot the accounts, and enter the balances. **(4)** Take a trial balance as of October 31, using a sheet of two-column journal paper.

Problem 6-B   A. K. Lein decides to open a men's clothing store under the name of The Southgate Store. The books of original entry include a sales journal, a purchases journal, and a combined cash journal. This problem involves the use of the sales journal and combined cash journal only. The following selected transactions were completed during the month of July:

July 1. Invested $10,000 in the business.
   2. Sold merchandise on account to J. D. Mead, $65.10, tax $3.26. Sale No. 304.
   5. Sold merchandise on account to B. A. Moore, $69.45, tax $3.47. Sale No. 305.
   6. J. D. Mead returned goods for credit. Sales price $16.40, tax 82 cents.
   9. Sold merchandise on account to H. C. Bock, $83.12, tax $4.16. Sale No. 306.
   13. Received $51.14 from J. D. Mead on account.
   14. Sold merchandise on account to R. G. Fear, $50.40, tax $2.52. Sale No. 307.
   19. A customer returned some merchandise purchased earlier in the day for cash. Sales price, $12.25, tax 61 cents.
   21. Received $87.28 from H. C. Bock on account.
   26. Sold merchandise on account to G. M. Decker, $30.60, tax $1.53. Sale No. 308.
   28. Sold merchandise on account to J. R. Metcalf, $18.80, tax 94 cents. Sale No. 309.
   30. Total cash sales for month, $681.50, tax, $34.08.

REQUIRED: (1) Record each transaction in the proper journal using the following accounts:

111 Cash	311 A. K. Lein, Capital
121 Accounts Receivable	411 Sales
241 Sales Tax Payable	041 Sales Returns and Allowances

For the sales journal, use a sheet of paper ruled like that shown at the top of page 152. For the combined cash journal, use a sheet of paper like that shown in the illustration on pages 160 and 161. (The Check No. column will not be used in this problem.) Number the pages of the journals. (2) Prove the combined cash journal by footing the amount columns; then total and rule this journal. (3) Prove the sales journal by footing the amount columns and determining that the totals of the debit and credit columns are equal in amount. Enter the totals and rule. (4) Open the necessary accounts using the four-column form of ledger paper. Post the sales journal and combined cash journal entries for July, foot the accounts, and enter the balances. (5) Take a trial balance as of July 31, using a sheet of two-column journal paper.

Problem 6-C   Helen M. Harris operates a retail business under the name of The HMH Store. She keeps a purchases journal, a sales journal, and a two-column general journal as books of original entry. The four-column form of general ledger is used. Individual accounts with customers and suppliers are not kept in ledger form; however, the purchase invoices and sales tickets are filed in such a manner that the amounts due to suppliers and due from customers may be determined at any time. All charge sales are payable by the tenth of the following month. The trial balance taken as of March 31, 19—, is reproduced at the top of page 271.

NARRATIVE OF TRANSACTIONS FOR APRIL

Apr. 1. (Friday) Paid the rent for April in advance, $650.
   2. Paid the following bills:
      Gas and electric bill, $49.60.
      Telephone bill, $29.85.
   4. Received Invoice No. 81 dated April 1 from G. B. Jenkins, 13 Holly Drive, St. Louis, MO 63048, for merchandise purchased, $225. Terms, 30 days net.
   4. Sold merchandise on account to W. N. St. John, 10204 Whitlock, St. Louis, MO 63114, $29.25, tax $1.46. Sale No. 51.
   6. Sold merchandise on account to the Breckenridge Inn, 1351 Dunn Road, St. Louis, MO 63135, $90.75, tax $4.54. Sale No. 52.
   8. Sundry cash sales, $196, tax $9.80.

THE HMH STORE
Trial Balance
March 31, 19—

Cash.................................	111	4,926.00	
Accounts Receivable....................	121	7,410.00	
Merchandise Inventory..................	131	48,400.00	
Store Equipment.......................	181	2,540.00	
Accounts Payable......................	231		7,743.42
Sales Tax Payable.....................	241		169.24
Helen M. Harris, Capital...............	311		14,403.34
Helen M. Harris, Drawing...............	031	3,000.00	
Sales.................................	411		106,300.00
Sales Returns and Allowances............	041	935.00	
Purchases.............................	511	58,700.00	
Purchases Returns and Allowances.........	051		468.00
Rent Expense..........................	611	1,950.00	
Advertising Expense.....................	621	530.00	
Heating and Lighting Expense............	631	275.00	
Telephone Expense.....................	641	158.00	
Miscellaneous Expense..................	651	260.00	
		129,084.00	129,084.00

Apr. 9. Paid the following suppliers on account:
Chatman Bros., $165.30.
Sexton & Co., $274.20.

11. Received the following remittances to apply on account:
Marriott Hotel, $83.25.
J. W. Weiler, $40.
Ms. B. K. Cheek, $62.70.

12. Received Invoice No. 82 dated April 9 from Rose & Stroble, Columbus, OH 43216, for merchandise purchased, $385. Terms, 30 days net.

13. Paid $169.24 to State Treasurer for March sales tax.

13. Made sales on account as follows:
No. 53, Ms. M. J. Calais, Baden, MO 63147, $96.15, tax $4.81.
No. 54, Marriott Hotel, Lambert Field, St. Louis, MO 63134, $63, tax $3.15.
No. 55, Ms. J. P. Stephan, 4148 Parc Chalet, St. Louis, MO 63114, $77, tax $3.85.

14. Paid $29 for newspaper advertising.

15. Sundry cash sales, $156.75, tax $7.84.

16. Helen M. Harris withdrew $500 for personal use.

18. Made sales on account as follows:
No. 56, C. L. Beggs, 318 E. Claymont, St. Louis, MO 63011, $79.10, tax $3.96.
No. 57, Ms. R. E. Morris, 3818 Connecticut, St. Louis, MO 63111, $34.80, tax $1.74.
No. 58, Breckenridge Inn, 1351 Dunn Road, St. Louis, MO 63135, $82.66, tax $4.13.

Apr. 19. Received Invoice No. 83 dated April 16 from Chatman Bros., Cincinnati, OH 45227, for merchandise purchased, $252.40. Terms, 30 days net.

20. Gave the Breckenridge Inn credit for $14.70 for merchandise returned. (Sales price, $14, tax 70 cents.)

21. Received credit from Chatman Bros. for $19.60 for merchandise returned.

22. Sundry cash sales, $173.40, tax $8.67.

23. Received Invoice No. 84 dated April 22 from Sexton & Co., Detroit, MI 48237, for merchandise purchased, $95.20. Terms, 30 days net.

25. Made sales on account as follows:

No. 59, J. W. Weiler, 332 Portica, St. Louis, MO 63017, $49.95, tax $2.50.

No. 60, Marriott Hotel, Lambert Field, St. Louis, MO 63134, $82.56, tax $4.13.

25. Allowed credit for $4.83 to C. L. Beggs for merchandise returned. (Sales price, $4.60, tax 23 cents.)

27. Paid Edison Bros. $75.45 on account.

27. Received $137.38 from Breckenridge Inn to apply on account.

28. Purchased store equipment on account from the Stern Fixture Co., 800 N. 7, St. Louis, MO 63101, $150. Terms, 60 days net.

28. Paid freight and drayage on merchandise purchased, $30.

30. Sundry cash sales, $164.50, tax $8.23.

30. Helen M. Harris withdrew $450 for personal use.

REQUIRED: (1) Journalize the April transactions. Total the purchases journal and rule; foot the sales journal, enter the totals, and rule. Prove each page of the two-column journal by footing the debit and credit columns. (2) Open the necessary general ledger accounts, using the trial balance on page 271 as a guide. Record the April 1 balances as shown in the March 31 trial balance, complete the individual posting from the two-column journal, and complete the summary posting from the purchases and sales journals. Enter the account balances. (3) Take a trial balance using a sheet of two-column journal paper.

Problem 7-A   Ms. F. M. Nations is a dealer in mirrors and glassware. In accounting for notes received from customers in return for extensions of time in paying their obligations, she uses a notes receivable register similar to the one reproduced on pages 172 and 173. Following is a narrative of transactions involving notes received from customers during the current year:

Mar. 7. Received from George Lucas a 60-day, 7% note (No. 1) for $800 dated March 5 and payable at First National Bank, Willow Springs.

Apr. 27. Received from John J. Neel a 90-day, 6% note (No. 2) for $600 dated April 26 and payable at Second National Bank, Lemay.

May   4. Received a check for $809.33 from George Lucas in payment of his note due today plus interest.

  20. Received from Edward F. Ford a 60-day, 8% note (No. 3) for $650 dated May 19 and payable at Meachem Park Trust Company, Meachem Park.

July 18. Received a check for $658.67 from Edward F. Ford in payment of his note due today plus interest.

  25. Received a check for $609 from John J. Neel in payment of his note due today plus interest.

Sept. 3. Received from W. P. Clark a 90-day, 7% note (No. 4) for $900 dated September 2 and payable at Kirkwood State Bank, Kirkwood.

Dec.   2. Received a check from Kirkwood State Bank for $905.75 in payment of the W. P. Clark note due yesterday plus interest less a $10 collection charge.

REQUIRED: **(1)** Prepare entries in two-column journal form to record the foregoing transactions. Foot the amount columns as a means of proof. **(2)** Make the required entries in a notes receivable register to provide a detailed auxiliary record of the notes received by Ms. F. M. Nations.

Problem 7-B   J. C. Hess operates a department store. Sometimes he finds it necessary to issue notes to suppliers to obtain extensions of time for payment of their accounts. Unless otherwise stated, all such notes are made payable at the Jefferson County Bank, Jefferson. Following is a narrative of transactions involving notes issued by Mr. Hess during the current year:

Feb.   1. Borrowed $1,000 from the bank on a 90-day, 8% note (No. 1).

Mar.   7. Issued a 60-day, 7% note (No. 2) for $625 to Black & Decker Co.

Apr. 21. Issued a 60-day, 6% note (No. 3) for $720 to J. E. Andrews & Sons.

May   2. Issued a check for $1,020 to the bank in payment of note due today plus interest.

  6. Gave Black & Decker Co. a check for $7.29 in payment of the interest and a new note (No. 4) for $625, due in 60 days, with interest at 7%, in settlement of the note due today.

June 20. Issued a check for $727.20 to J. E. Andrews & Sons in payment of note due today plus interest.

July   1. Borrowed $3,000 from the bank on a 90-day, 8% note (No. 5).

  5. Issued a check for $632.29 to Black & Decker Co. in payment of note due today plus interest.

Sept. 29. Gave Jefferson County Bank a check for $60 in payment of the interest and a new note (No. 6) for $3,000, due in 60 days with interest at 8%, in settlement of the note due today.

Nov. 28. Issued a check for $3,040 to the bank in payment of note due today plus interest.

REQUIRED: **(1)** Prepare entries in two-column journal form to record the foregoing transactions. Foot the amount columns as a means of proof. **(2)** Make the required entries in a notes payable register, similar to the one reproduced on pages 176 and 177, to provide a detailed auxiliary record of the notes issued.

There are no Practical Accounting Problems for Chapter 8.

Problem 9-A   Ward Wentworth is in the business of retail heating and cooling. Merchandise is sold for cash and on account. On the next page is a reproduction of the Trial Balance columns of his work sheet for the year ended December 31.

REQUIRED: Prepare a ten-column work sheet making the necessary entries in the Adjustments columns to record the following:

(1) Merchandise inventory, end of year, $20,406.40.
(2) Accruals:
    Interest accrued on notes payable, $29.34.
    Accrued bank credit card expense, $165.40.
(3) Prepaid expenses:
    Prepaid insurance unexpired, $448.
    Supplies on hand, $96.
(4) Depreciation:
    Store equipment, 10% a year, $704.
(5) Uncollectible accounts expense:
    Increase allowance for doubtful accounts $128 to provide for estimated loss.

Problem 9-B   Refer to the work sheet for Ward Wentworth (based on Problem 9-A) and from it prepare the following financial statements:

(1) An income statement for the year ended December 31.
(2) A balance sheet in account form as of December 31.

WARD WENTWORTH
Work Sheet
For the Year Ended December 31, 19—

Account	Acct. No.	Trial Balance Debit	Trial Balance Credit
Marshall & Ilsley Bank.................	111	8,745.44	
Petty Cash Fund......................	112	100.00	
Accounts Receivable....................	121	9,158.40	
Allowance for Doubtful Accounts..........	012		79.55
Merchandise Inventory.................	131	17,164.80	
Prepaid Insurance.....................	141	896.00	
Supplies..............................	151	288.00	
Store Equipment......................	161	7,040.00	
Accumulated Depreciation—Store Equipment	016		704.00
Notes Payable........................	211		3,500.00
Accrued Interest Payable...............	221		
Accounts Payable.....................	231		10,674.70
Sales Tax Payable.....................	241		828.00
FICA Tax Payable.....................	251		540.00
Employees Income Tax Payable..........	261		590.00
FUTA Tax Payable....................	271		86.00
State Unemployment Tax Payable........	281		122.60
Accrued Bank Credit Card Expense.......	291		
Ward Wentworth, Capital..............	311		42,317.69
Ward Wentworth, Drawing.............	031	12,000.00	
Expense and Revenue Summary..........	321		
Sales................................	411		82,296.00
Sales Returns and Allowances...........	041	286.40	
Purchases............................	511	57,970.00	
Purchases Returns and Allowances........	051		294.90
Rent Expense.........................	611	4,800.00	
Advertising Expense....................	612	624.00	
Salaries Expense......................	613	19,200.00	
Payroll Taxes Expense.................	614	1,320.00	
Insurance Expense.....................	615		
Supplies Expense......................	616		
Depreciation Expense..................	617		
Uncollectible Accounts Expense..........	618		
Charitable Contributions Expense.........	619	400.00	
Bank Credit Card Expense..............	621	1,827.60	
Miscellaneous Expense.................	622	168.00	
Interest Expense......................	711	44.80	
		142,033.44	142,033.44

Note: Problems 9-B and 10-A are also based on Ward Wentworth's work sheet. If these problems are to be solved, the work sheet prepared in Problem 9-A should be retained for reference until after they are solved, when the solutions of all three problems may be submitted to the instructor.

Problem 10-A   Refer to the work sheet for Ward Wentworth (based on Problem 9-A) and draft the general journal entries required:

(1) To adjust the general ledger accounts so that they will be in agreement with the financial statements.

(2) To close the temporary owner's equity accounts on December 31.

(3) To reserve the accrual adjustments as of January 1.

**Problem 10-B
(Complete cycle
problem)**

Kathy Dirkers operates a merchandising business as a sole owner. She calls her business "Kathy's Boutique." She keeps a purchases journal, sales journal, combined cash journal, and general ledger. While a petty cash fund is maintained, no payments are made from the fund in December. For her combined cash journal, she uses nine-column paper (9 columns divided — 3 left, 6 right) with headings arranged as follows:

Bank
  (1) Deposits Dr.
  (2) Checks Cr.
  (3) Purchases Discount Cr.

General
  (4) Debit
  (5) Credit
  (6) Accounts Payable Dr.
  (7) Accounts Receivable Cr.
  (8) Sales Cr.
  (9) Sales Tax Payable Cr.

The four-column form of ledger ruling is used. Individual accounts with customers and suppliers are not kept in ledger form; however, the purchase invoices and sales tickets are filed in such a manner that the amounts owed to suppliers and due from customers can be determined at any time. At the end of the eleventh month of this year, her trial balance appeared as shown on page 277.

NARRATIVE OF TRANSACTIONS FOR DECEMBER

Dec. 1. (Thursday) Purchased merchandise from Borowsky Bros., Cedar Rapids, IA 52401, $1,800, Invoice No. 21, dated November 30. Terms, 6/10, n/30.

  2. Paid the December rent, $900. Check No. 64.

  2. Paid the telephone bill, $48. Check No. 65.

  3. Paid Curlee Co. $1,685 in full of December 1 balance. Check No. 66.

  5. Sold merchandise on account to M. T. Clark, 901 Clayton Rd., St. Louis, MO 63117, $150, tax $7.50. Sale No. 121.

  6. Purchased merchandise from the James Co., Jamestown, NY 14701, $1,320. Invoice No. 22, dated December 5. Terms, 30 days.

  7. Received $225 from Vernelle Cone in full settlement of her account.

KATHY'S BOUTIQUE
Trial Balance
November 30, 19—

Clayton Bank	111	14,093.70	
Petty Cash Fund	112	100.00	
Accounts Receivable	121	12,711.70	
Allowance for Doubtful Accounts	012		194.90
Merchandise Inventory	131	58,240.00	
Prepaid Insurance	141	1,330.00	
Supplies	151	224.00	
Store Equipment	181	5,320.00	
Accumulated Depreciation — Store Equipment	018		1,064.00
Notes Payable	211		3,360.00
Accrued Interest Payable	221		
Accounts Payable	231		4,507.60
Sales Tax Payable	241		926.20
Employees Income Tax Payable	251		334.90
FICA Tax Payable	261		278.40
FUTA Tax Payable	271		79.30
State Unemployment Tax Payable	281		106.70
Accrued Bank Credit Card Expense	291		
Kathy Dirkers, Capital	311		94,525.75
Kathy Dirkers, Drawing	031	12,600.00	
Expense and Revenue Summary	321		
Sales	411		234,304.00
Sales Returns and Allowances	041	353.90	
Purchases	511	176,960.00	
Purchases Returns and Alllowances	051		395.10
Purchases Discount	052		308.00
Rent Expense	611	9,900.00	
Advertising Expense	612	6,750.00	
Salaries and Commissions Expense	613	36,200.00	
Payroll Taxes Expense	614	2,483.80	
Miscellaneous Expense	615	501.25	
Insurance Expense	616		
Supplies Expense	617		
Depreciation Expense	618		
Uncollectible Accounts Expense	619		
Bank Credit Card Expense	621	2,577.30	
Interest Expense	711	39.20	
		340,384.85	340,384.85

Dec. 8. Paid Borowsky Bros. $1,692 in settlement of their invoice of November 30, less 6% discount. Check No. 67.

8. Received $222.45 from LaVerne Becht in full settlement of her account.

9. Sold merchandise on account to Isabel Godair, Fenton, MO 63026, $57.30, tax $2.87. Sale No. 122.

Dec. 9. Received a notice from Clayton Bank that $352.25 had been deducted from the account of Kathy's Boutique, representing a discount of 3 percent on the amount net of returns of BankAmericard and Master Charge vouchers that had been deposited during November.

10. Purchased merchandise from the Thayer Mfg. Co., Kansas City, MO 64019, $483.20. Invoice No. 23, dated December 9. Terms, 30 days.

12. Sold merchandise on account to Fae Underwood, Irondale Estates, St. Louis, MO 63101, $150.40, tax $7.52. Sale No. 123.

13. Issued Check No. 68 to Clayton Bank, a U.S. Depositary, in payment of the following taxes:

(a) Employees' income tax withheld during November....		$334.90
(b) FICA tax:		
On employees (withheld during November)........	$139.20	
On the employer.............................	139.20	278.40
Total		$613.30

14. Sold merchandise on account to Marian Bock, 873 Cliff St., Ferguson, MO 63135, $145, tax $7.25. Sale No. 124.

15. Issued Check No. 69 payable to State Treasurer for $926.20 for November sales tax.

17. Kathy Dirkers withdrew $300 for personal use. Check No. 70.

19. Gave Fae Underwood credit for $52.50 because a part of the merchandise sold her on the twelfth was returned. (Sales price, $50, tax $2.50)

20. Sold merchandise on account to M. T. Clark, 901 Clayton Rd., St. Louis, MO 63117, $85, tax $4.25. Sale No. 125.

21. Purchased merchandise from Barbie Brooks, Inc., Cincinnati, OH 45202, $1,096.50. Invoice No. 24, dated December 20. Terms, 8/10, n/30.

22. Received $105.42 from Fae Underwood for balance of Sale No. 123.

23. Paid bill for advertising, $300. Check No. 71.

26. Sold merchandise on account to Joan Aach, 195 Johnson St., St. Louis, MO 63130, $225.75, tax $11.29. Sale No. 126.

26. Purchased merchandise from Borowsky Bros., Cedar Rapids, IA 52401, $1,541.90. Invoice No. 25, dated December 23. Terms, 2/10, n/30.

26. Received a check for $100 from M. T. Clark to apply on account.

27. Sold merchandise on account to Fae Underwood, Irondale Estates, St. Louis, MO 63101, $235.50, tax $11.78. Sale No. 127.

27. Sent the Thayer Mfg. Co. a check for $200 to apply on account. Check No. 72.

28. Sold merchandise on account to Linda Boyd, 812 Sixth St., Kirksville, MO 63501, $92.50, tax $4.63. Sale No. 128.

28. Purchased store equipment from the Mattoon Supply Co., Mattoon, IL 61938, $520. Terms, 60 days net.

29. Received $60.17 from Isabel Godair in payment of Sale No. 122.

29. Received credit from Borowsky Bros. for $60 because a part of the merchandise purchased on the twenty-sixth was returned by agreement.

29. Sold merchandise on account to Isabel Godair, Fenton, MO 63026, $122.50, tax $6.13. Sale No. 129.

Dec. 30. Sundry cash and bank credit card sales for month, $14,414.80, tax $720.74.

30. Issued Check No. 73 payable to Payroll for $2,606.70.

PAYROLL STATEMENT FOR MONTH ENDED DECEMBER 31

Total wages and commissions earned during period..........		$3,300.00
Employees' taxes to be withheld		
(a) Employees' income tax...........................	$495.30	
(b) FICA tax @ 6%..................................	198.00	693.30
Net amount payable to employees......................		$2,606.70
Employer's payroll taxes:		
(a) FICA tax @ 6%..................................		$ 198.00
(b) UC taxes —		
State @ 2.7%...............................	$ 89.10	
Federal @ 0.5%.............................	16.50	105.60
Total...		$ 303.60

(In addition to recording the amounts withheld from employees' wages for income tax purposes and for FICA tax, the social security tax imposed on the employer should also be recorded.)

REQUIRED: **(1)** Journalize the December transactions. **(2)** Open the necessary general ledger accounts and record the December 1 balances, using the November 30 trial balance as the source of the needed information. Complete the individual and summary posting from the books of original entry. **(3)** Take a trial balance of the general ledger accounts. **(4)** Prepare a ten-column work sheet making the required adjustments from the information given below. Number the pages of the journals as follows:

Purchases Journal........ Page 34
Sales Journal........... Page 46
Combined Cash Journal.. Pages 49–51

(a) Merchandise inventory, end of year, $81,900.

(b) Accruals:
Interest accrued on notes payable, $33.60.
Accrued bank credit card expense, $357.65.

(c) Prepaid expenses:
Prepaid insurance unexpired, $886.
Supplies on hand, $70.

(d) Depreciation:
Store equipment, 10% a year, $532.

(e) Uncollectible accounts expense:
Increase allowance for doubtful accounts $295.90 to provide for estimated loss.

(5) Prepare an income statement for the year ending December 31 and a balance sheet in report form as of December 31. **(6)** Record the adjusting entries in the combined cash journal and post. **(7)** Record the closing entries in the combined cash journal and post. **(8)** Place "no balance" symbols in the accounts that are in balance after the adjusting and closing entries have been posted. **(9)** Take a post-closing trial balance. **(10)** Record the necessary reversing entries as of January 1 in the combined cash journal. Place "no balance" symbols in the accounts that are closed.

Appendix

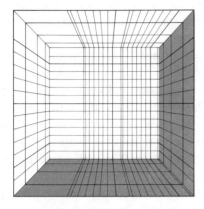

COMPUTER-BASED ACCOUNTING SYSTEMS – DESIGN AND USE

Structure of accounting systems

The design of a system of forms, records, and reports depends in large measure on the nature of the business by which the system is used. The number of transactions to be recorded in a given time period has much to do with the planning and arrangement of the chart of accounts and of the procedures for gathering and processing transaction information. Physical location of factory buildings, warehouses, stores and offices, and the transaction volume at each location also influence the design of an accounting system.

The nature of the business, the plan of organization, the kinds of transactions to be recorded and summarized, the transaction volume, and the location of physical facilities together comprise the *structure* of an accounting system. All of these factors together make careful systems planning essential.

The language of computer-based systems

The original or *source documents* for many kinds of business transactions have been presented in this textbook. The source document is always the key record in a computer-based accounting system just as it is in a manual accounting system. Whether a source document is prepared by hand or by machine, the data it contains must be collected and the recording process started by people.

Some modern businesses are quite large, and this relative size affects their accounting systems. Modern systems for relatively large businesses include computer equipment (hardware) that operates without human guidance other than pressing one or more buttons. The use of such equipment in an accounting system makes it a *computer-based accounting system*.

Computer-based accounting has brought about the development of a new language as well as new procedures. In computer-based accounting, facts and figures such as ledger account titles, dollar amounts, and physical quantities are known as *data*. The use of these data in different ways for different business purposes is known as *data processing*. Accounting involves the processing of data in several different forms. In fact, the original preparation of the source document for a business transaction is a form of data processing. Likewise, the recording of transactions in books of original entry, posting to ledger accounts, taking trial balances, and preparing financial statements are also forms of data processing.

Those who use computer equipment to process accounting records must apply accounting principles to each step. The same principles of debit and credit apply whether the work is done with computer equipment, with conventional accounting machines, or by the manual bookkeeper. Equipment and machines reduce routine manual work, increase the speed of producing records, and permit more accurate financial reporting.

Data processing is usually described in two ways. The processing of business transactions by means of simple office machines with card punches or tape writers attached is known as *integrated data processing* (IDP). The processing of business transactions by means of an electronic computer is known as *electronic data processing* (EDP).

Accounting systems review

No one can design and install an accounting system for a business that will function properly without a thorough knowledge of the operations of that business. When a business is first established this may not be possible. What is more, expansion of a business into new areas of operation, new personnel, or increased transaction volume may cause its accounting system to become inadequate.

For any one of the foregoing reasons, a business may decide to review its accounting system on an almost continuous basis, and to change one or more parts of the system at frequent intervals. Accounting systems review subdivides into three essential phases: **(1)** systems analysis, **(2)** systems design, and **(3)** systems implementation.

Systems analysis

Systems analysis has three major objectives:

(a) The determination of business needs for information.
(b) The determination of sources of such information.

(c) The shortcomings in the accounting systems and procedures presently in use.

The first step in systems analysis usually is a review of the organizational structure and the job descriptions of the personnel involved. The second step in systems analysis usually is a study of forms, records, and reports, and the processing methods and procedures used by the business. In this connection, a *systems manual*, which details instructions to employees and procedures to be followed, is extremely valuable to the systems analyst if it is available. The third step in systems analysis is to project management's plans for changes in such operational matters as sales volume, products, territories, salesmen, or customers into the near future.

Systems design

Accounting systems design changes are the result of systems analysis. A good systems designer needs to know the relative merits of various types of computer hardware, and be able to evaluate the various alternatives open to the business, which may or may not involve computer hardware.

Creativity and imagination are important attributes of a successful systems designer. The following general principles also are important:

(a) The value of information produced by an accounting system should never be less than the cost of obtaining it, and preferably the value should be greater than the cost.

(b) Any accounting system needs sufficient built-in internal control to safeguard business assets and protect data reliability.

(c) Any accounting system needs to be flexible enough to absorb data volume increases and changes in procedures and data processing techniques without disruption of the system.

Systems implementation

A newly created or revised accounting system is worthless without the ability to carry out, or implement, the recommendations of the systems analyst. The new or revised forms, records, reports, procedures, and hardware recommended by the systems analyst must be installed, and obsolete items must be removed. Each and every employee who will have a hand in operating the system must be thoroughly trained and adequately supervised until the new system is operating smoothly.

A major systems change, such as from a manual accounting system to a computer-based accounting system, usually is spread over a rather long period of time. For a while during the changeover period, the old and new systems must function side by side at least in part, and care must be taken to avoid seriously affecting the reliability of the data produced by the system(s).

Flowcharts

One of the major tools of the systems analyst in the design of computer-based accounting systems is called the *flowchart*. In a flowchart, the major steps to be undertaken in processing a particular accounting transaction or series of closely related accounting transactions are shown in graphic form. The symbols most commonly used in preparing flowcharts are:

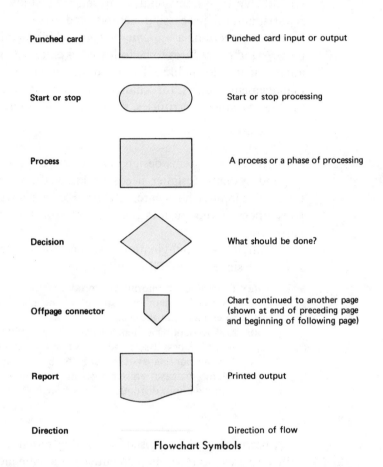

Flowchart Symbols

Flowcharts usually are prepared to be read from left to right and from top to bottom, with the direction of the flow being shown by lines and arrows. A brief description of each step in processing usually is written inside each flowchart symbol. When one or more decisions are required at some stage in data processing, the questions to be answered usually are printed inside or next to each decision symbol. Most decisions involve comparison of two data items. If the items match, the decision is to go on with the process; if the two items do not match, the decision usually is to retrace some of the previously completed steps in the process.

The process involved in manually posting information from employee check stubs to a payroll register is shown in the flowchart on page A-5.

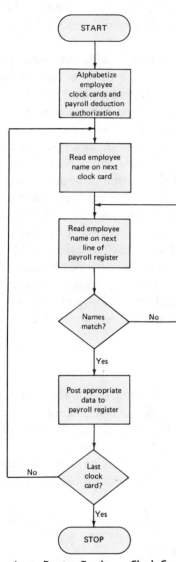

START

↓

Alphabetize employee clock cards and payroll deduction authorizations

↓

Read employee name on next clock card

↓

Read employee name on next line of payroll register

↓

Names match? → No

↓ Yes

Post appropriate data to payroll register

↓

Last clock card? → No

↓ Yes

STOP

Flowchart—Posting Employee Clock Cards and Deduction Authorizations to Payroll Register

This flowchart correlates with the discussion on pages 75–77 in Chapter 4. The employee doing the work begins by arranging the completed clock cards and payroll deduction authorization forms in alphabetical order and clipping the related forms together for each employee. (The clock cards were in clock number or social security number order.) The name on the first clock card and the name on the first line of the payroll register are examined. If they match, the appropriate data is posted to the payroll register. If they do not match, each succeeding line of the register is examined until the right one is found. After posting the appropriate data to the right line, the name on the next clock card is matched to the register and the process is repeated until all clock cards have been posted. This assumes that there is only one clock card and set of related payroll deduction authorization forms per employee, and that each time a new employee is hired, a new clock card is prepared, related payroll deduction authorization forms are completed, and the payroll register listing of employees is revised. Otherwise, the flowchart would have to be extended to include the necessary correctional steps.

The amount of detail shown in a flowchart depends upon its purpose and the amount of detail desired. In implementing a computerized version of the payroll system illustrated above, information concerning hardware would have to be added, and more detailed information about adding new employees, dropping old employees, etc., would have to be included. The punched card symbol for input or output and the report symbol for printed output would then be pressed into use, as well as the connector symbol for flowcharts occupying two or more pages.

In a computer-based payroll system, the flowchart would be the basis for the development of the computer program. Each labeled symbol in the flowchart would constitute a programming step. A collection of computer programs is known as a *software* package.

The write-it-once principle as a labor-saving device   A source document, such as a purchase invoice or a sales ticket, usually is prepared manually by handwriting or typing on the document at the time of the transaction. The first step in computer-based accounting is the preparation of a punched card or a section of magnetic tape by a machine operator from a source document. (Optical character recognition (OCR) equipment that can read data from source documents directly into computers is rapidly emerging.)

If the operator types the source document on an office machine with a card punching or tape encoding attachment, the card or tape is being prepared at the same time that the source document is being typed. If the office machine used is not an integrated data processing machine, the card or tape must be prepared later as a separate operation.

The process of recording the basic information about a business transaction in a form that makes later hand copying unnecessary has been called the *write-it-once principle*. This first step in computer-based accounting makes it possible to save labor in completing the later steps of the accounting cycle. Once a punched card or a magnetic tape has been prepared by a machine operator or a source document has been "read" directly into the computer, the recorded information can be used over and over again when and where needed. The only further human effort needed is to feed the cards or tape into computer equipment. This equipment then performs automatically the functions of journalizing, posting, taking trial balances, preparing financial statements, and adjusting and closing ledger accounts.

Importance of locating errors in the write-it-once operation

If errors in the punching of cards, encoding of magnetic tape, or preparation of source documents are not discovered before the cards, tape, or documents are fed into computer equipment, such errors will be repeated in each step of the automated accounting cycle.

Designers of computer-based accounting systems have recognized the seriousness of the error problem. Errors in computer-based systems are normally located in either of two ways:

(a) Transaction information is verified as soon as it has been recorded.
(b) Automatic error-locating procedures built into the computer equipment are used later on in the accounting cycle.

Verifying transaction information already punched into cards is a process of running the cards through manually operated machines a second time. A different machine operator reads the information from the source document and goes through the same punching motions as did the original operator. If each punching stroke hits a hole in the card, the card passes right on through the machine. If a punching stroke hits a solid section of card, an error is indicated, and the machine notches the edge of the card next to the error. Notched cards are set aside and corrected later.

Businesses that find errors very difficult to control may decide not only to verify source document information before cards are processed but also to use automatic error-locating procedures later in the accounting cycle. Computer equipment also may be set up to locate certain errors electronically. When such errors are so located, an error light on the equipment usually goes on, and if the computer operator is not able to remedy the difficulty, the equipment stops running.

Basic phases of automated data processing

The automated processing of any data in the completion of the accounting cycle consists of five basic phases. These five phases are common to all computer equipment, regardless of manufacturer. They are:

(a) Input   (d) Arithmetic and logic
(b) Control   (e) Output
(c) Storage

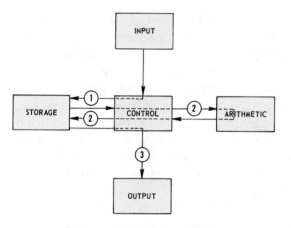

Diagram of Basic Computer System

A diagram of a basic computer system is shown at the left.

Input. In order that computer equipment may complete the accounting process, the source document may have to be rewritten in a form that the equipment can interpret. Information about a business transaction in a form acceptable for use in automated data processing equipment is known as *input*. Any acceptable means for presenting this information to a computer is known as an *input device*.

Control. *Control* is the nerve center, or "action central" of the computer-based accounting system. It is like the central hall in a home or the lobby of a hotel. People must pass through the lobby of a hotel to get to their rooms. In the same way, transaction information must be routed through control in each step of automated data processing. Transaction information received as input is sent by control to storage, as shown by the flow line labeled "1" in the diagram above.

Storage. Transaction information stops in *storage* to await further use in computer-based accounting. Storage is often called the CPU (central processing unit) by computer people. Because storage holds information for future use just as does the human mind, it is often referred to as "memory." But unlike the human mind, storage must be told in great detail what to do with each item of transaction information that it holds. A detailed list of steps to be followed in completing the computerized accounting cycle is known as a *program*. A person who designs programs is called a *programmer*. The detailed work of arranging transaction information in the most efficient manner for computer processing is called *programming* and is usually preceded by a flowchart, as mentioned earlier.

Arithmetic and Logic. The primary work of computer-based accounting is done in the *arithmetic and logic* phase. Transaction information is routed from storage through control to arithmetic and logic. In the arithmetic phase, addition, subtraction, multiplication, or division is performed as needed; and the result is returned by control to storage. This round trip is shown by the flow line labeled "2" in the basic computer system diagram. The logic phase can compare two numbers and tell whether the first number is smaller than, equal to, or larger than the second number. This feature is useful in controlling inventories and expenses.

Output. When ledger account balances, financial statement items, or other data are desired, they are obtained from the automated data processing system in the output phase. Business information in a form acceptable for human use is known as *output*. Any acceptable means for converting coded machine information into English is known as an *output device*.

Business information requested by management from the data processing system is routed from storage through control to output, as shown by the flow line labeled "3" in the basic computer system diagram. Output devices are prepared which are used later to print in English the particular business information requested, or output is produced directly on a high-speed printer attached to the CPU.

Input and output may be and often are handled by the same physical equipment, called I-0 equipment by computer people.

The punched card as an input device

At present, the punched card is the most frequently used initial input device. One form of punched card is the IBM (International Business Machines Corporation) card, illustrated at the top of page A-9.

Utility companies, oil companies, magazine publishers, and mail order houses use punched cards as statements of account. The federal government and many large private companies use punched cards for payroll checks and other remittance checks.

The small figures on the IBM card show that it has 80 columns, numbered from left to right. The large figures on the card show that it has ten rows, numbered 0 to 9 inclusive from top to bottom. In addition, as the above illustration shows, the blank space at the top of the card provides room for two more rows, called the "twelve row" and the "eleven row."

As shown by the punches in the illustration, a single numerical digit may be formed by punching a small hole in a column at one of the ten posi-

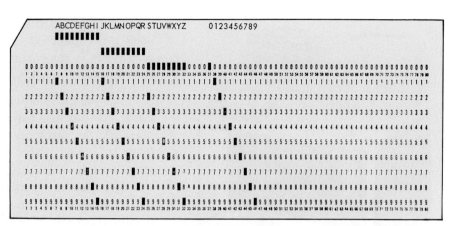

Standard IBM Card

tions numbered zero through nine A single letter or symbol may be formed by punching two holes in a column. One of these holes is punched through a position numbered one through nine. The other hole is punched through a position numbered twelve, eleven, or zero, as shown in the illustration above. The three top rows on the card are called the "zone" rows, and a hole punched in one of these rows is called a "zone" punch.

Planning the Use of the Punched Card. The first step in the use of a punched card as an input device is to plan the arrangement of the information on the card. A punched card that is to be used as a statement of account will contain the following information:

(a) Customer's name and address	**(e)** Current sales to the customer
(b) Customer's account number	**(f)** Amount received on account
(c) Billing date	**(g)** Sales returns and allowances
(d) Customer's previous balance	**(h)** Customer's new balance

Each item of information requires that several holes be punched into the card. An estimate is made of the longest group of letters or numbers required for each of the eight items to be placed on any statement of account. The punched card (or cards if two are needed) is then subdivided into eight groups of columns of sufficient size.

A group of columns used for a single item of information on a punched card is known as a *field*. There is a field for the customer's name and address, and a field for each of the other seven items of information.

Punching Information Into the Punched Card. After the information for preparing a customer's statement of account has been provided by the computerized accounting system, a machine operator enters this information into a machine which in turn punches information holes into the card. One field on the card is used for each of the eight information items.

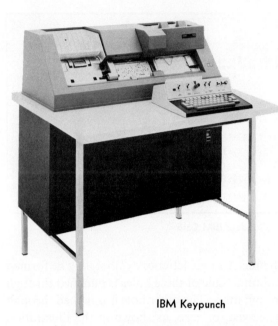

IBM Keypunch

A machine used to punch information holes into punched cards from source documents is known as a *keypunch*. An IBM keypunch machine is illustrated here.

Verifying the Information on the Punched Card. As soon as a batch of cards has been punched, the cards are checked in an attempt to avoid errors. A machine that looks exactly like a keypunch and is used to find punching errors is called a *verifier*. As mentioned earlier, another operator reading from the same source document as the keypunch operator enters the data into the verifier. The IBM verifier machine "feels" each card electronically to determine whether the correct holes have been punched. Each correct card is notched in a special "verify" position. If the verifier machine "feels" a missing hole or a hole in the wrong position, it notches a special "error" position on the card and the keyboard on the machine locks up.

Printing the Information on a Punched Card. The punched information on each IBM card is printed on a two-part statement card consisting of a statement and a stub. The printing is done by running the punched cards through an automatic printing machine that lists, totals, and prints information previously punched onto cards. This machine is called a *tabulator* or *high-speed printer*. The information may either be printed on the same punched card from which it comes or on a separate sheet of paper.

Completing a Punched Card Statement of Account. After each of the two-part statement cards has been tabulated, the customer's account number and balance due are punched into the stub portion of the card. The statement card is then ready to be mailed to the customer. A completed two-part statement card is illustrated at the top of the next page.

Sorting Customer Remittance Stubs. When the customer receives a statement like the one illustrated on page A-11, the stub is detached and returned with the remittance. When a remittance arrives, the amount received is keypunched into the stub that comes with the remittance. The stubs are then grouped into piles and run through a machine which sorts them by customer's account number.

A machine that automatically groups all punched cards of a similar kind and arranges them in some order is called a *sorter*. The stubs received

Punched Card Statement of Account

from customers are placed in the hopper of the sorter. The sorted stubs drop into pockets. There is a "reject" pocket for cards that the machine is unable to sort.

Posting Customer Remittance Stubs. The final process in accounting for customer remittances is to run the stubs through the printer or tabulator in account number order. This machine process posts the remittances to individual customers' ledger account cards and determines the new account balances.

The same basic operations are followed in processing punched card checks, except that cash payment transactions are involved rather than cash receipt transactions. The transaction information must still be keypunched, verified, printed, sorted, and posted. These are basic data processing operations in computer-based accounting systems.

Magnetic tape as an input device

Magnetic tape usually is used as a repeat input device in EDP systems. It is prepared for input by depositing small magnetized spots on reels of tape. This tape comes from the factory coated with a magnetic metal substance.

The chief advantage of magnetic tape is the speed with which it can be used as input. It is easy to carry and compact to store.

Magnetic ink symbol numbers as input devices

As discussed in Chapter 3, the American Bankers Association recommends the use of symbol numbers printed in magnetic ink on each bank check. The use of these magnetic ink symbol numbers permits the automated processing of checks.

The use of magnetic ink symbol numbers in the processing of bank checks is called *magnetic ink character recognition*. The common abbreviation for this process is *MICR*. A bank check with magnetic ink symbol numbers printed across the bottom of the check is illustrated below:

No. 43   ST. LOUIS *County National* BANK   80-459 / 810

CLAYTON (ST. LOUIS) MO. *May 5* 19 77

PAY TO THE ORDER OF *Millburg Pharmacy* $15 42

Fifteen 42/100 ~~~~~~~~~~~~~~ DOLLARS

J. A. McManus

⑆0810⑈0459⑆ 042⑆ 121 3⑈

Bank Check with Magnetic Ink Symbol Numbers

Note that the symbol numbers at the bottom of the check use a style that is different from regular Arabic numerals. This is because these numbers are read by a device that "feels" the surface area of each number and recognizes its shape. Regular Arabic numerals, especially 2, 5, 6, and 9, are too much alike to be easily distinguished one from the other by an electronic reading machine.

Encoding Symbol Numbers on Bank Checks. Magnetic ink symbol numbers are printed on checks using special printing machines. A machine for printing magnetic ink characters on checks is called an *encoder*.

Encoding may be done by the company that prints the blank checks, or by the bank that supplies the blank checks to its depositors.

Clearing Encoded Bank Checks Through the Federal Reserve System. The first series of encoded numerals in the check illustration (0810-0459) is adapted from the ABA number in the upper right-hand corner of the check. Notice that the number 80, which represents the State of Missouri, has been dropped from the encoded symbol number. This is because 0810 locates the bank in the Eighth Federal Reserve District (08) and the Greater St. Louis area (10), and the State of Missouri is understood.

The Federal Reserve system sorts checks encoded with magnetic ink symbol numbers as follows:

Step 1. The bank in which the check is deposited forwards it to the Federal Reserve clearing house in its district.

Step 2. The Federal Reserve clearing house sorts the check along with other checks received from banks in its district on special sorting equipment using the first two encoded symbol numbers (08 in the illustration).

This results in twelve batches of checks for the twelve Federal Reserve districts.

Step 3. Each Federal Reserve clearing house forwards the checks drawn on banks in other Federal Reserve districts to the proper districts. In this process, the check illustrated on the previous page is forwarded to the Eighth Federal Reserve District clearing house in St. Louis.

Step 4. The clearing house in St. Louis sorts on the next two encoded symbol numbers (10 in the illustration) for distribution of the checks to regional clearing houses. Since the bank on which the illustrated check is drawn is a Greater St. Louis bank, this check is not forwarded to a regional clearing house.

Step 5. Each district or regional clearing house sorts on the next four symbol numbers (0459 in the illustration) for distribution to individual banks. These four symbol numbers are individual bank numbers.

Step 6. Batches of sorted checks are forwarded to the banks on which they were drawn. The illustrated check is sent to St. Louis County National Bank.

Processing Encoded Bank Checks in Individual Banks. The second series of encoded numerals on the illustrated check (121-077-3) is the account number of the individual depositor at the bank. The depositor's bank sorts its own checks by account number. It uses the same type of MICR sorting equipment as that used in the Federal Reserve clearing houses. This equipment can sort as many as 90,000 checks per hour.

In smaller banks, checks sorted by depositor's account number are posted by using conventional bank posting machines. Larger banks having encoders of their own print the amount of each check in magnetic ink under the signature line. Encoding amounts of individual checks makes it possible to sort and post electronically to depositors' ledger accounts in one operation.

OCR Readers as Input Devices. As mentioned earlier, the use of optical character recognition (OCR) machines to "read" directly from source documents into computers is a growing practice, especially in conjunction with the major credit-card systems discussed in Chapter 6. Special type is required, but it is not as stylized as MICR type. The only requirement is that all characters be printed at right angles and that all curves and diagonal lines be eliminated.

The control phase in automated accounting

The control phase of an electronic system receives electronic commands from input devices and sees that they are carried out. Each command refers to some item of transaction information which is in storage. The control phase searches storage locations one by one in carrying out commands from input devices and keeps track of the location of each command as it is carried out. This avoids skipping program steps.

The storage phase in automated accounting

In manual accounting, the journal, the ledger, and the trial balance are methods of temporarily storing transaction information. This information is stored permanently on the financial statements.

In computerized accounting, means of storage must be used which make it possible to complete the accounting cycle automatically. Means of storing journal entries, ledger account balances, and trial balance information must be found. Any means of storing accounting information in between the steps of the computerized accounting cycle is known as a *storage device*.

External Storage Devices. Storage devices physically removed from a computer system from which data can be fed into the system when desired are known as *external storage devices*. Both punched cards and magnetic tape are able to retain transaction information for long periods of time. For this reason, as well as the fact that they can be physically removed from the system, these input devices are used also as data (external) storage devices. (Magnetic disks, contained in a "phonograph-type" unit, are also used as external storage devices.)

Externally Stored Journal Entries. External storage devices may be used either for temporary storage or for permanent storage of transaction information. Punched cards are excellent storage devices for journal entries. This is because a separate punched card can be used to record each debit element of a journal entry and a separate punched card can be used to record each credit element of a journal entry. The cards can then be machine sorted by ledger account titles for machine posting.

Journal entries may also be stored on magnetic tape. However, reels of tape cannot be sorted in the same way that punched cards are sorted. Journal entries on reels of tape must be machine posted in the order in which they were recorded. This is the same order in which journal entries would be posted manually. The only advantage of machine posting is that it is faster and relatively free of error.

Internal Storage Devices. The internal storage phase of a computer system is contained within the machinery. The storage phase receives instructions from control, which have been passed on from input. These instructions are of four types:

(a) Take data from input
(b) Send data to arithmetic and logic
(c) Receive data from arithmetic and logic
(d) Send data to output

Devices for temporarily storing accounting information within a computer are known as *internal storage devices*.

Internally Stored Ledgers. Internal storage devices are used in computerized accounting to keep ledger accounts up-to-date. Each account in the ledger is assigned a storage address. Debits and credits are fed in on punched cards or reels of tape. Control instructs input to transfer a debit or a credit amount into storage from a card or tape reel.

The incoming debit or credit amount must go to a storage address different from the address assigned to the related ledger account. Since this address is needed only for the current posting operation, it is not permanently assigned. However, the accountant must keep a chart of storage addresses (corresponding to a chart of accounts) in order to know at all times which addresses are assigned and which are open.

Automatic Posting. Automatic posting requires the following steps:

Step 1. Control instructs input to read the old balance of the ledger account from a master magnetic ledger tape into its assigned address in storage.

Step 2. Control instructs storage to transfer the old balance of the ledger account from its assigned address to the arithmetic and logic unit.

Step 3. Control instructs storage to transfer the related debit or credit amount, which has just come into storage from a punched card or transaction tape to arithmetic and logic.

Step 4. Control instructs arithmetic and logic either to add the debit amount to or subtract the credit amount from the old balance of the account.

Step 5. Control instructs storage to receive the new ledger account balance from arithmetic and logic and to store it in the assigned storage address for the particular ledger account. This is the same address in which the old ledger account balance was stored.

Step 6. Control instructs storage to transfer the new ledger account balance out to an updated master magnetic ledger tape.

In a computer-based accounting system, when a new item is stored electronically in the same internal storage address as a previous item, the new item replaces the old item at that address.

To illustrate the automated posting process, suppose that the cash account is assigned storage address number 10. The beginning cash balance, a debit of $1,200, becomes input by means of a punched card and is sent to address number 10 by the control unit. Suppose also that a debit to the cash account, in the amount of $50, is placed in input by means of another punched card and is sent by control to address number 100 for temporary storage.

The posting process will proceed as follows:

Step 1. Control instructs storage to transfer the beginning cash balance of $1,200 from address number 10 to arithmetic and logic.

Step 2. Control instructs storage to transfer the $50 debit to the cash account from address number 100 to arithmetic and logic.

Step 3. Control instructs arithmetic and logic to add the $50 cash debit to the beginning balance of $1,200.

Step 4. Control instructs storage to receive the new cash balance, $1,250, and to store it back in address number 10, the address temporarily assigned to the cash account.

Limitations of Internal Storage. The illustration of automated posting demonstrates that internal storage may be used both for temporary storage of debits and credits to ledger accounts and for semipermanent storage of ledger account balances. A small business having relatively few ledger accounts could get along with a rather small amount of internal storage. However, a large business having a great many ledger accounts would need a rather large amount of internal storage. Internal storage either must be large enough to handle the ledger accounts and the posting operations of the computer-based accounting system in which it is used, or ledger account balances will have to be stored externally on magnetic tape, punched cards, or magnetic disks.

The arithmetic and logic phase in automated accounting

The arithmetic and logic phase of an electronic system receives instructions from control to add, subtract, multiply, or divide, or to compare two numbers. Arithmetic and logic works with only two numbers at a time, having received them from different storage locations. To avoid returning subtotals or partial products to storage, however, arithmetic and logic has a temporary electronic storage unit of its own. The electronic storage device in the arithmetic and logic phase of a computer system used to store subtotals and partial products for further processing is known as an *accumulator*.

The output phase in automated accounting

In many ways, the output phase in automated accounting is just the reverse of the input phase. Punched cards and magnetic tape have already been described as input devices and as storage devices. Cards and reels of tape may also be used effectively as output devices.

Upon request, control will instruct storage to punch out cards or to write on magnetic tape any information desired. This might be journal entries, ledger account balances, trial balances, or financial statements. The cards or tapes must then be converted to English language information.

The Tabulator as an Output Device. The tabulator has already been discussed in connection with the use of the punched card. As indicated, it can list, total, or print journal entries, ledger account balances, trial balances, or financial statements whenever desired. The tabulator prints a line at a time and can handle up to 90 lines a minute.

The High-Speed Printer as an Output Device. High-speed printing machines are now available into which punched cards, magnetic tape, or electronically readable source documents may be fed. These machines are capable of printing in excess of 900 lines of information per minute.

Index

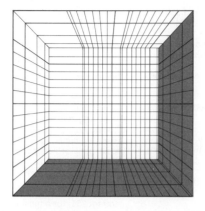